POSTCARD HISTORY SERIES

Racine

On the front cover: **MONUMENT SQUARE, C. 1930.** Racine's public square was laid out in 1836 when the original town site was platted. During the pioneer years, it was known as Hay Market Square because farmers would bring loads of hay or firewood to the square for sale. On July 4, 1884, the Civil War soldier monument was dedicated and, from then on, the square has been known as Monument Square. The Venetian Theatre (right), built in 1928 for a modest $1 million, was one of the finest show houses ever built in Racine. The 2,100-seat atmospheric theater was built with a plaster art decor of Italian Renaissance design with statuary. It was razed in 1977. The Racine County Courthouse (left) was razed in 1931 after a replacement was built. Just to the north, the building with the roof sign and flag pole was Zahn's Department Store, an upscale popular store known for finer quality clothes and other merchandise. Directly across the square is the old Manufacturers National Bank Building. (Author's collection.)

On the back cover: **RACINE HARBOR, C. 1860.** This rare early view of Racine's inner harbor truly captures the beauty of Racine and shows why it was dubbed the "Belle City of the Great Lakes," the French word *belle* meaning "beautiful." The artist's view was looking southeast from Erie Street just below where Saint Patrick's Church stands today. The bridge to the left, which is in line with Wisconsin Avenue, was later replaced with a bridge on Main Street. The building next to the bridge was the Dutton and Raymond grain warehouse. Next to the Dutton warehouse are the railroad depot and switching yards of the Racine and Mississippi Rail Road Company. The bridge that crossed the river at Second Street is also shown. It was later replaced by the State Street Bridge. (Author's collection.)

POSTCARD HISTORY SERIES

Racine

Gerald L. Karwowski

ARCADIA
PUBLISHING

ISBN 978-0-7385-5062-6

Published by Arcadia Publishing
Charleston, South Carolina

Printed in the United States of America

Library of Congress Catalog Card Number: 2007924317

For all general information contact Arcadia Publishing at:
Telephone 843-853-2070
Fax 843-853-0044
E-mail sales@arcadiapublishing.com
For customer service and orders:
Toll-Free 1-888-313-2665

Visit us on the Internet at www.arcadiapublishing.com

For my wife, Marie, who has contended with the piles of historical memorabilia that I continuously bring home; and for my children Lisa, Aria, and Erica, who have totally supported their father's love of local history.

Contents

ACKNOWLEDGMENTS

This book would not have been possible, first of all, without the help and support of my wife, Marie A. Karwowski, and my daughters, Lisa, Aria, and Erica.

I also want to acknowledge and thank the following organizations and individuals who provided assistance in the research and creation of this book: The Racine Public Library reference desk staff members have been an asset on this project—their expert help and, at times, their tolerance have been truly appreciated; the Racine Heritage Museum has been a very helpful resource as well, and a special thank you goes to director Chris Paulson and archivist Richard Ammann; the Burlington Historical Society and especially Don Vande Sand for his expert help and encouragement—for a fabulous local history Web site, visit www.burlingtonhistory.org; Preservation-Racine Incorporated, for sharing its records about the landmarks and historic buildings in the area; special thanks go to Vivian Merlo, Roberta Fiene, Don Rintz, Barbara Walter, Mary Whitman, Margo Drummond, and Racine historian Bob Johnson; photo-journalist and author of *Wright In Racine*, Mark Hertzberg, for sharing his extensive knowledge of architect Frank Lloyd Wright and the buildings he designed in Racine; the University of Wisconsin-Parkside's archives and Area Research Center; and archivist Nicholas Weber.

In addition, I appreciate the encouragement and help of Arcadia editor, Jeff Ruetsche, and the other Arcadia employees who contributed to the publishing of this book.

Lastly, but perhaps most basically, this book would not have been possible at all without the local amateur and professional Racine historians and photographers who, throughout the years, have gathered and documented the endless trail of historical facts and photographs for future generations to enjoy.

All the images in this book are from the postcard collection of the author who has been and is a devoted Racine collector for the past 40 years.

Introduction

Racine's story begins in 1833 when a Native American treaty cleared the way for settlers to move into southeastern Wisconsin to start cultivating what was considered wilderness at the time. This caught the eye of Racine's founder, Capt. Gilbert Knapp, who had explored the mouth of the Root River earlier during his commission as a lake captain and found it to be an ideal site for a harbor and settlement. In November 1834, Knapp staked a claim for about 141 acres north and south of the Root River. He then built a small crude cabin near what is today State Street and Lake Avenue. The area and settlement, first called Port Gilbert in honor of its founder, came to be known simply as Root River until 1836 when the name Racine was chosen.

Racine is the French word for "root," which in turn is the English translation of the river's Native American name, Schip-i-coten or Chippecotton. Knapp's financial partners, Gurdon Hubbard and Jacob Barker, have been memorialized on Racine's north side with streets named after them. Early in its history, Racine became known as the "Belle City of the Lakes" because of its natural beauty. *Belle* is a French word meaning "beautiful."

The settlement was incorporated as a village in 1841 and became a city in 1848 with a population of about 3,000. Throughout the following decades, Racine became one of the largest manufacturing cities in Wisconsin. Like most lakeshore cities in the Midwest, it started as a grain shipping center and evolved into a mecca of manufactured goods to supply the markets of the growing new lands west of the Mississippi River.

During the postcard era of the 1900s, the city began to expand rapidly and, with the thousands of new people calling Racine home, there was a need for new schools, churches, and public buildings. Many of these changes are documented in postcard form. New factories were built and the added industry fueled the economy. As the city matured, the streets were being paved and streetcars and automobiles began replacing the horse and buggy. Old frame buildings were replaced by attractive and larger brick or stone buildings. With photographers capturing all these transitional stages on film, they printed them and sold them for communication or curiosity with little thought of leaving a visual history of the growth and changes of the city. These publishers did their best to manufacture sellable new cards showing the ever-changing landscapes. Many of these landmark buildings still punctuate the streets and blocks of Racine.

The city's oldest surviving industry, CNH Case-New Holland (formerly J. I. Case Company) was founded in 1842 by Jerome Increase Case when he began manufacturing a primitive ground hog threshing machine. The company is still a world leader in the manufacture of agricultural machinery.

By the Civil War, manufacturing was well-rooted in Racine with the main pattern of industry continuing to center around wagons and farm-related machinery. The term "made in Racine" became a mark of excellence known all over the world. During the late 19th century, other new and nationally important businesses were founded. The Horlick Food Company, organized by William and James Horlick in 1875, manufactured a food product for infants and invalids. In 1883, William discovered and patented the world's first powdered milk food, which he called malted milk. Samuel C. Johnson began his business in 1886 with the manufacture of parquet flooring. Needing a finish that would hold up to the harsh soaps of the day, the company began experimenting with wax. This need later led them to South America for carnauba wax. Johnson's Wax continued to grow and expand its product lines and today the firm is a global leader in the manufacture of household products.

The world-renowned Johnson office buildings were the creation of architect Frank Lloyd Wright. The administration building, completed in 1939, is constructed of red brick and stone and has 43 miles of glass but no windows. Wright said, "The building was tailor made for the Johnson company." Wright also called the building an architectural interpretation of modern business at its best design, to be as inspiring a place to work in as any cathedral ever was to worship in. One of the seven art wonders of America is the brick and glass tower research center also designed by Wright and added to the complex in 1950.

Western Printing Company started out as a small, storefront printing shop in 1907 and grew to be a leader in the manufacturing of children's books. The company revolutionized the children's book market creating lines of wholesome reading for millions of young minds. Its Golden Books became a part of American life. Also, beginning in 1933, it produced story material for decades based on the characters of Walt Disney productions. The millions of wonderful literary artifacts produced by Western Printing Company are a reminder of the Racine's contributions to American literature.

After the turn of the 20th century, automobiles began to set the pace of American industry and American life and Racine was soon marketing a few models of its own, including Case and Mitchell automobiles. Racine's involvement in the evolution of the American automobile, however, had begun much earlier. In 1873, Racine became the birthplace of an early self-propelled car, a steamer built by the Reverend James W. Carhart of Racine. He designed and operated the first light self-propelled highway vehicle in the United States and probably one of the first in the world. He named it Spark. Powered by a two-cylinder steam engine, it was steered by a lever and had a top speed of five miles per hour.

At the 1908 International Automobile Exposition held in Paris, France, Carhart was addressed as the "Father of Automobiles" and received a cash award and a certificate of honor for his invention. Racine became a magnet for inventive people like Carhart. Their inventions fueled the manufacturing growth in the city and in recent years Racine has been hailed as "Invention City."

Racine was also the birthplace of high-speed electric motors used in products like the blender, drink mixers, and sewing machines and became known as the "Factional Electric Motor Capital of the World."

Like many other cities of the early 20th century, Racine was a melting pot of ethnic groups. However, Racine's population boasted a one-third Danish descent. That fact and the famous kringle pastry, which is shipped far and wide, also gave Racine nicknames like "Kringleville." The West Racine area, known as Little Denmark, was the Danish stronghold. But Racine had people of many other cultural backgrounds. Together this ethnic and manufacturing diversity has put Racine on the world map.

Racine is easy to find on any map. It is sandwiched between two major cities, Chicago and Milwaukee. Everyone knows that the best part of any sandwich is the unforgettable filling in the middle.

One

Harbor Scenes

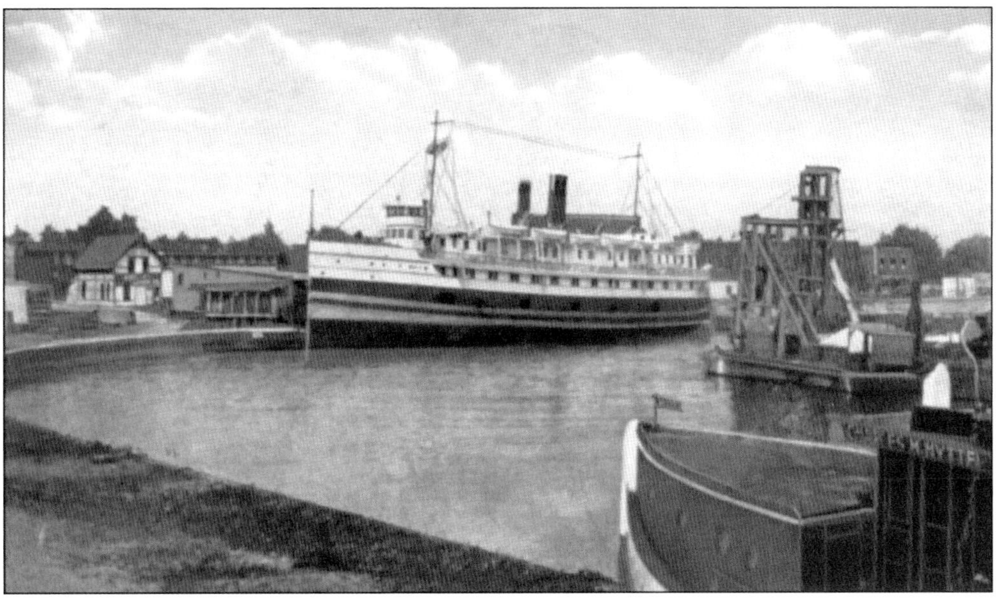

Inner Harbor Scene. Large steamships docking along the Root River near the Main Street Bridge were daily occurrences as they picked up passengers and freight. The Racine harbor was the lifeblood of the city throughout its early history. The little village celebrated a major event on July 16, 1844, when the steamship *Chesapeake* tied up at the new Racine docks. According to an early history, "This was the first steamer that had ever entered any artificial harbor in Wisconsin." By the 1860s, railroads and, after 1900, motorized trucking took their toll on the steamship lines. By 1916, the only bulky freight that came to Racine by water was coal. Passenger ships continued for about a decade longer. The small frame building with the gable roof located just left of the docked steamship was the old Coast Guard life saving station. The structure was moved to the corner of Dodge and North Wisconsin Streets when the new Coast Guard building was constructed about 1903. The historic building was razed in 1967.

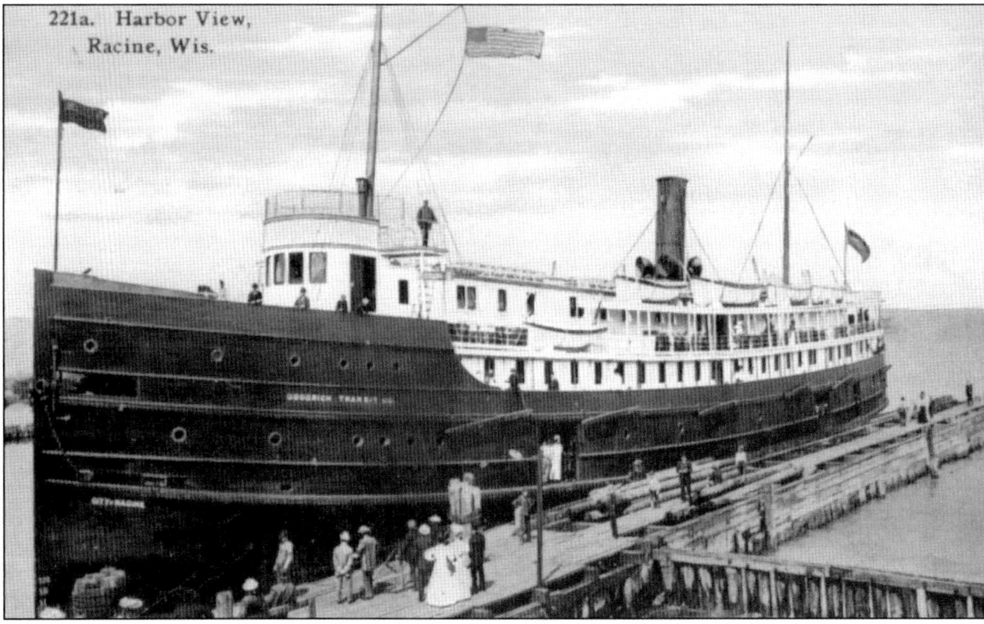

DOCKED AT SOUTH PIER. One of the Goodrich Transportation Company's fleet, the S.S. *City of Racine*, is shown docked at Racine's south pier. The S.S. *City of Racine* was a propeller-driven steamer built in Manitowoc, by H. B. and G. B. Burger in 1888 and 1889. It was launched in April 1889 with a tonnage of 1,041.02. The ship was totally rebuilt in 1909 and was renamed S.S. *Arizona*, which last operated as a passenger steamer in 1926.

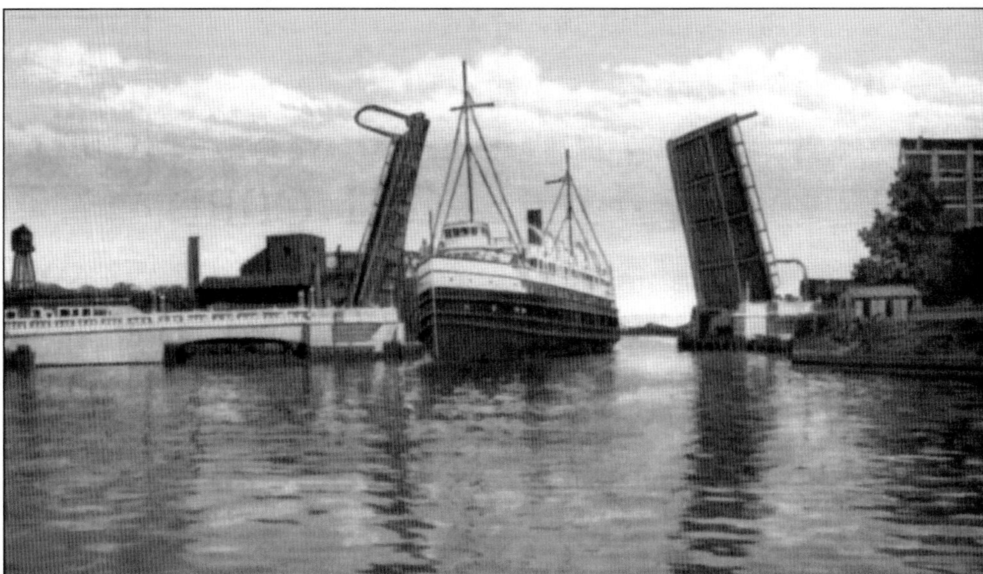

STEAMER ENTERING INNER HARBOR. Scene looking east as a Goodrich Transportation Company ship passes through the Main Street Bascule drawbridge. The Goodrich lines ran regular schedules between Milwaukee and Chicago and would stop in Racine to pick up passengers and freight. Beginning around 1840, Racine was well on the way to being a leading Lake Michigan port. The inner harbor and Root River shoreline on any given day would be jammed with boats and ships of all sizes.

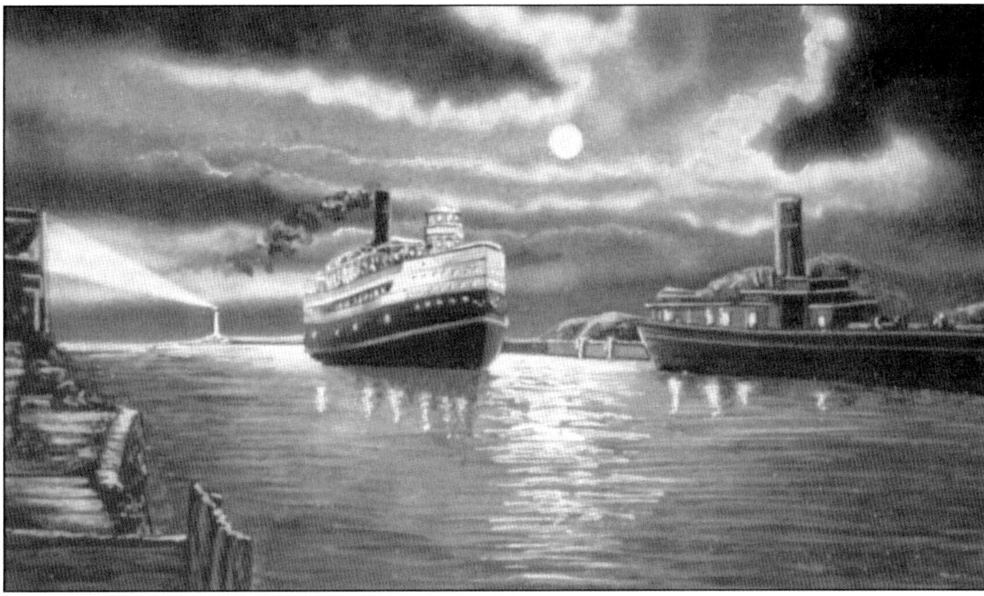

HARBOR SCENE AT NIGHT. In the early 1900s, night photography was very hard to bring about. Postcard photographers and publishers would take their daylight views and have them colored during the printing process to create night scenes. In many night photographs there would be a day scene of the same view. This card shows a night view of a Goodrich steamship entering Racine harbor. The north and south piers each had navigation lights. Access into the docking area was almost a straight line.

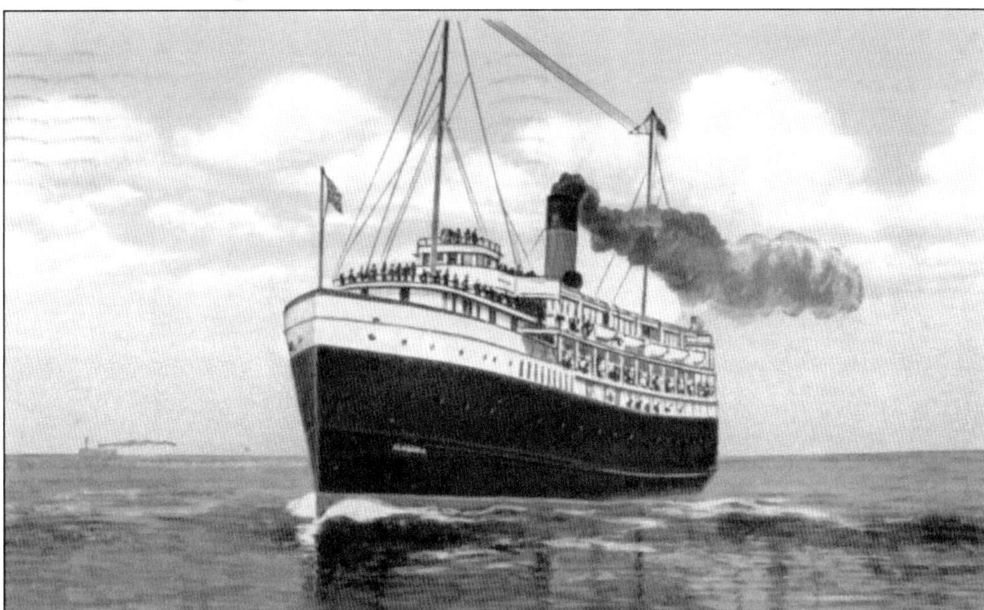

EXCURSION STEAMER S.S. *ALABAMA*. The majestic steamships of the Goodrich Transportation Company were known for their distinctive red smoke stacks. These ships looked like the RMS *Titanic* as they moved into the small, narrow channel of the Root River making their way to the dock. For decades, it was very common for Racine residents to spend day excursions on Lake Michigan enjoying the sites and shorelines along the Chicago and Milwaukee route.

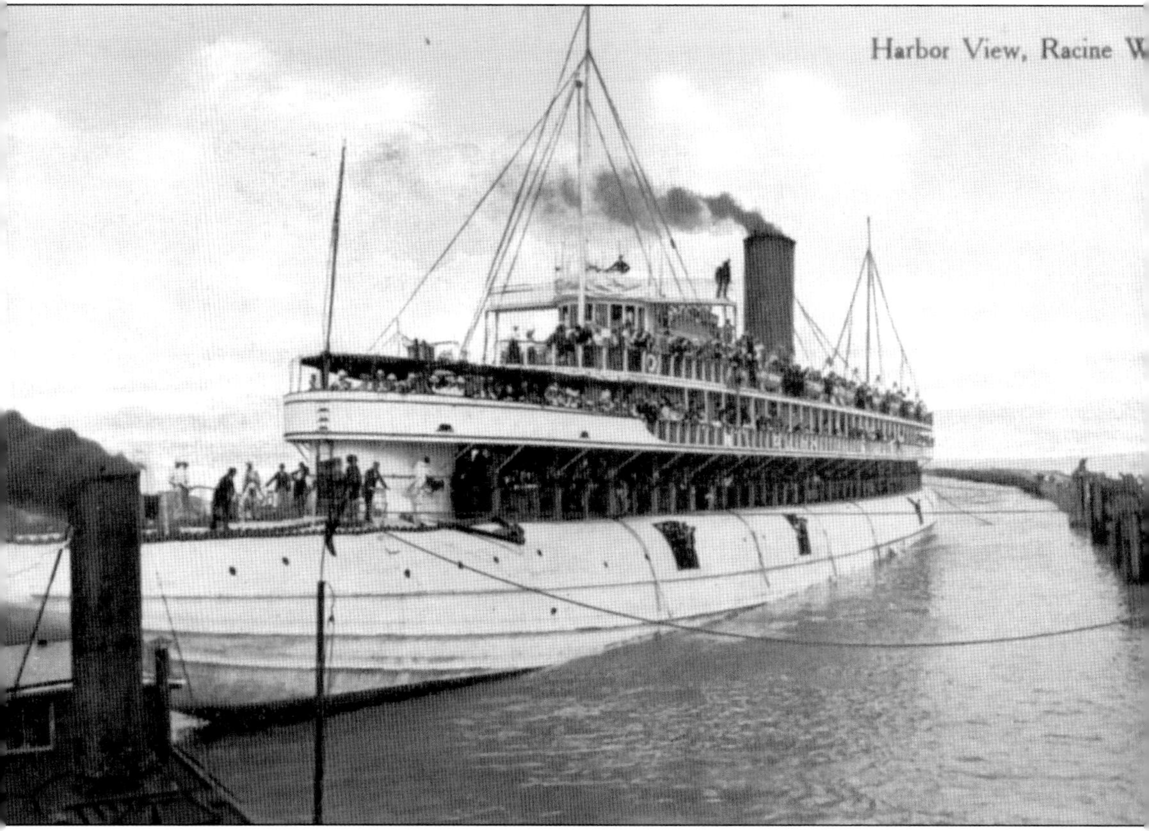

Steamer Docking in Racine. The whaleback steamship S.S. *Christopher Columbus* is shown docking along the south pier east of the Main Street Bridge. The steel whaleback was a single-screw steamer built in 1892 and 1893 as a passenger ship for the Colombian Exposition that was held in Chicago. The ship was 362 feet in length and was driven by an 18-foot propeller that developed an amazingly fast cruising speed of 20 miles per hour. At the close of the exposition, the steamer became an excursion ship on the Chicago-Milwaukee route that also stopped in Racine. There were only 43 whaleback ships ever built and only the S.S. *Christopher Columbus* was a passenger ship. It was last operated in 1932 and was cut up for scrap in 1937.

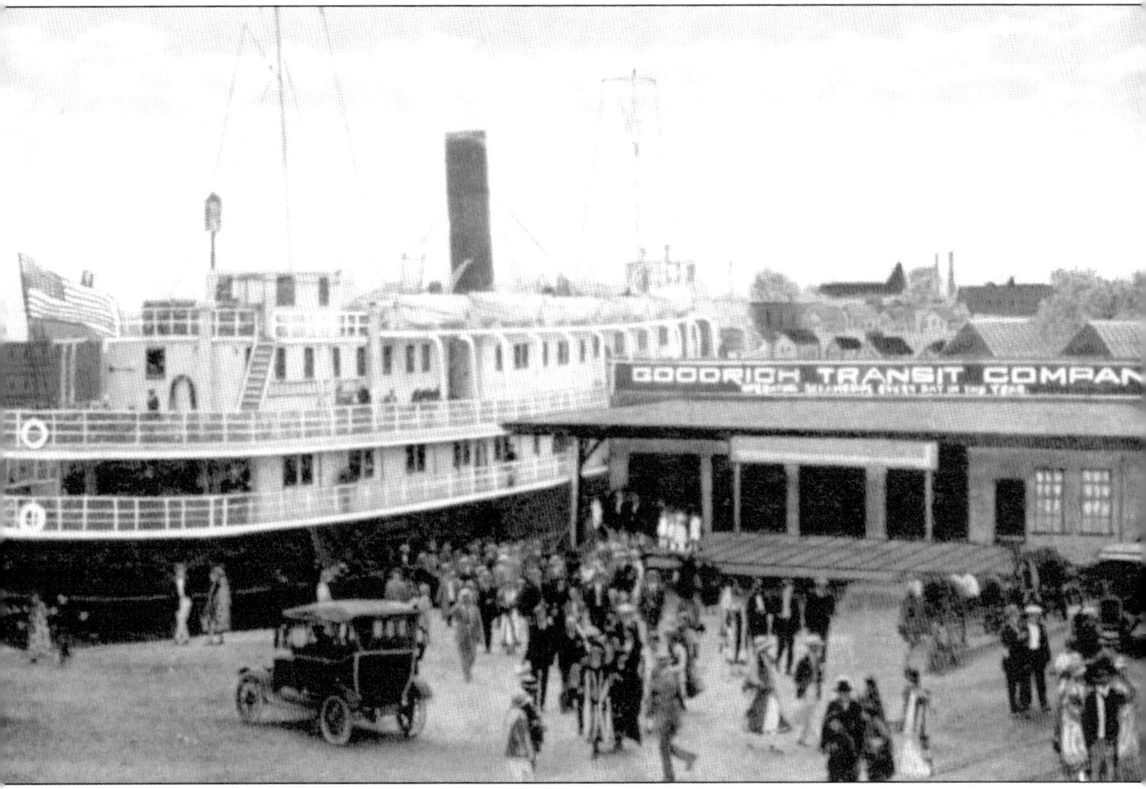

GOODRICH BOAT DOCK. This view shows a lot of activity at the Goodrich Transit Company docks located on the north side of the Root River just west of the Main Street Bridge about 1920. In the 1950s, this area was occasionally used by docked naval ships and residents were invited aboard on ship tours. The area was also used as a shipping dock for large limestone boulders being shipped out of Racine from the huge limestone quarry located at Three Mile Road and Douglas Avenue. The Goodrich ships and buildings have disappeared and the naval ships rarely dock in Racine any more, but the stone quarry is still in operation at its same location.

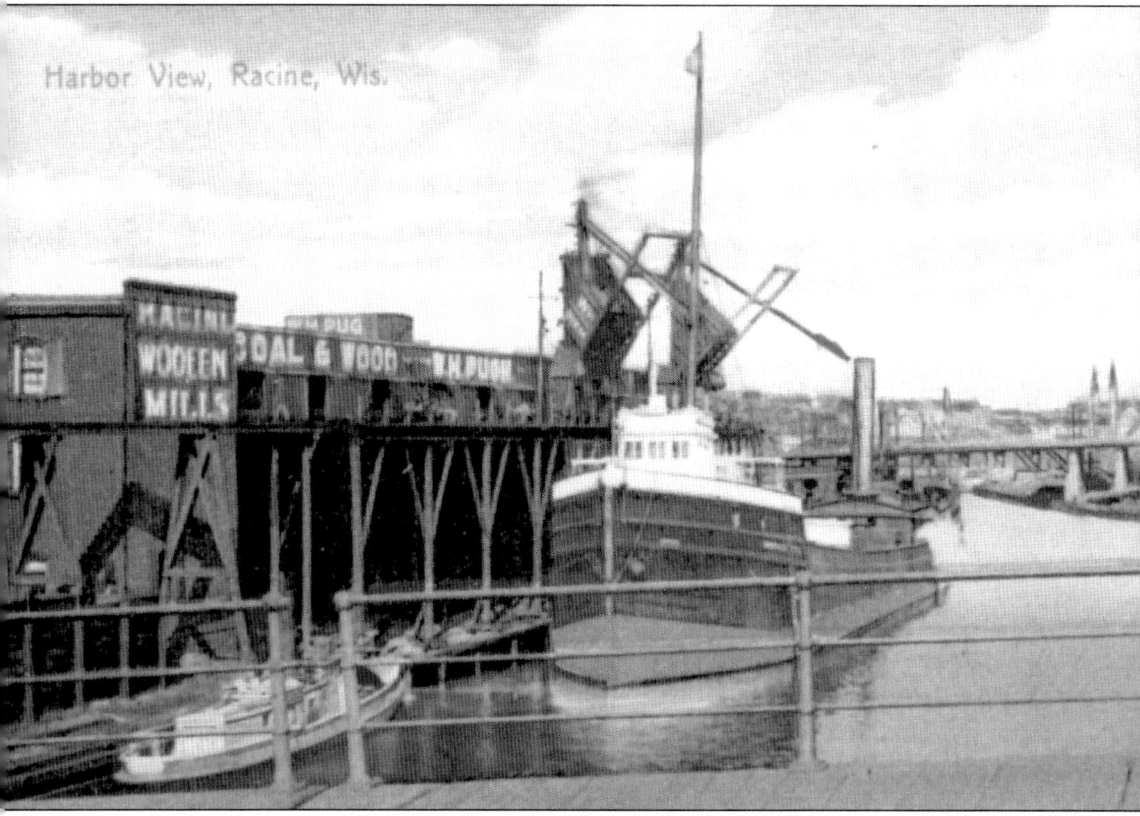

RIVER VIEW FROM FOURTH STREET BRIDGE. This rare double view is looking north from the Fourth Street Bridge toward State Street about 1908. The large lake coal hauler is docked at one of the William H. Pugh Coal Company's storage sheds on the west side of the Root River. These large coal ships could not navigate a turn and the river was too shallow beyond the Fourth Street Bridge, so most of Racine's coal yards were located close to the mouth of the Root River. To the right is a small factory building that housed the Racine Economy Spring

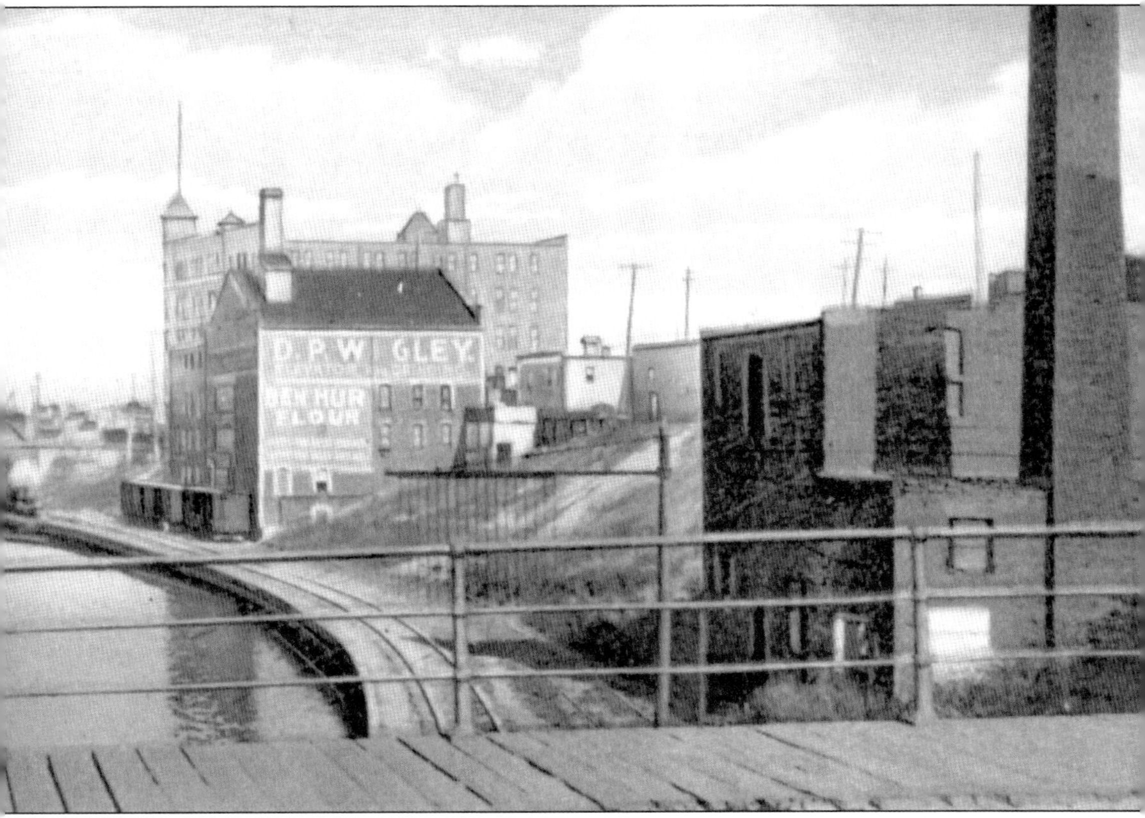

Company at the time, followed by the D. P. Wigley feed mill and Dr. Shoop's Family Medicine Company's building (back right). The Chicago, Milwaukee and St. Paul Railroad tracks ran along the riverbank. It was very common to see dozens of flat cars loaded with J. I. Case Company tractors and threshing machines ready to be shipped out. When the railroad abandoned this section of track, the rails and track bed were replaced by a paved service road. Currently this is a docking area for large pleasure boats.

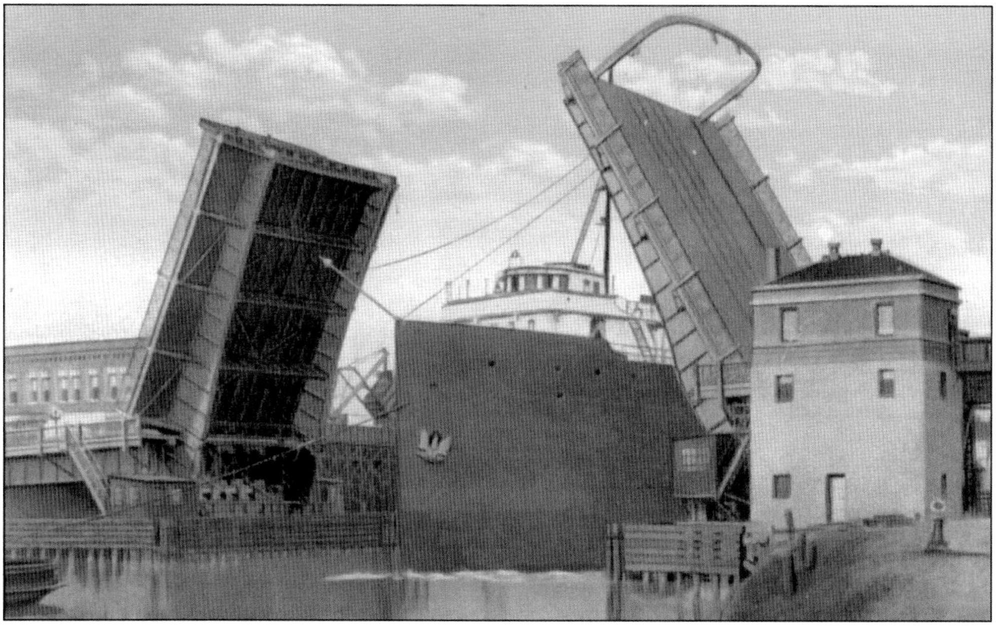

STATE STREET BRIDGE. A gigantic coal ship is squeezing its way through the relatively new State Street Bridge around 1922. Constructed in 1921 and 1922 at a cost of $375,000, this bascule double leaf bridge replaced the outdated 1885 steel swing bridge. The span was 60 feet wide, which allowed four lanes of traffic with the center lanes designed for streetcar use. The bridge was replaced in 1988 with a single leaf design.

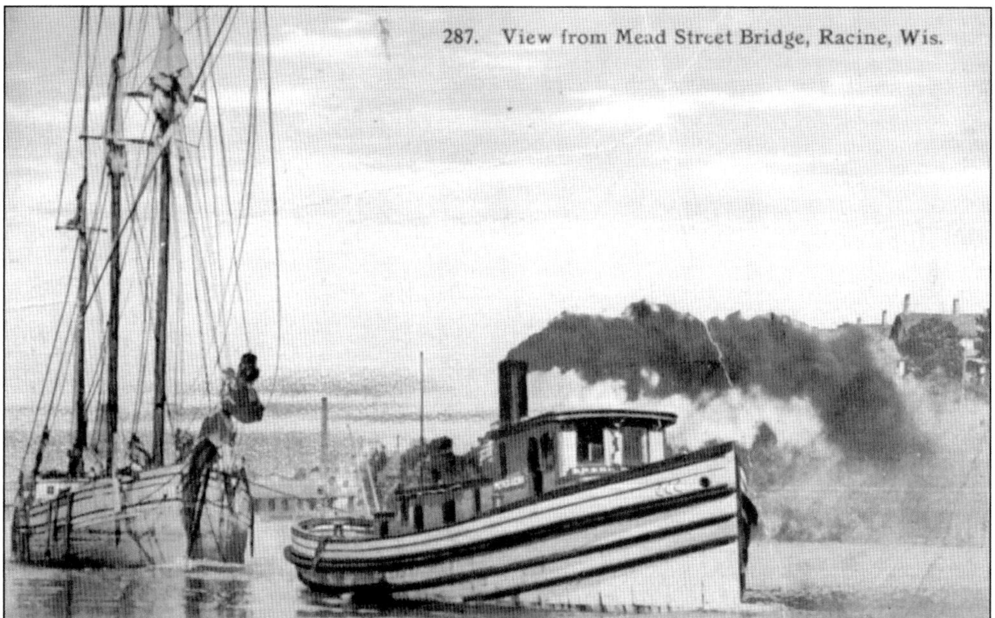

VIEW FROM MEAD STREET BRIDGE. Tugboats towing sailing ships out to open water were a common sight for many decades along the Root River. At times, the river shoreline would be choked with small ships docked two or three abreast. This view is from the Mead Street (now Marquette Street) Bridge around 1908.

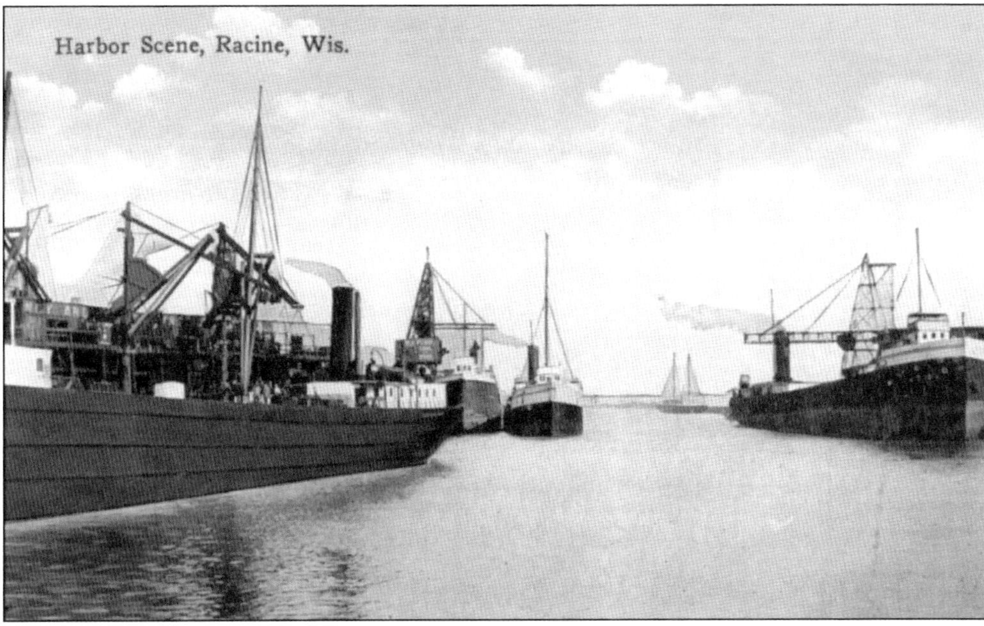

HARBOR SCENE. This view is looking east about 1913 from the Main Street Bridge when large coal vessels, docked at the coal yards, were a regular sight. Because Racine was a major manufacturing center, there was always a large demand for coal. The Root River shoreline near the mouth of the river was lined with coal yards with hefty stockpiles year round. By the 1950s, the coal yards began to disappear as fuel oil and natural gas became the common energy sources.

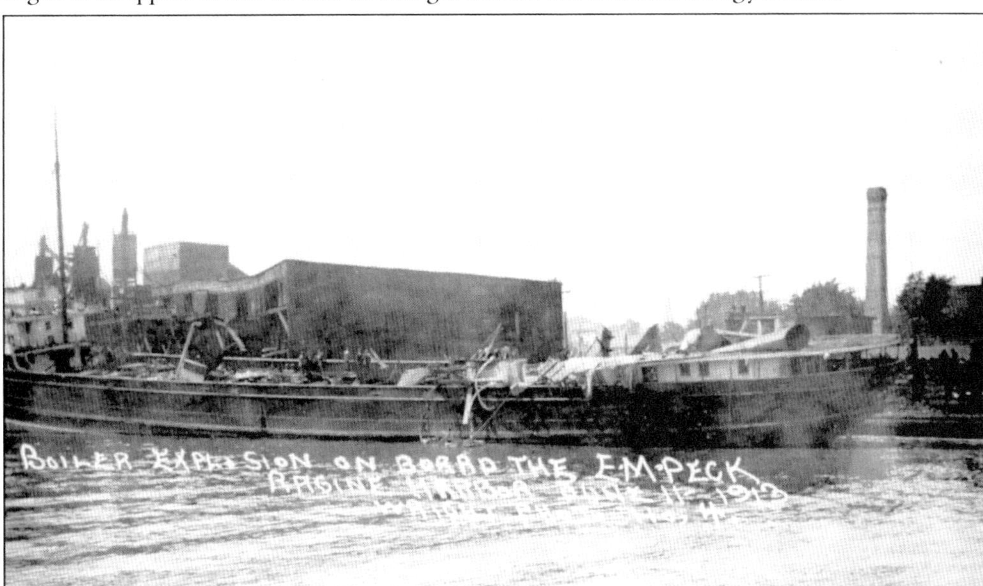

BOILER EXPLOSION ON BOARD S.S. *E. M. PECK*. An awful maritime accident occurred on Wednesday, June 11, 1913, when the boiler of the steamship S.S. *E. M. Peck* exploded a few hundred feet east of the Main Street Bridge. The ship was delivering a load of coal to the William H. Pugh Coal Company. Six men were killed at the scene and one died later at the hospital. The boiler was thrown through the Bauman and Murphy coal shed over 200 feet away. Other pieces were found scattered blocks away from the scene.

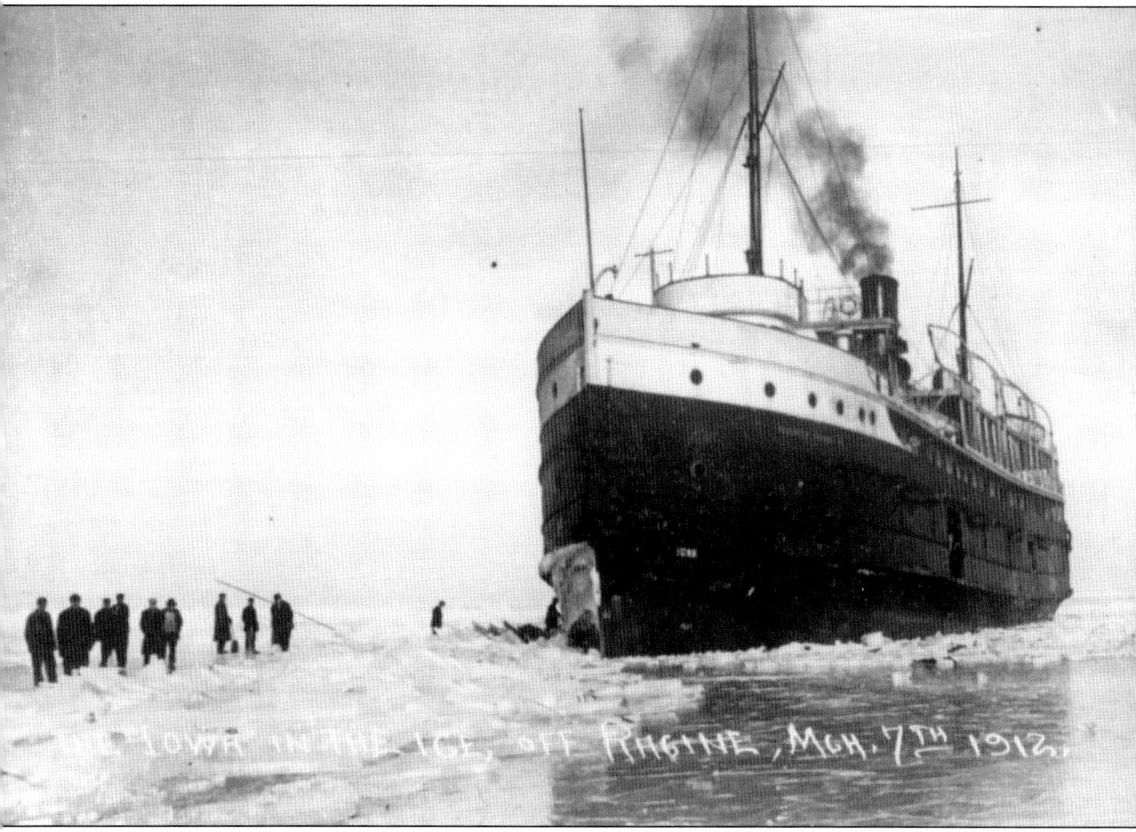

S.S. *IOWA* IN ICE. Throughout marine history, ships on the Great Lakes would occasionally become icebound. The weather on March 7, 1912, was very harsh and it was said that Lake Michigan had completely frozen over. This view documents the Goodrich ship S.S. *Iowa* stuck in the ice near Racine. On another occasion, the ship was beached south of Racine. The S.S. *Iowa*'s streak of bad luck ended in 1915 when the ship attempted to make its way through some heavy ice blocking the Chicago harbor. There was a strong southeast wind moving the ice that caught the steamer and crushed it. A total loss, the steamer sank, but all of the crew were saved by walking ashore over the ice.

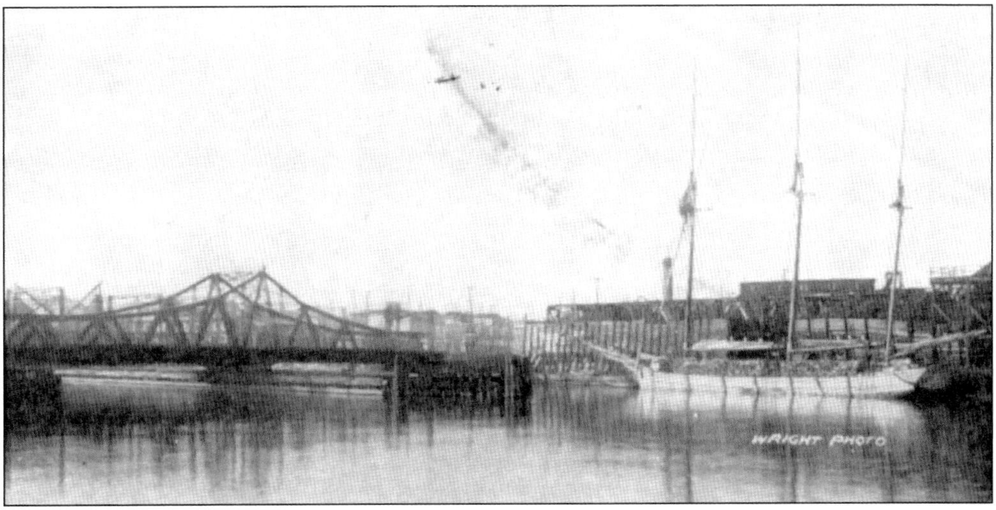

HARBOR NEAR MAIN STREET BRIDGE. When this view was taken about 1911, sailing ships still mastered the Great Lakes. This ship was docked on the north side of the river just east of the Main Street Bridge. The total number of vessels that had been registered in Racine was more than 300. During the summer of 1914, the last active Racine sailing ship, the *J.B. Newland*, was sold by her owner, Capt. C. Nalied, and that chapter of Racine's marine history came to a close.

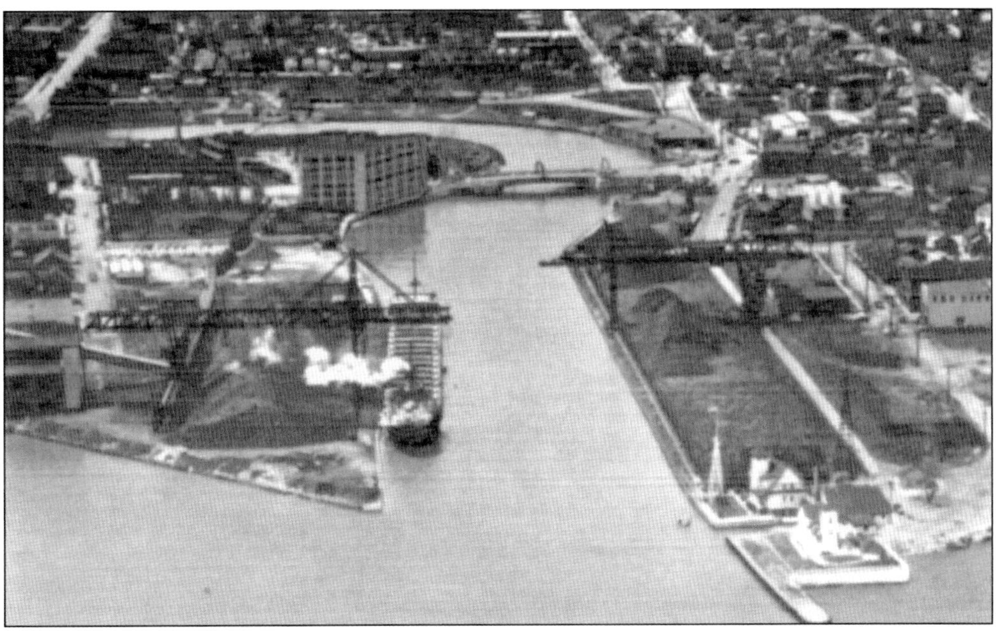

MOUTH OF ROOT RIVER. This aerial view shows the mouth of the Root River and docks around 1940. The coal crane to the right belonged to the William H. Pugh Coal Company. Next to the Main Street Bridge is the Terminal building. It has been razed and a new building now sits on the site. The entire south side of the Root River has been redeveloped into Gaslight Pointe. The 1866 harbor lighthouse and the old Racine Coast Guard station buildings seen at bottom right are now privately owned.

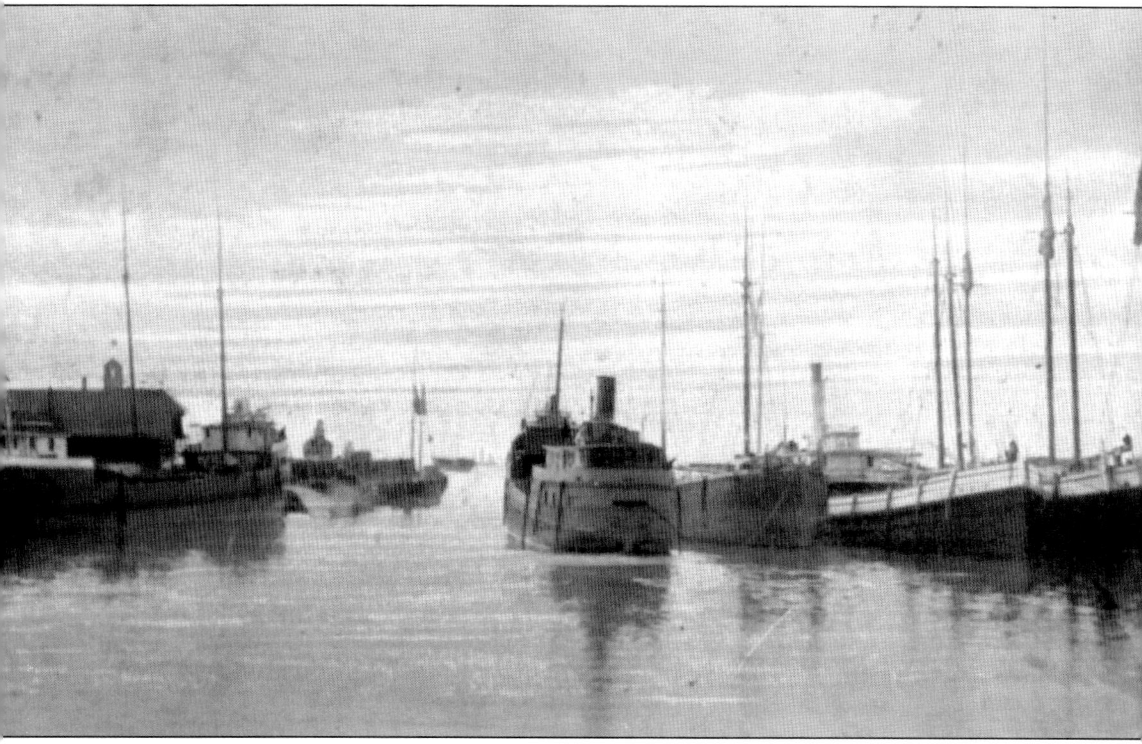

HARBOR TRAFFIC JAM. This view looks east from the Main Street Bridge about 1905. It shows the Root River's mouth clogged with small lake vessels. Harbor space has always been limited and captains had to be creative at times. Because the Root River became shallow beyond the Marquette Street Bridge, few ships ever ventured that far upriver. There were a number of boathouses on the banks of the river as far as Herrick Avenue (now Memorial Drive) with most clustered near the Sixth Street Bridge. These structures mainly housed small pleasure craft. Fishing tugs were docked between the State Street and Fourth Street bridges during the 1950s. Large spools of fishing nets could be seen scattered among the fishermen's shanties just south of State Street for decades.

Two

STREETSCAPES

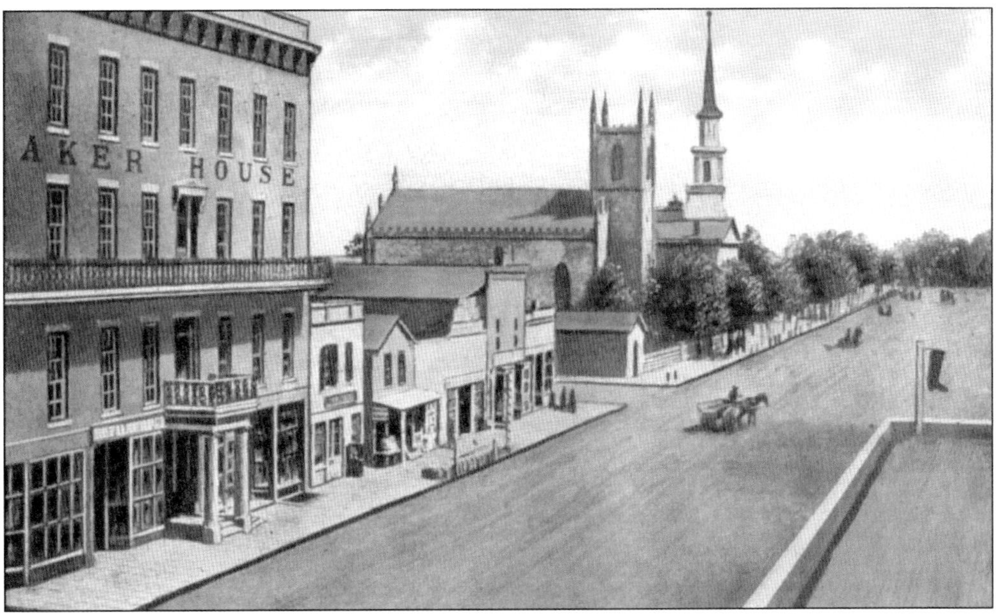

EARLY MAIN STREET. This photograph, one of the earliest views of Main Street, looks south toward the east side of Hay Market Square (now Monument Square). Taken around 1860, it was later reproduced as a postcard to illustrate the changes in downtown Racine. The Baker House hotel was located in the middle of the 400 block. The Episcopal Church with the square tower and the Church of the Good Shepherd with the tall steeple both faced the square. The Episcopal church burned down in 1866, but a replacement, built at Seventh and Main Streets, is still in use today. The Church of the Good Shepherd was razed in 1892 and replaced with the first Hotel Racine.

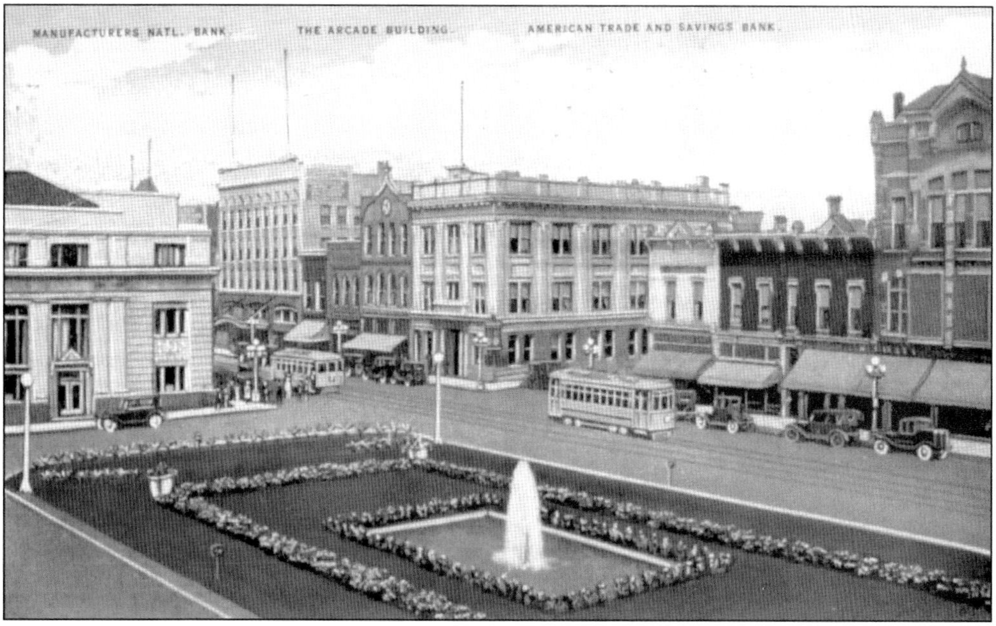

MAIN STREET AND THE SQUARE. This view looks northeast at Fifth and Main Streets and the north end of Monument Square around 1915. This postcard highlights the three major buildings in the view—Manufacturers National Bank, Arcade Building, and American Trade and Savings Bank. Today the Arcade Building facade has been totally restored and the old American Trade and Savings Bank building has recently been remodeled and is now the Racine Art Museum (RAM).

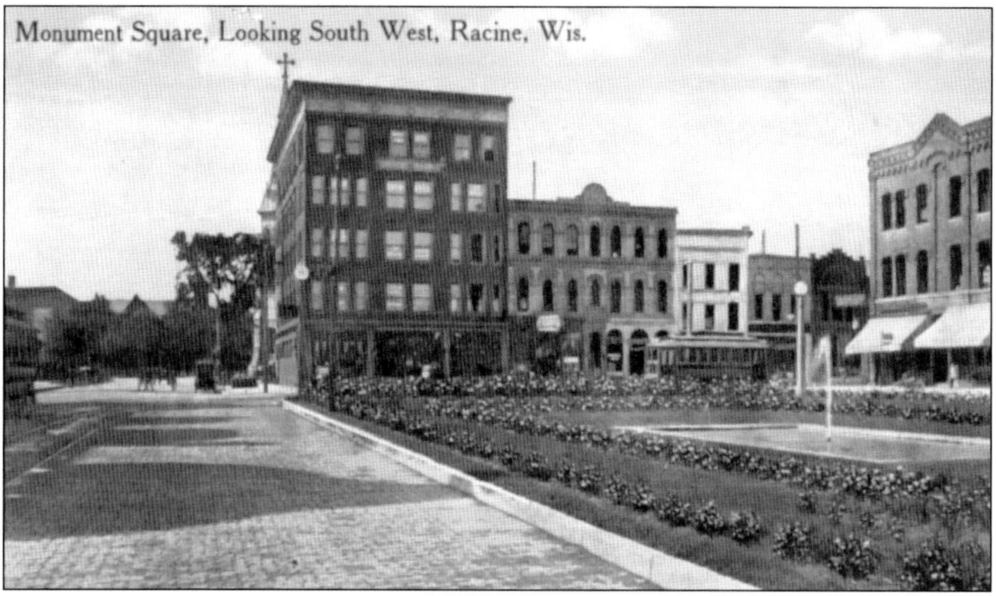

MONUMENT SQUARE LOOKING SOUTH. This view, taken about 1910, looks down a brick-paved Main Street toward Sixth Street and the south end of Monument Square soon after the square was landscaped. The city hired Jens Jensen, a well-known landscape architect, to oversee the design and plantings. The five-story building on the corner, designed by C. A. Dichaut, was built about 1899 as the Robinson Building and has been standing with few changes for more than a century.

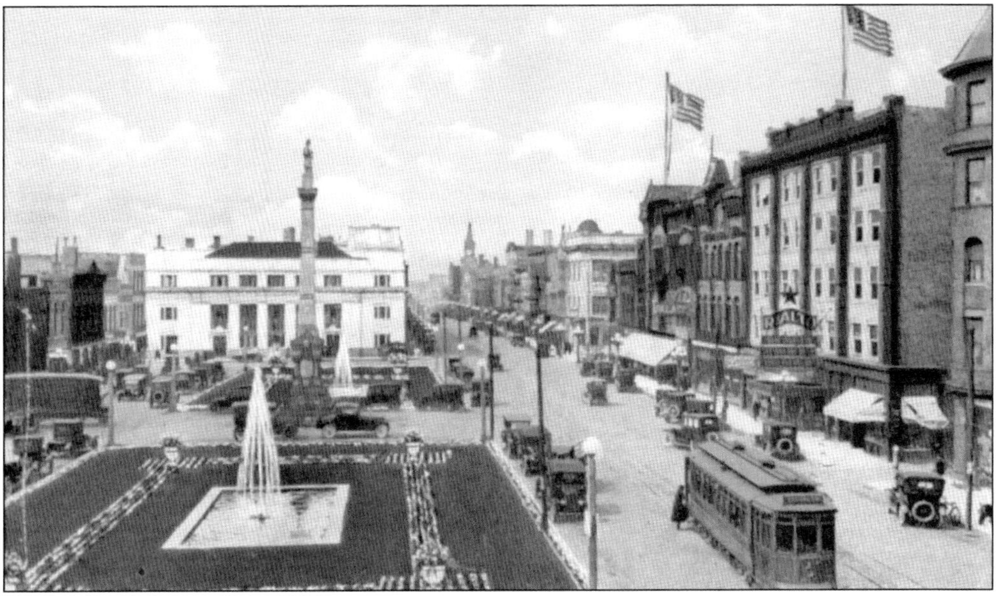

Monument Square Looking North. Taken between 1915 and 1920, this view looks across Monument Square along the east side of Main Street from the Robinson Building. The sights include the marquee of one of Racine's larger theaters, the Rialto. The theater entrance and lobby were located in the Baker Block with the auditorium built at the rear. During its early years, it was an active show house with stage shows and vaudeville. Many famous entertainers appeared live on stage as their shows traveled through the Midwest.

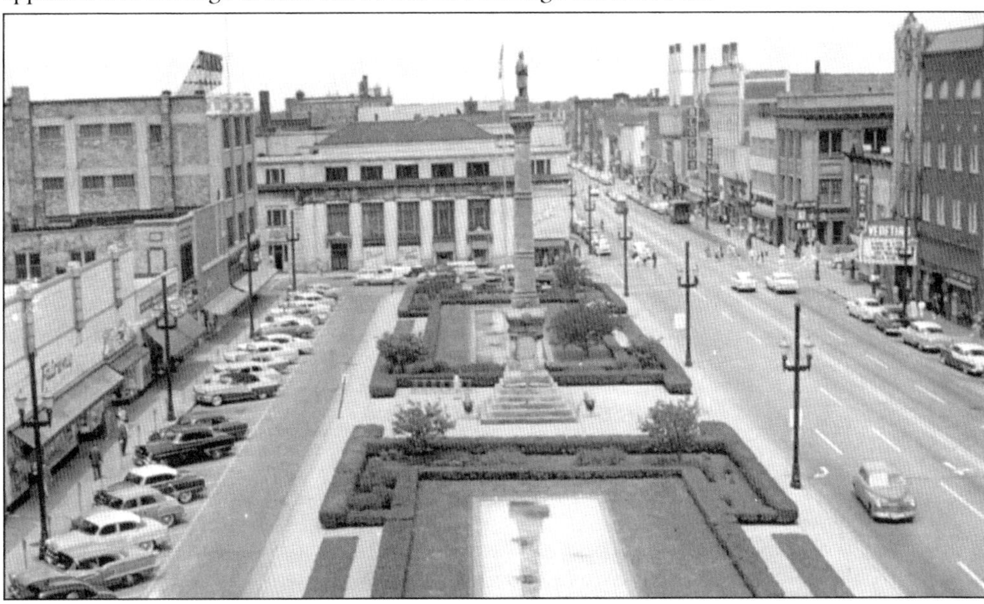

Bird's-Eye View of Monument Square. Racine's public square became Monument Square on July 4, 1884, when the Civil War soldier memorial was dedicated. During the second decade of the 20th century, the square was totally landscaped and beautified. This view shows the well-groomed square as it looked in the 1960s. To the right is the Venetian Theatre. To the left was a Fairway Store, which later became Wolf Brothers Clothing. Just north, the building with the roof sign and flagpole was Zahn's Department Store.

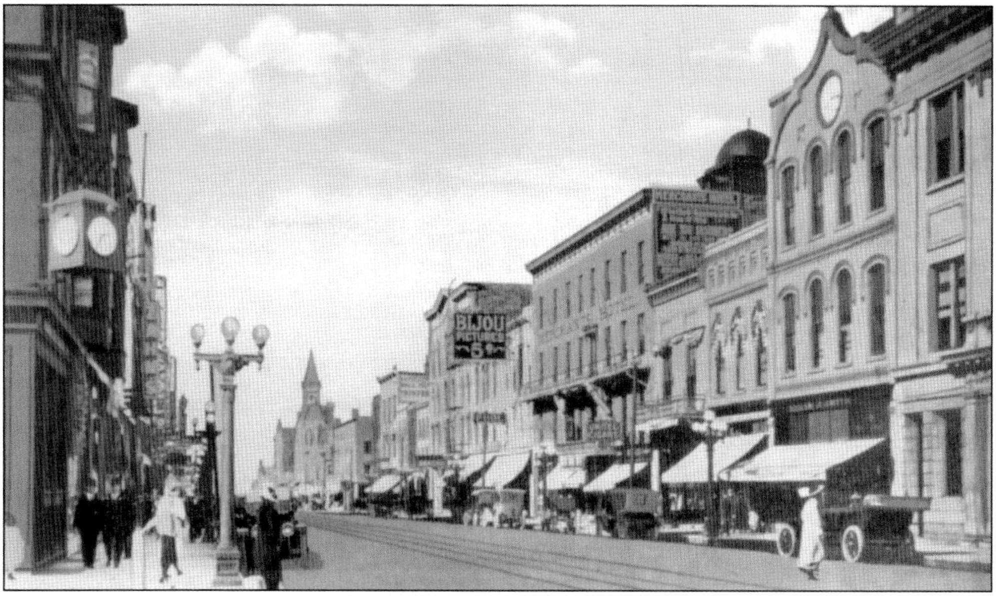

MAIN STREET FROM FIFTH STREET, *c.* 1912. This popular shopping area was lined with stores, banks, a hotel, theaters, and everything one would normally see on a Main Street in any large city in the United States. To the people of Racine, these stores were special because they were in a place they called home. Full page advertisements in the *Racine Daily Times* newspaper asked residents to follow the "Golden Rule of Trade" and spend their money in their hometown of Racine.

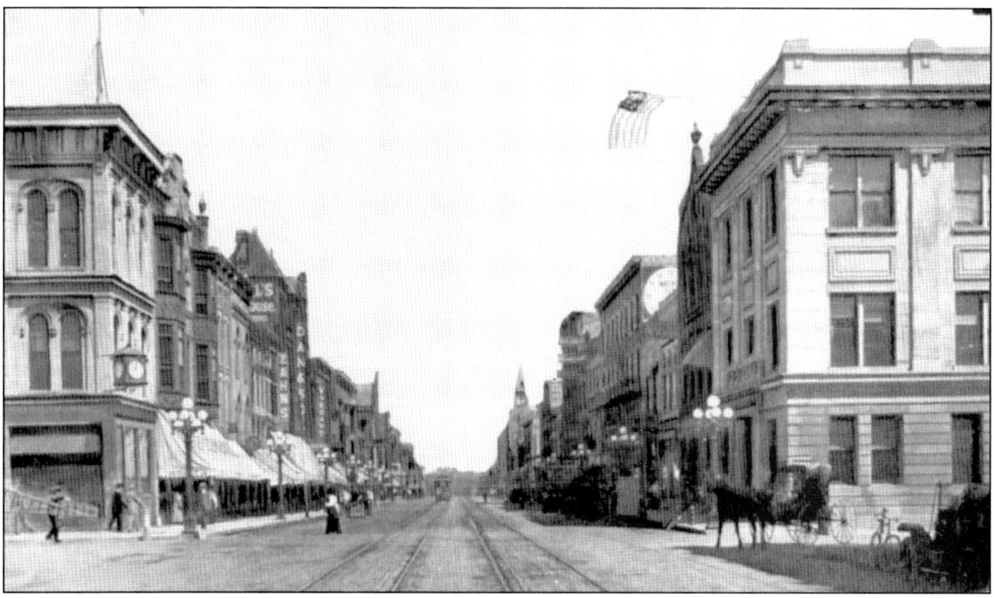

MAIN STREET LOOKING NORTH. This view, taken from the intersection of Fifth and Main Streets about 1908, shows the Commercial Savings Bank on the east side of the street. Directly across the street was Manufacturers National Bank (front left) with the clock. Continuing down the west side of the street are two of Racine's most popular stores of the period—Zahn's Dry Goods Store at 428 Main Street and Dan and Sol's Clothing Store at 424–426 Main Street. Zahn's Dry Goods Store later moved to 500 Monument Square where it stayed until it closed in 1981.

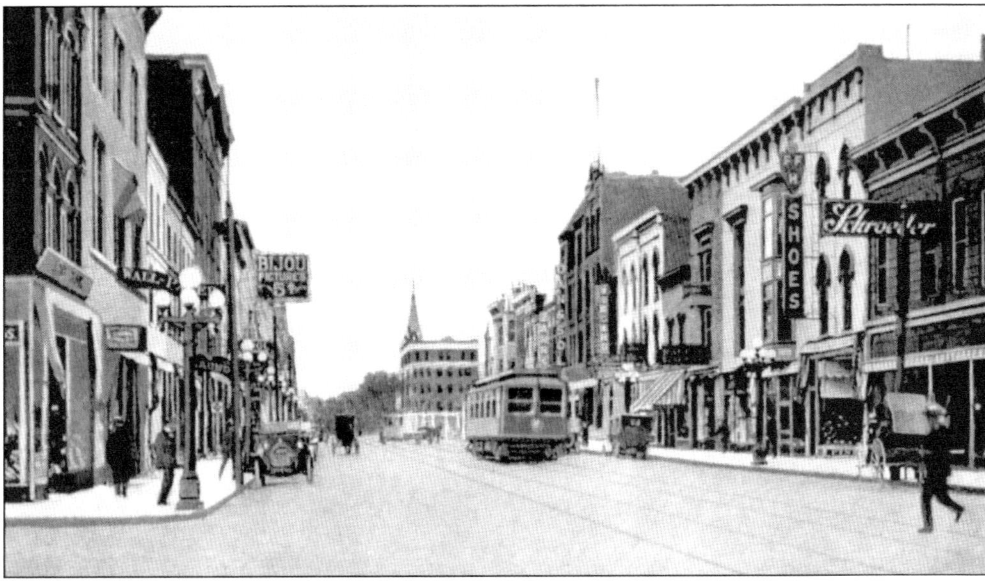

MAIN STREET FROM FOURTH LOOKING SOUTH. This view was taken about 1908 from Fourth and Main Streets looking south. On the west (right) side of the street was Schroeder Dry Good Store at 402–404 Main Street. Recently the entire facade was restored and the building now houses a frame shop. Down the block is Dan and Sol's Clothing Store, which was known for its elegant, pricey clothing. On the east side of the street was the Bijou Theatre with its sign advertising picture shows for 5¢.

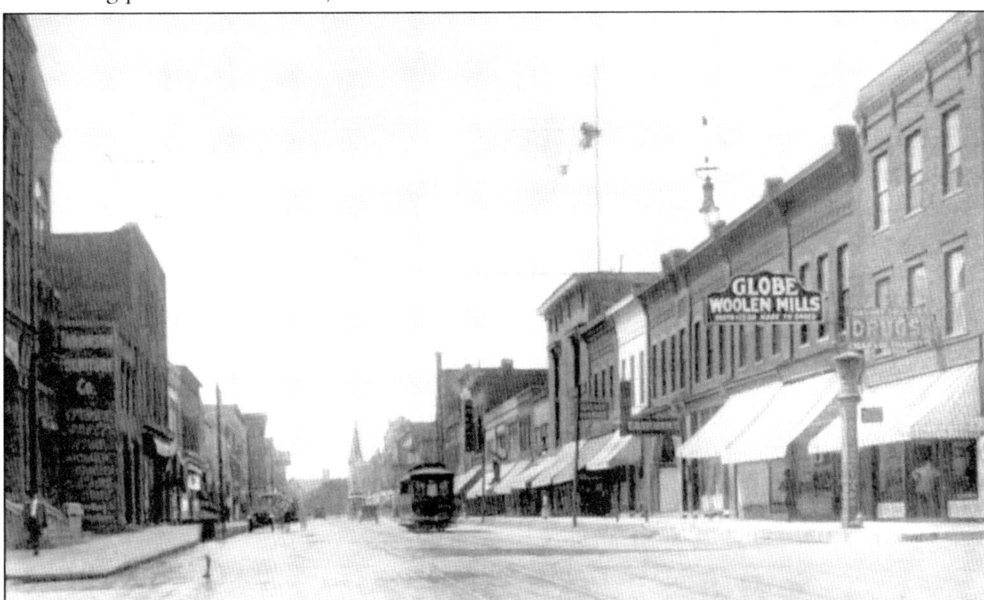

MAIN STREET FROM THIRD LOOKING SOUTH. This view looks south along the west side of Main Street from the corner of Third Street about 1907. Pokorny Drug Store was located at 300 Main Street with the pestle and mortar advertising post out front. Years later, the store was moved to 340 Main Street at the opposite end of the block. There it became one of the showplace drugstores in town. It sported a popular soda fountain, high back wooden booths, and beautiful tile work.

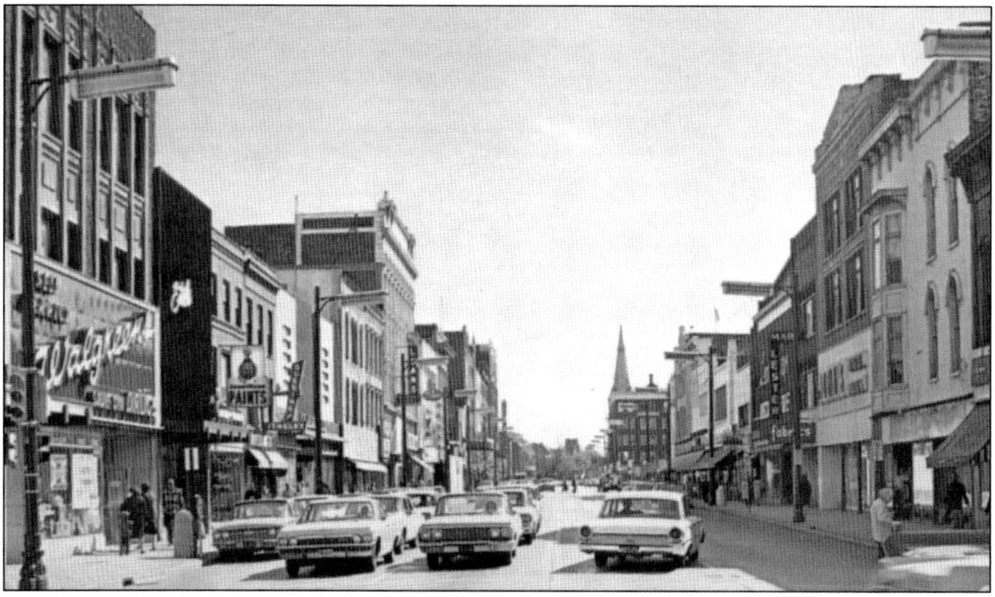

MAIN STREET IN THE 1960S. By the 1960s, new shopping centers were being built south and west of Racine. Large shopping centers such as Elmwood Plaza and Turnstyle were drawing customers out of the downtown area. After decades of decline, many of the buildings were razed or stood empty and were in dire need of repairs. Currently, entrepreneurs have restored many of the facades and opened small shops, and downtown Racine still survives with its old world charm.

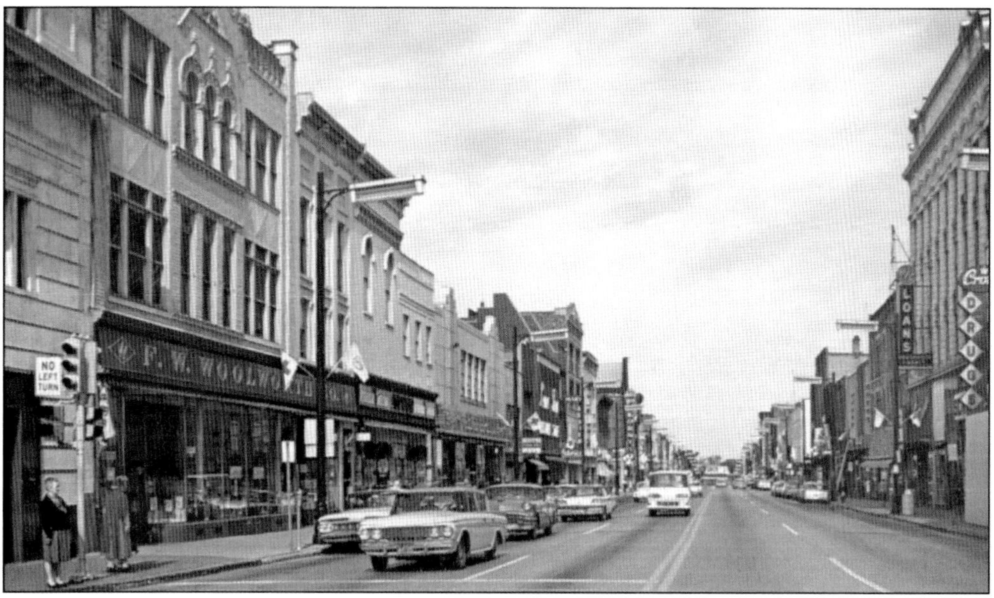

MAIN STREET, 1960S. Walking down Main Street today, many of the original storefronts are still seen. Like most larger cities in the nation, Racine had an F. W. Woolworth store. This scene shows what could be called dime store row—Woolworth's at 436–438 Main Street, S. S. Kresge at 430–432 Main Street, and Neisner Brothers at 424 Main Street. But like the Kenosha-built Rambler automobile shown in the foreground, many of Racine's old stores are now just part of history.

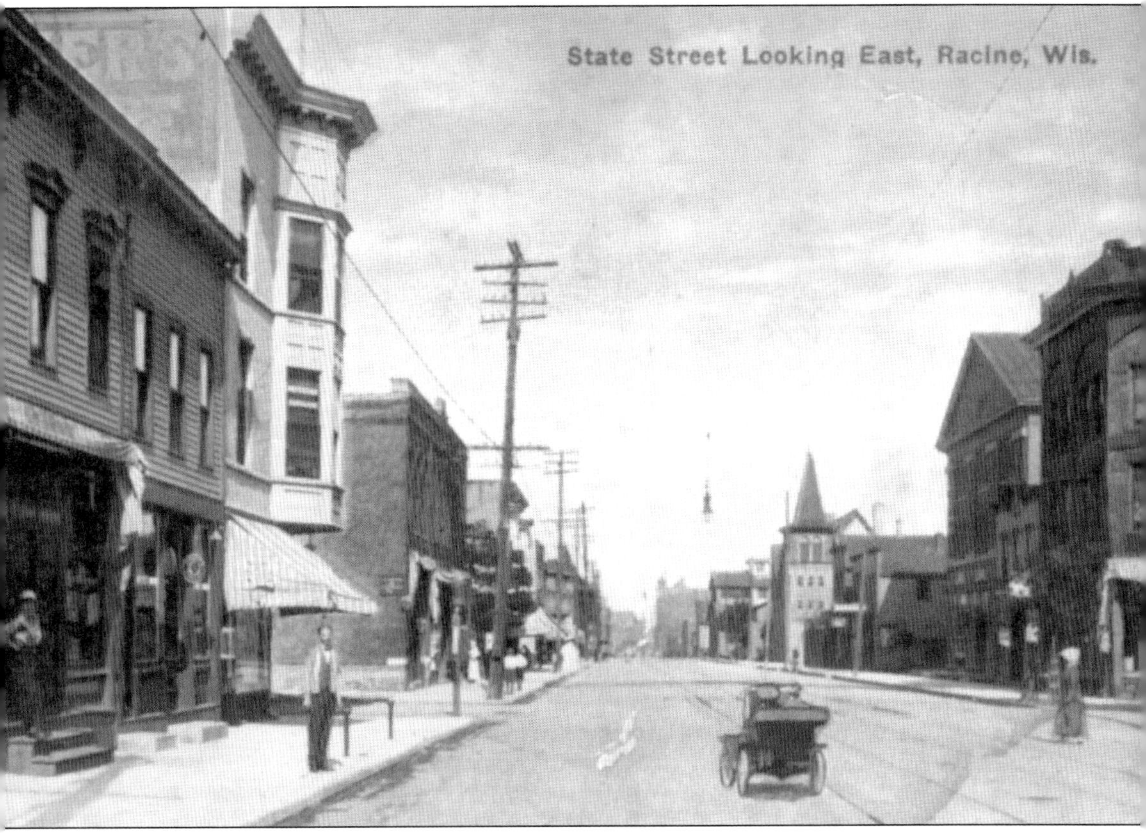

LOOKING EAST FROM STATE AND MARQUETTE. One of Racine's small secondary business sections was located along State Street, a north side artery west of downtown. Originally the area was known as Sagetown, named after the pioneer family that settled there. Around the 1890s, the district became a stronghold for residents of Danish descent and many of the stores offered clerks who also spoke Danish. This view, taken about 1910, looks east from Milwaukee Avenue (now Martin Luther King Drive) and shows State Street crossing Marquette Street. The three-story building with the lowered awning at the left was Dr. Fancher's drugstore, which was built in 1909. It was razed with other buildings on the small block for a park with a statue honoring Dr. Martin Luther King Jr. West of the drugstore was a small tavern. Because patrons would spit their tobacco juice on the walkways, the area was nicknamed "Slippery Corners." To the right front is Hotel Mohr. It was razed when the intersection was widened. Dania Hall is next to where Hotel Mohr was. Bethesda Evangelical Lutheran Church is on the next block.

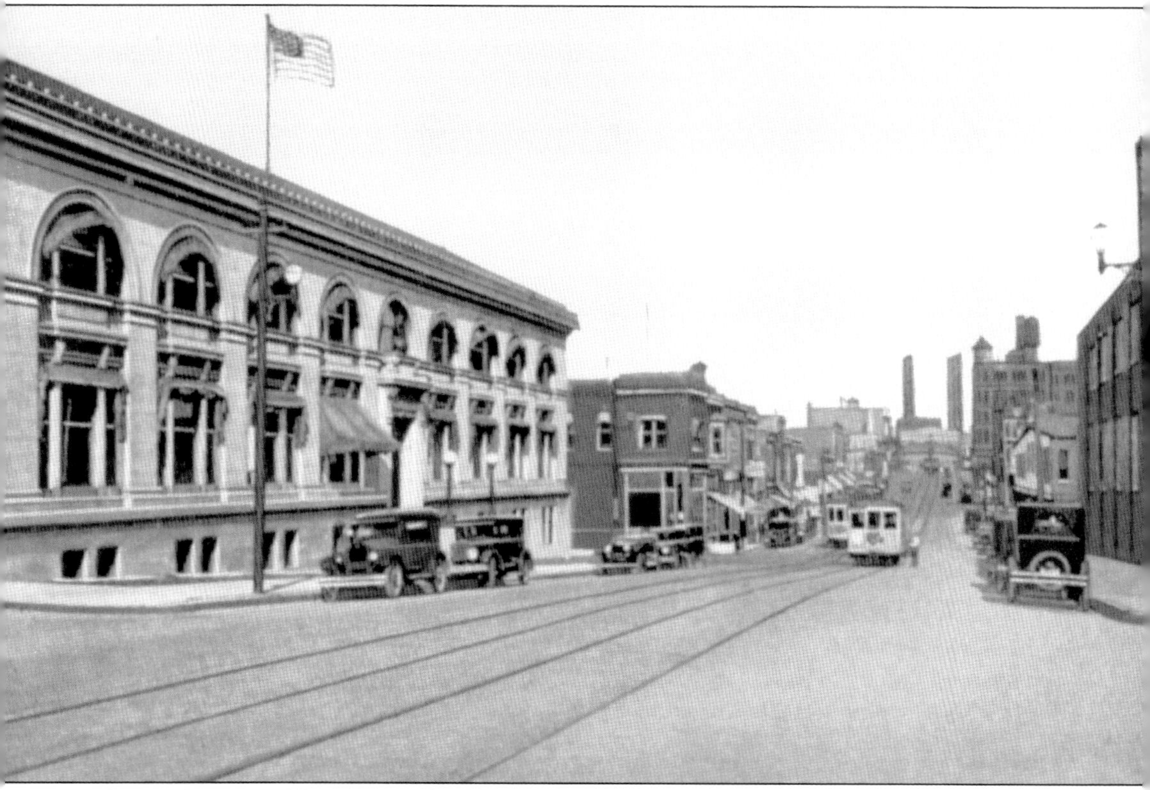

STATE STREET. Almost every building shown in this 1930s view of east State Street has been demolished. Surviving is the main office of the J. I. Case Company (now CNH Case-New Holland) at the left and a few buildings east of Erie Street. For years, a number of second-hand stores operated in the area. The most popular shop was Earl The Trader, which bought and sold for decades. Most of the structures were razed to create parking and green space around the J. I. Case Company complex. The J. I. Case Company was founded in Rochester in 1842, and in 1844, Jerome Increase Case moved his tiny threshing machine works to the village of Racine. In 1849, Case built a pretentious three-story brick building on Bridge Street. During the following decades the company's Main Works buildings covered acres in the heart of downtown Racine. The factory buildings were all razed and the Case Office Complex was built in the 1990s.

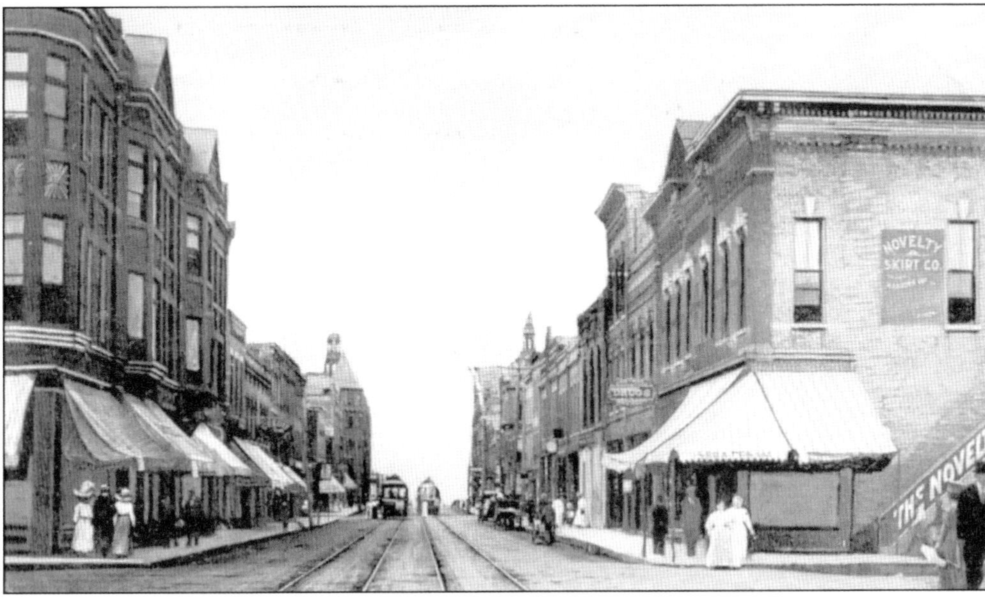

SIXTH STREET. This image looks east on Sixth Street across College Avenue about 1912. To the left is Racine's first YMCA, built in 1886. When the new YMCA building was constructed at 215 Fourth Street, the first building was sold to the Knights Of Pythias and became Racine's Pythian Castle. For decades, the Red Cross Drug Company operated its main store in the building. At the right is Leo Peil Grocery Store with the Novelty Shirt Company operating on the second floor. Many years later the same building was the home of the Mohr Jones Hardware Store.

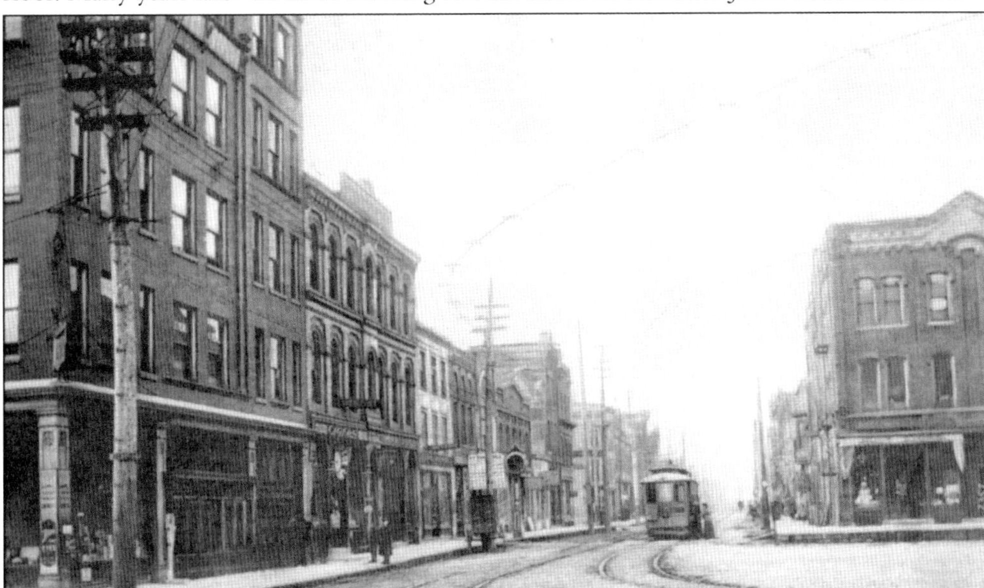

SIXTH STREET, LOOKING WEST. This view looks west on Sixth Street from Hotel Racine about 1907. The Sixth Street business district was a southwestern gateway leading in and out of downtown. Many shops handled dry goods, hardware, and other merchandise for farmers who were visiting the city to do business. Today a number of the restored buildings are occupied by the new art galleries and restaurants that have opened along this corridor. The fabulous Porters Furniture Store, located at 301 Sixth Street, has been an area anchor store for years.

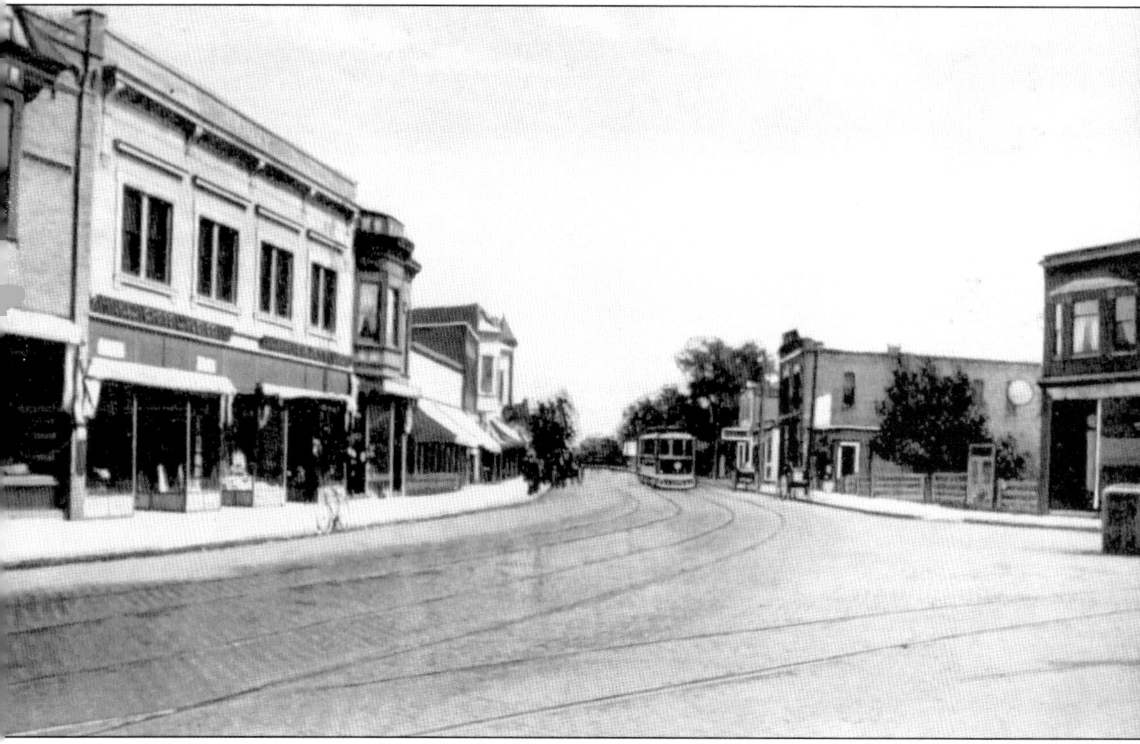

COLUMBIA CORNERS. For decades the business section where Washington Avenue and Fourteenth Street intersect was known as the Racine Junction. The name was coined because the area was close to where two major railroads crossed near Seventeenth Street a few blocks south of the corners. In 1909, a horse drinking fountain with a statue of Columbia was purchased by the Junction Business Men's Association and was placed at the Fourteenth Street intersection. The area was renamed Columbia Corners for a short time but was unable to shake the Racine Junction name. In 1910, a teamster driving one of R. R. Birdsall's teams damaged the drinking fountain. The base and pedestal were replaced, but the statue was set aside for repairs. Later vandals broke off her arms and it was decided not to replace the statue. This view shows the concrete base and the pedestal that held the statue at the far right. The old concrete fountain stood in the intersection for years as a flower planter. In 1928, the business district was renamed Uptown.

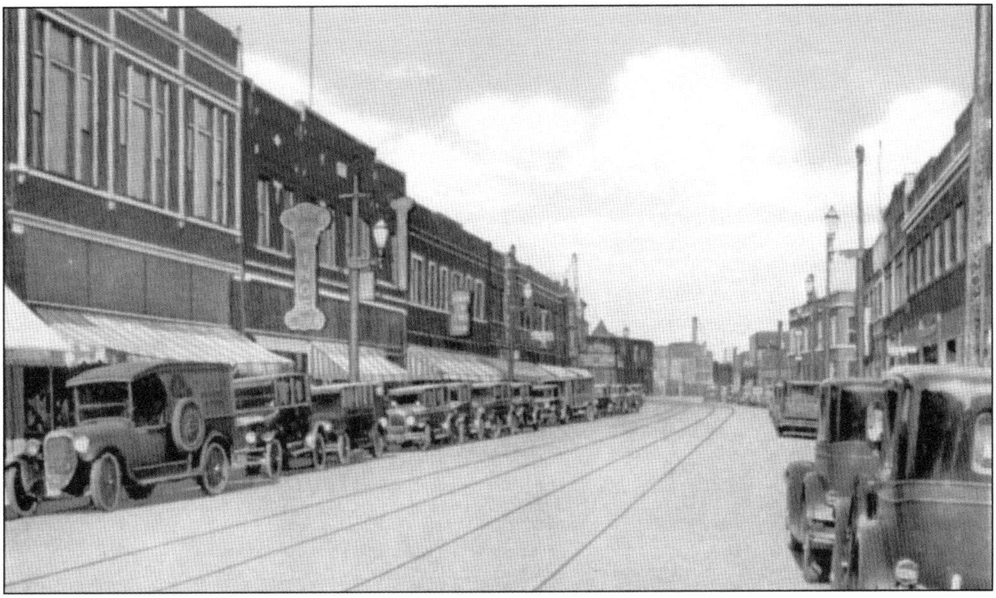

UPTOWN. Washington Avenue originally followed the Territorial Road. Starting downtown at Grand Avenue, it followed the high ground around the Root River valley until it intersected with the west end of Twelfth Street. From that point, it headed west across Racine County. On a sharp curve where Washington Avenue intersected with Fourteenth Street, a few small stores were built. As the city expanded, the area became known as the Racine Junction, then Columbia Corners, and finally Uptown. This view is looking east on the 1500 block in the late 1920s.

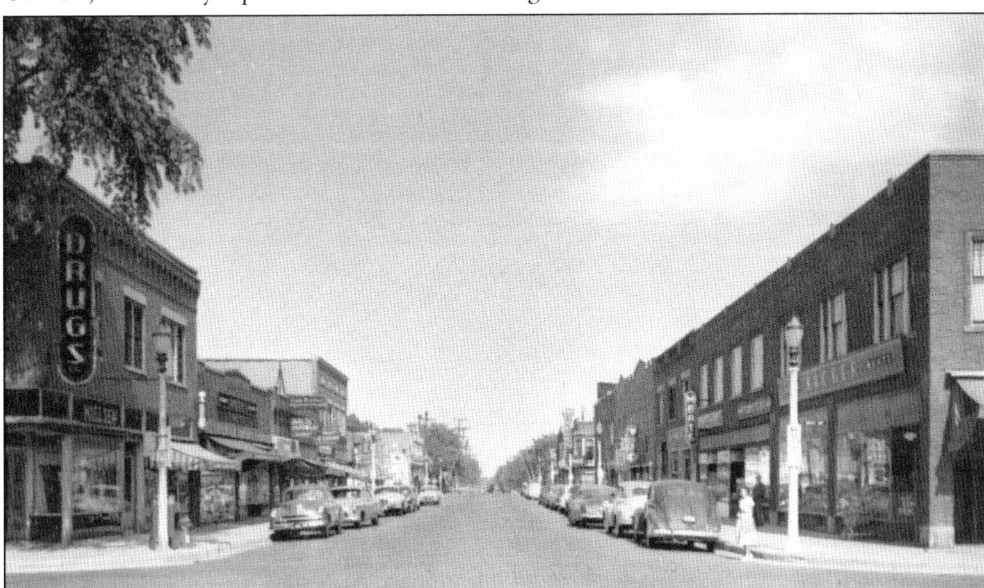

WEST RACINE. The brick-paved Washington Avenue looks east from the intersection of Hayes Avenue during the 1950s. Most of the buildings were constructed during between 1910 and 1930. In recent years, one entire block between Grove Avenue and West Boulevard was razed for redevelopment. At the right is a Kroger Foods Store, which is now Nelson's Variety Store. With wood floors and scattered dime-store merchandise, Nelson's is known for its ambiance and old world charm.

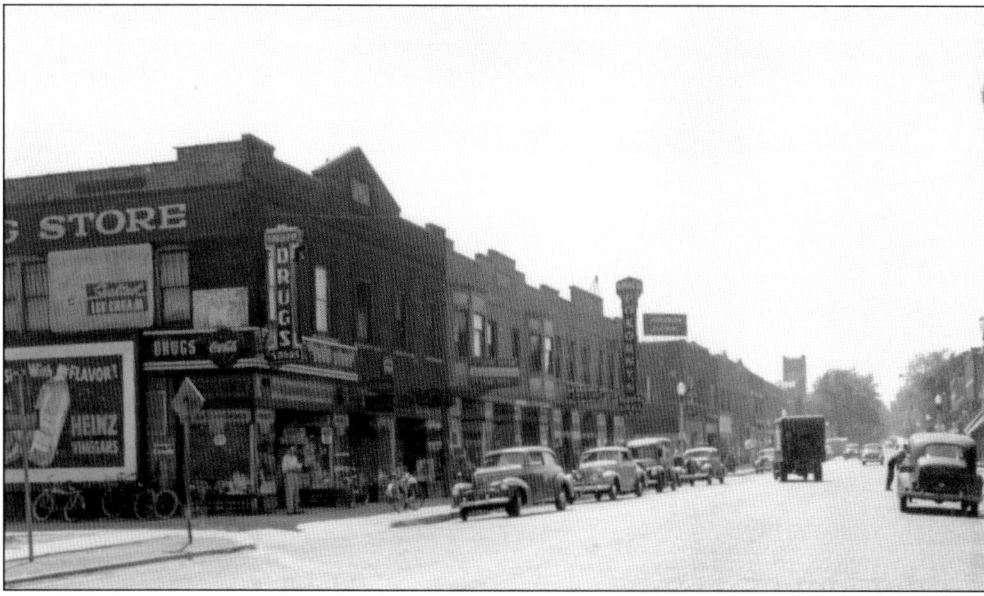

Business Section West Racine. In the late 1890s, a small business section started to grow on Washington Avenue just west of Mound Cemetery. The first business in the area was a pioneer inn and tavern located on the southwest corner of Grove and Washington Avenues. This tavern would be an oddity today because West Racine has been a dry area for decades. This view is looking west on Washington Avenue from West Boulevard. The first block shown in this view was razed in recent years.

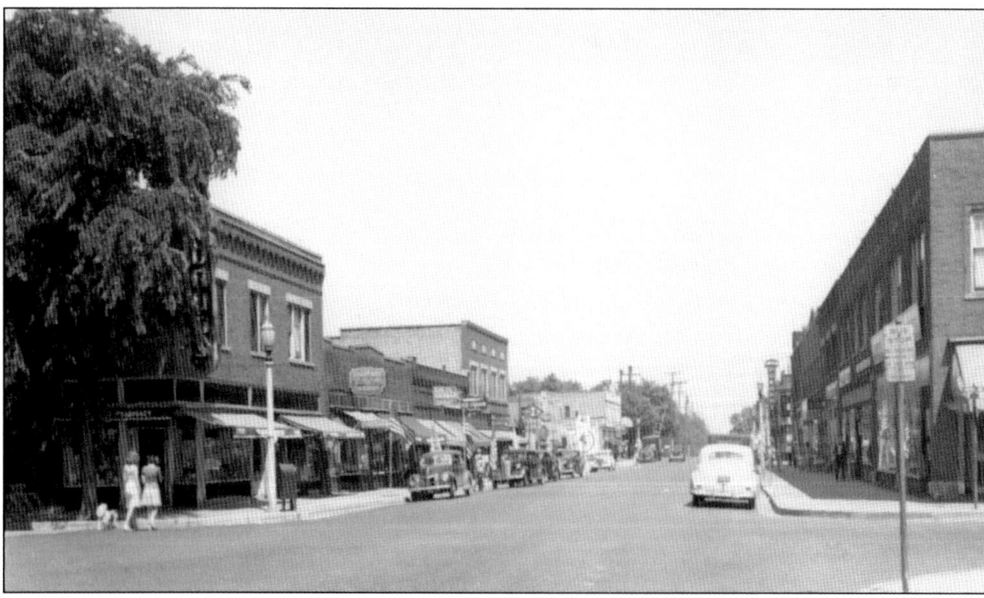

View of West Racine, c. 1940. This view looks east on Washington Avenue from the intersection of Hayes Avenue about 1940. There were barbershops, meat markets, grocery stores, and three drugstores. It was also the home for a number of quality bakeries that made the famous Danish pastry kringle. For decades, West Racine businessmen hosted Western Days with parades and contests all done in a western style. Store owners and clerks would wear western clothing while assisting customers during the annual sidewalk sales.

Three

PUBLIC BUILDINGS AND LANDMARKS

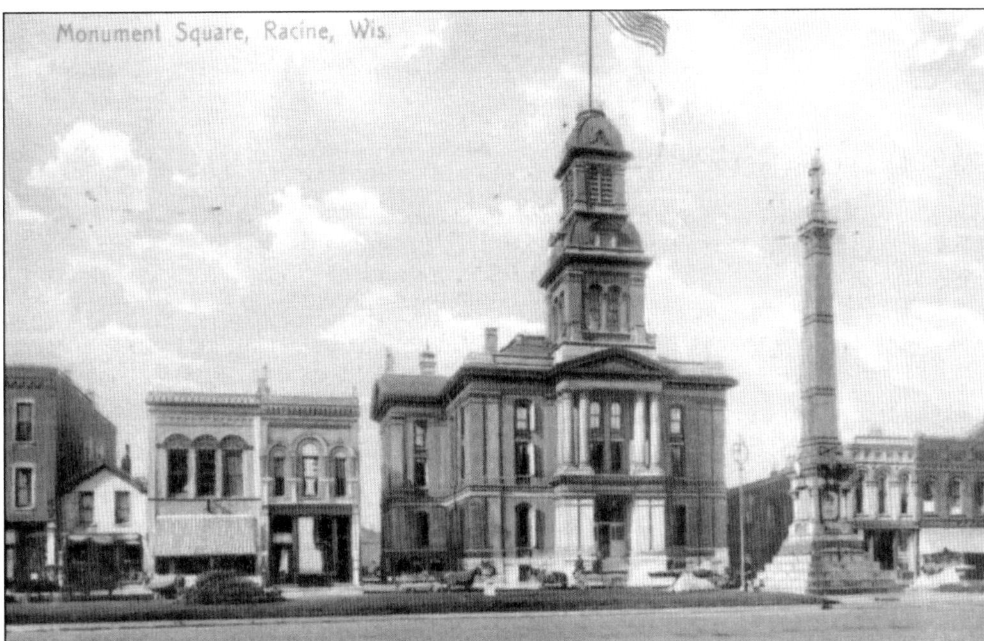

RACINE COUNTY "CENTENNIAL" COURTHOUSE. In the 1870s, Racine County had outgrown its small wooden frame courthouse. Plans were developed to build a new massive brick and stone structure on the same site in 1876. When construction began, the thrifty Racine county board asked the City of Racine for permission to move the outdated 1839 structure to the public square and allow the county officials to use it while the new structure was being built. When the new substantial structure was completed, its pretentious size and tower dominated the public square. It was razed in the 1930s after the present skyscraper-style courthouse was built.

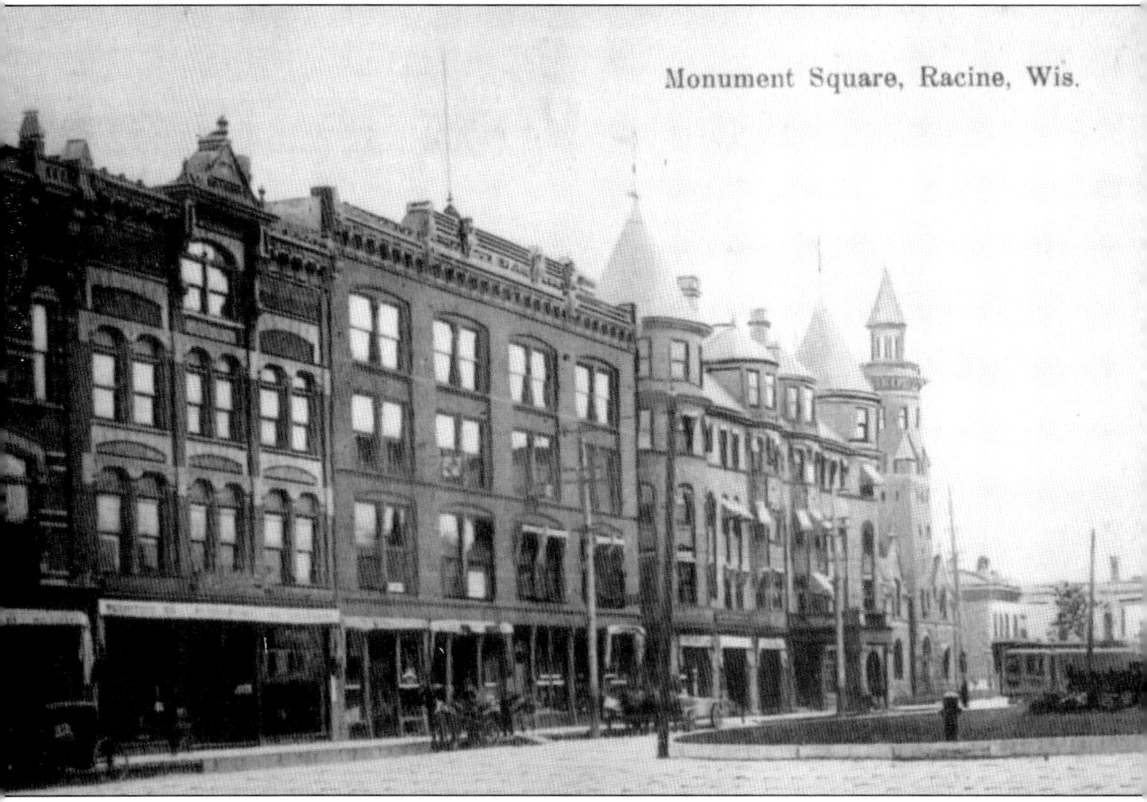

MONUMENT SQUARE. This rare panoramic view of Monument Square in 1909 shows downtown Racine maturing attractively. The original photograph was probably taken with an Al-Vista Panoramic Camera made by the Multiscope and Film Company of Burlington. Peter Angsten started production of the camera that he invented in 1897 in Burlington's vacant Union (now

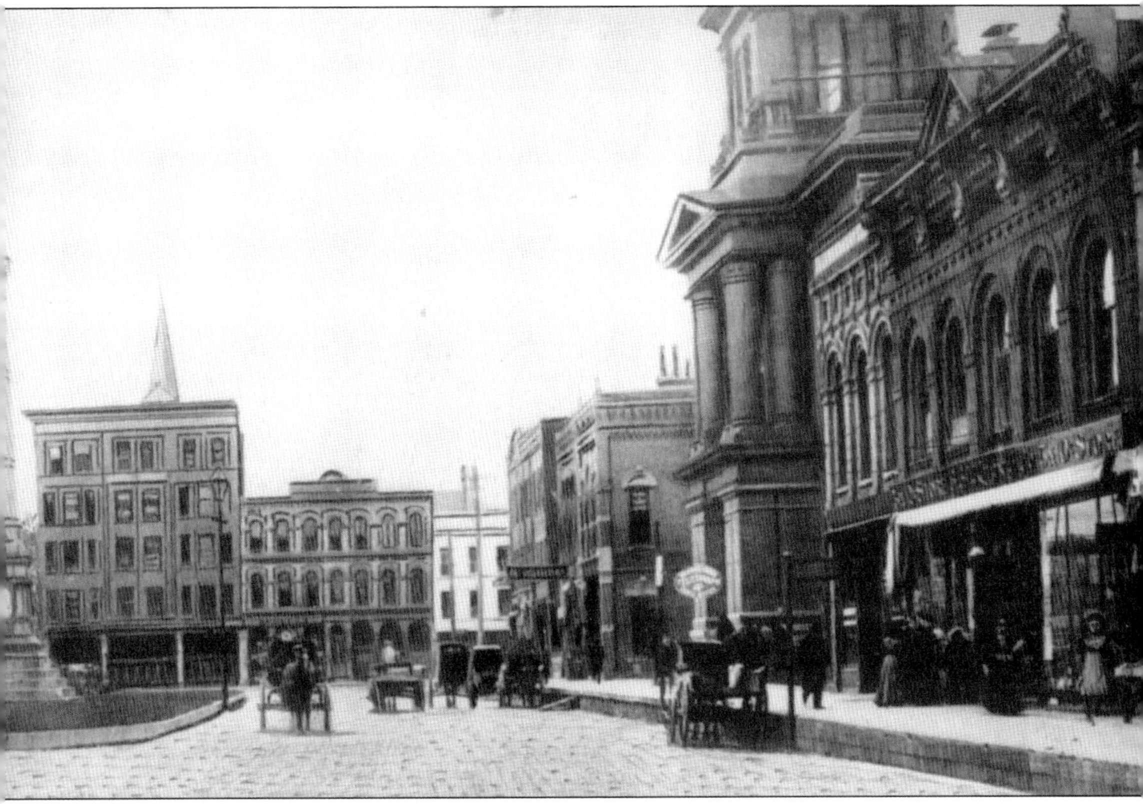

Lincoln) School building. Racine's E. A. Bishop Postcard Publishing Company produced about a dozen known double card views. Most double cards were cut in half and used for two mailings, which makes complete cards rare and desirable.

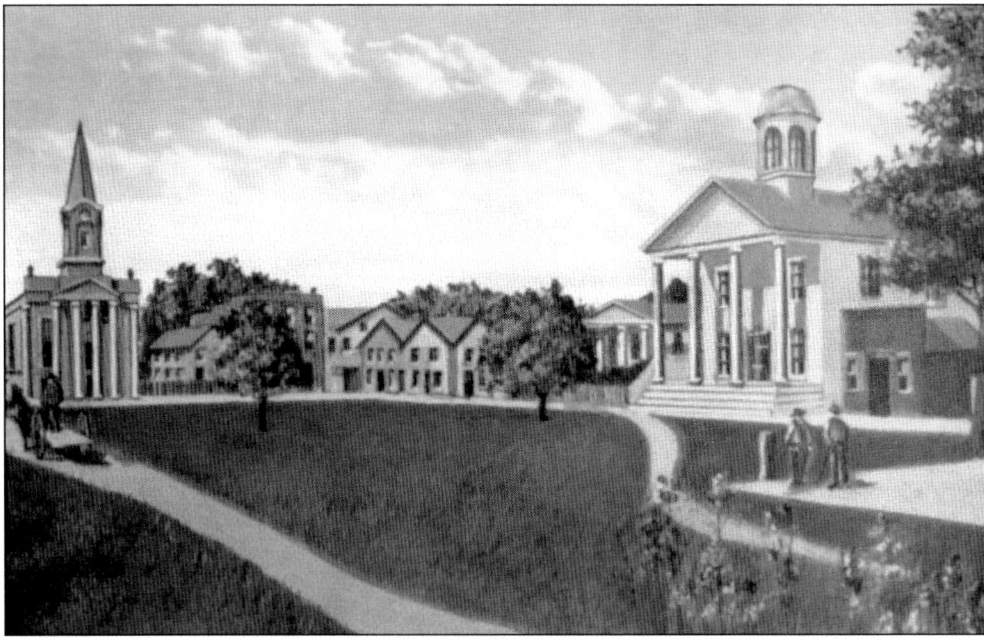

PUBLIC SQUARE. This old photograph reproduction was produced by the E. A. Bishop Postcard Company, Racine's largest postcard publisher. It was copied from a late-1850s view of Racine's public square. It shows the first Greek Revival style Racine County courthouse built in 1839 (right) and the First Baptist church (left).

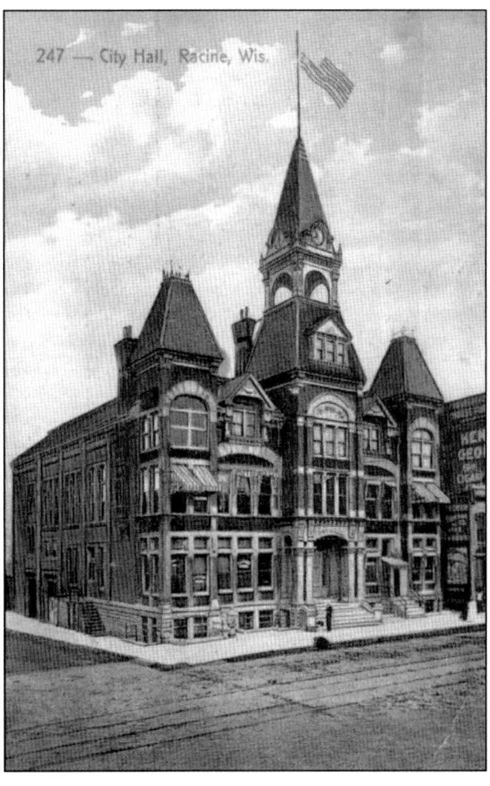

FIRST CITY HALL. By 1883, this new red brick building with arches and ornamental brick occupied the southeast corner of Third and Main Streets. The interior framework was constructed of wood and was considered a fire and safety hazard. In 1931, when a Works Progress Administration grant was issued to Racine for building a new city hall, the city took full advantage and built a modern building for government offices. The old building, razed in the 1930s, was later replaced by a one-story modern strip of storefronts.

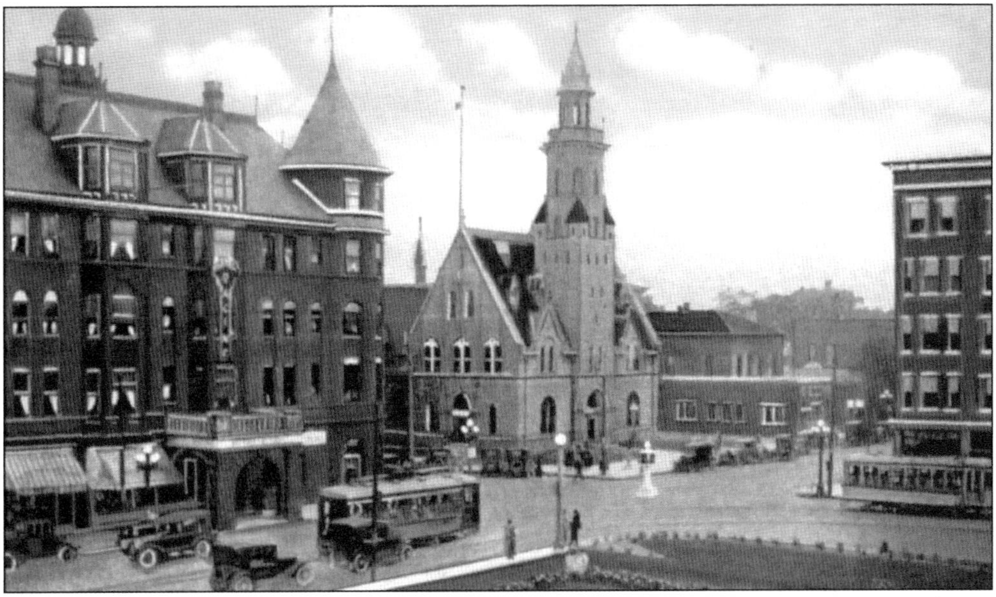

First Post Office Building. In 1897, the city's first building designed and built specifically for a United States Post Office was constructed at Sixth and Main Streets. After it was completed, the building was criticized by local residents because the architecture looked more like a church than a public building. It was razed and replaced with the present post office building. An atypical ring of stone with serpent heads surrounding the tower was saved from the old building and sited at the Racine Zoo.

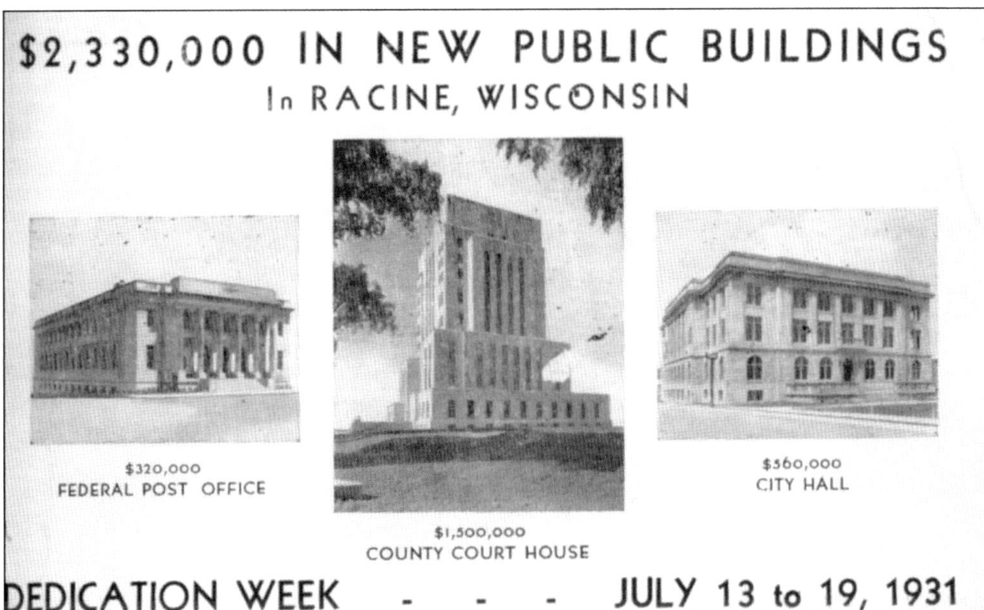

New Public Buildings, 1931. When Racine's new set of public buildings was completed, this postcard notice was printed to remind people that the dedication week would be from July 13–19, 1931. Few cities in the United States could boast of having three major public buildings all constructed at the same time. As of this publishing, all three of these buildings are still standing and being used for the purposes they were built for.

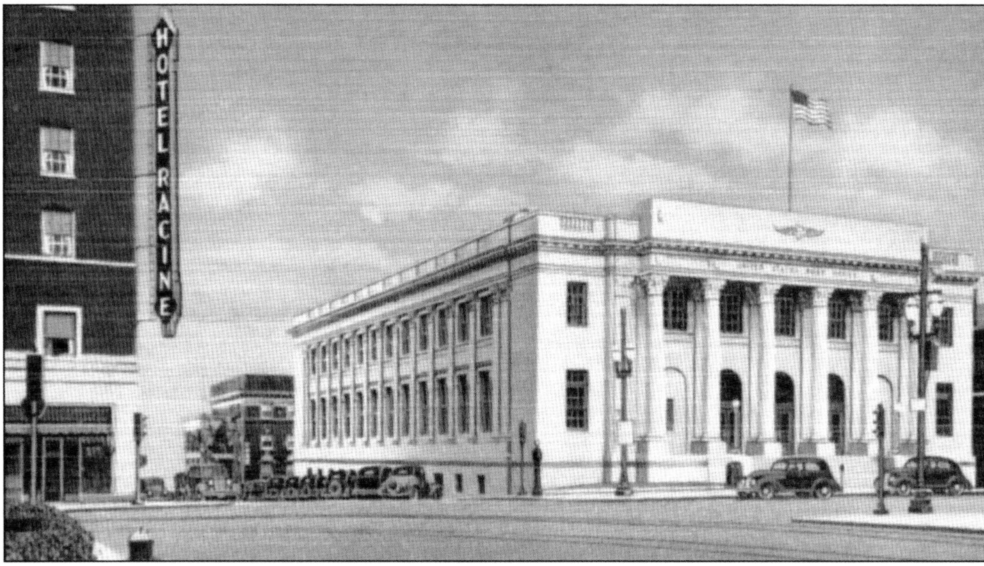

United States Post Office. The U.S. Post Office building in Racine, with its imposing neoclassical facade, Corinthian columned portico, and monumental size, symbolically speaks of the prestige of the federal government. Its location at the southeast corner of Monument Square and Main Street gives it visibility to visitors. Completed in 1931, the building was constructed through the efforts of Congressman Henry Allen Cooper to bring work to Racine during the Great Depression. The building was designed by James A. Wentmore, supervising architect of the U.S. Treasury Department.

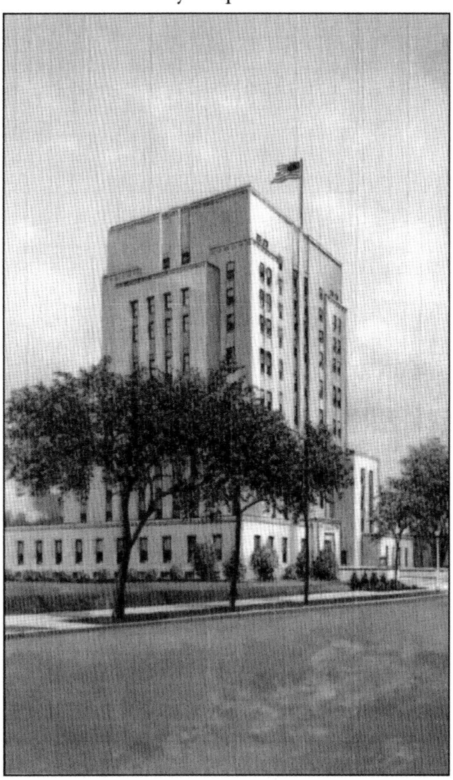

Racine County Courthouse. This stately 11-story structure, designed by the renowned Chicago architects Holabird and Root, was completed in 1931 at the cost of over $1 million. It is still the tallest building in Racine County, towering over surrounding buildings. The exterior walls are decorated with low-relief carvings created by Swedish sculptor Carl Milles. The ornamental designs illustrate the agricultural and industrial life of Racine's history. The actual stone carving was done by John Magnus Johnson. This project was Carl Milles's first American commission.

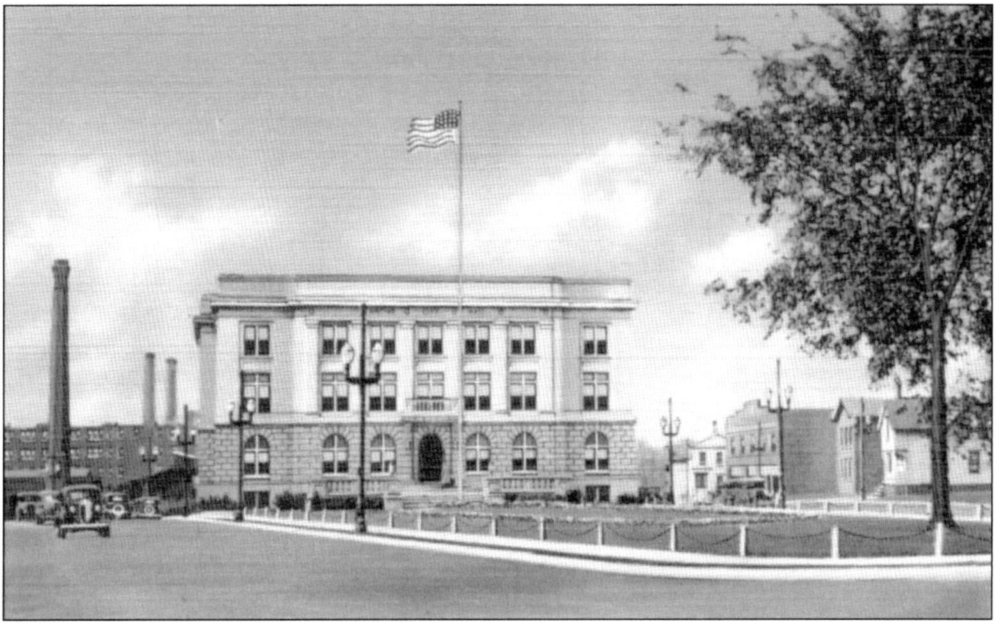

CITY HALL. On April 5, 1930, the Racine Common Council authorized the issuance of $350,000 in bonds for a new city hall. By the time it was completed, the building cost about $500,000. Original plans called for a 40-foot bell tower, but it was not added due to cost. The neoclassical designed structure was made of Indiana limestone. Dedication of the latest city hall was in July 1931, along with the new Racine County Courthouse and United States Post Office.

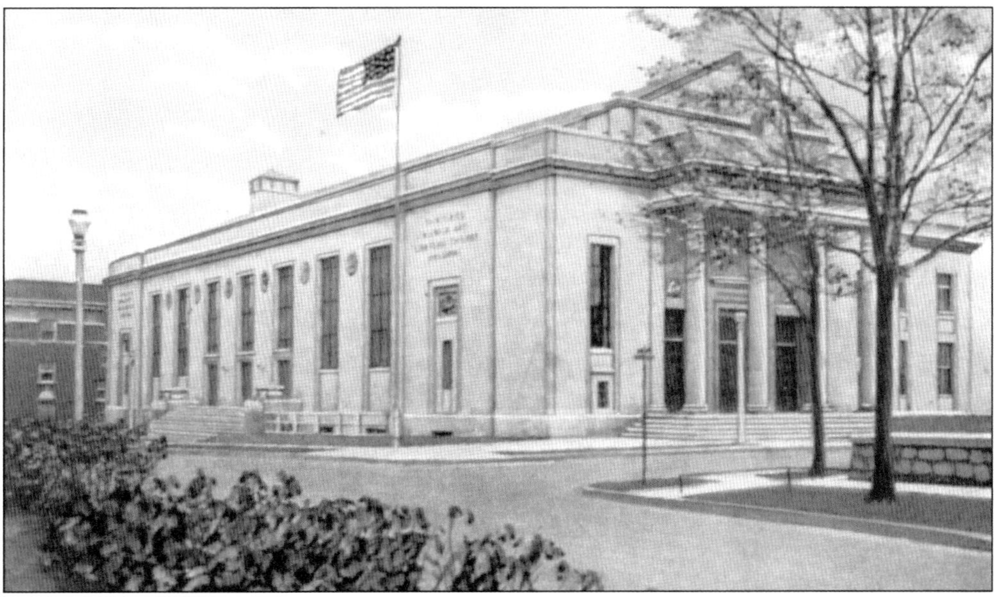

MEMORIAL HALL. When Memorial Hall was built in 1924, it was intended to be a symbol of gratitude for those who served in World War I. It was built of Indiana limestone in a neoclassical style designed by Chicago architect Howard Van Dorn Shaw. The contractor was the Bondgard-Christensen Construction Company whose partners at the time were Peter Bondgard, William Christensen, and Peter Brown Sr. Thomas Riley Marshall, a former vice president of the United States, spoke at the laying of the cornerstone on Memorial Day, May 31, 1924.

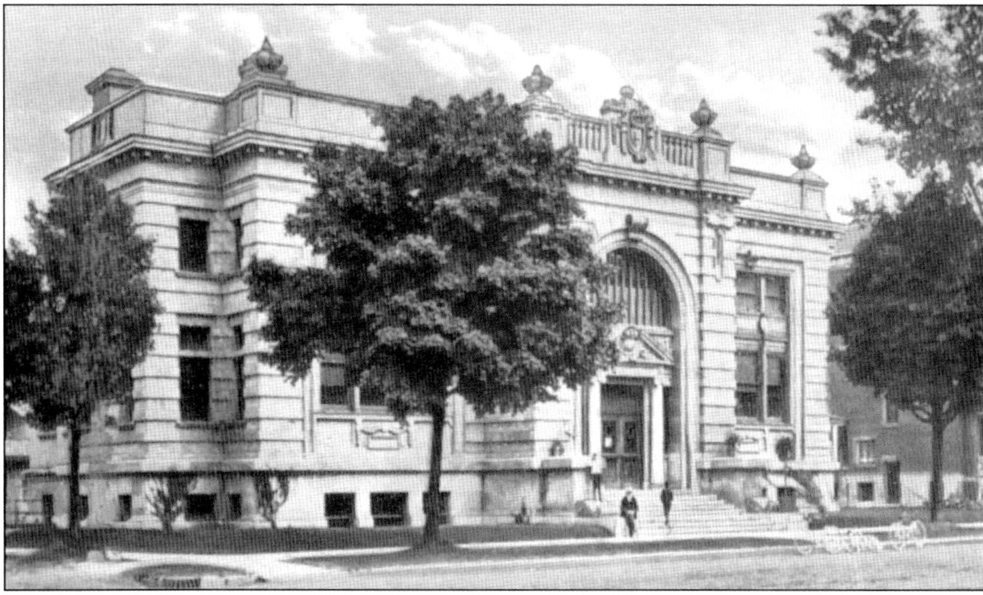

CARNEGIE LIBRARY. Racine's Carnegie Library was built in 1904 at the corner of Seventh and Main Streets. It served as a library until Racine built its current lakefront library in 1958. For many years, Racine had a small historical room in the Racine County Courthouse. The ever-growing collection and the fact that county government needed the space set in motion the idea of using of the Carnegie Library building as Racine's historical museum. It opened in May 1962 and is currently the home of the Racine Heritage Museum.

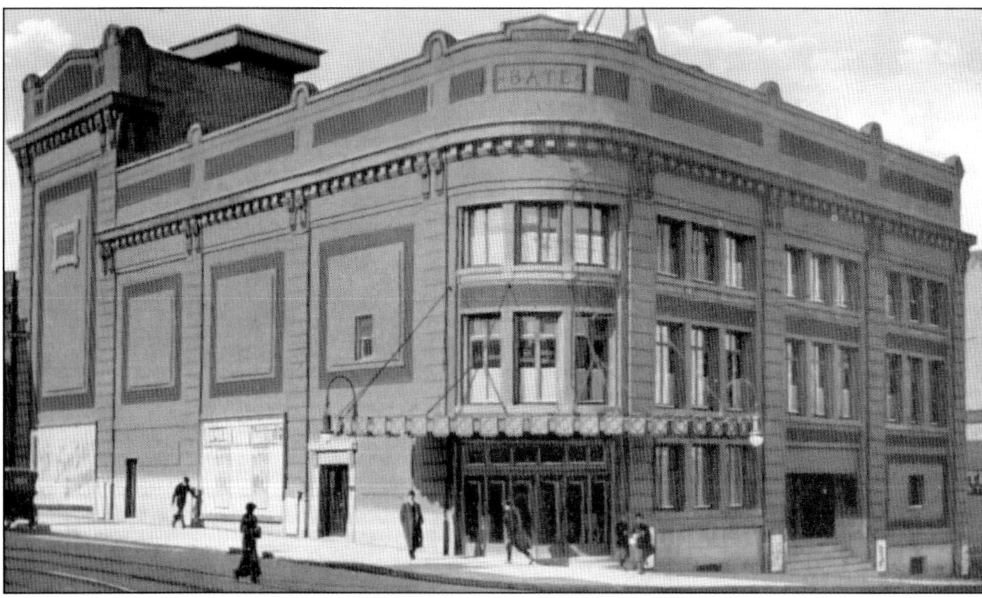

ORPHEUM THEATRE. The Orpheum Theatre was located at the northwest corner of State and Main Streets. The elegant show house was built in 1911 at a cost of $60,000 by the Racine Investment Company and was leased to the Orpheum Amusement Company. It was a source of entertainment for thousands of people who enjoyed vaudeville, opera, stage plays, and movies. When it closed in 1951, it was called the Main Street Theatre. It stood vacant for years and vandals brought its grand history to a close. In 1958, the building was razed.

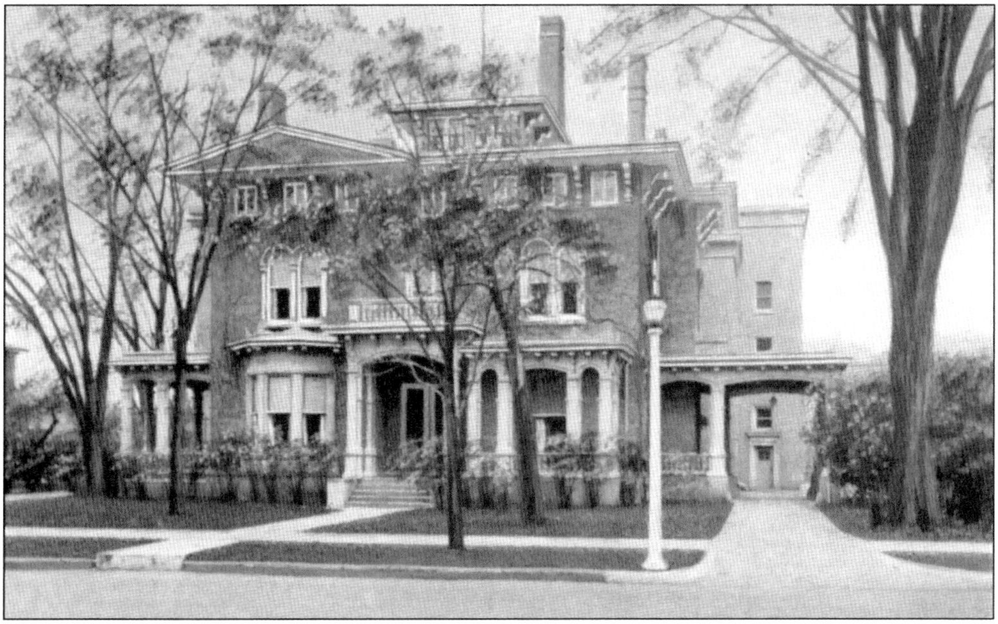

MASONIC CLUB. The present home of the Racine Masonic Club located at 1012 South Main Street was originally built as a home for businessman Henry S. Durand in about 1856. This grand, cream brick, Italianate mansion crowned with a cupola was purchased by the Masons in 1920 from the estate of Frederick Robinson. The Masons soon undertook a major restoration of the building. A large addition was added and the whole complex was dedicated in 1923.

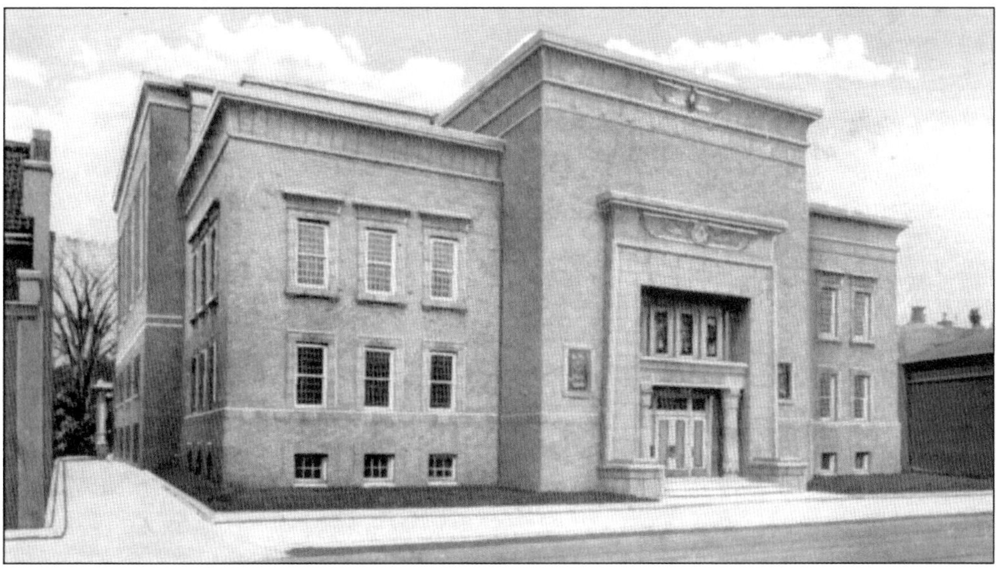

MASONIC TEMPLE. In the 1920s, this country was fascinated with the excavations going on in Egypt's Valley of the Kings. With the discovery of King Tut's tomb in 1922, a new form of Egyptian architecture became popular. The Masons hired local architect Edmund B. Funston to design an addition to the building. Funston drew on Egyptian details such as battered walls and papyrus columns. Scarabs and hieroglyphics were used as ornamentation and the winged disc of the Egyptian temple incorporated the Masonic symbol. The building is located at 1015 Wisconsin Avenue.

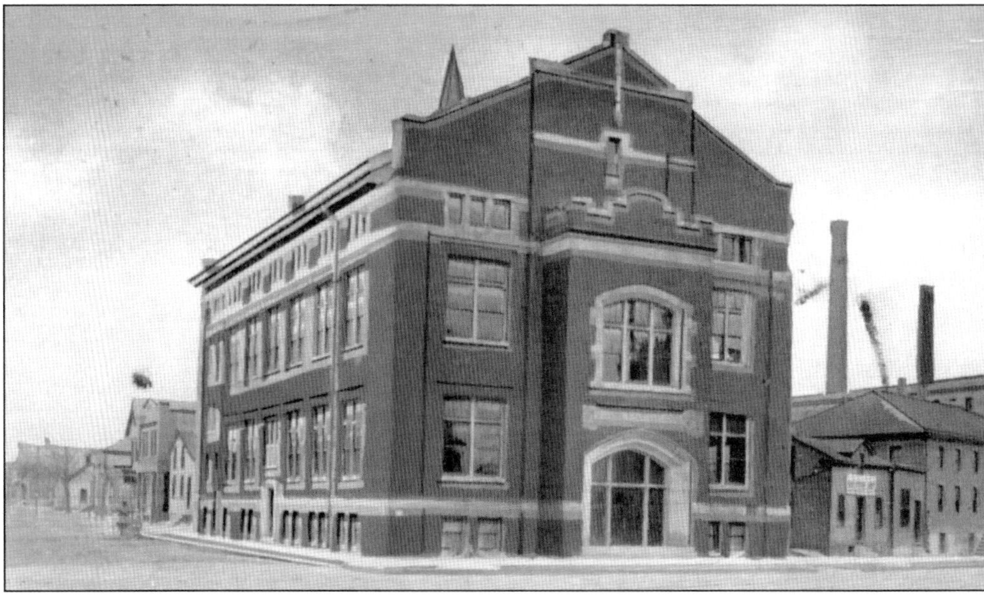

DANISH BROTHERHOOD. This brick and stone building, constructed in 1911 at the corner of Seventh Street and Grand Avenue, served as the home of the Danish Brotherhood Society. Racine Lodge No. 4 of the Danish Brotherhood was founded in 1882. Its purpose was to perpetuate memories of Denmark through cultural activities like a drama club, singing, sports, and drill teams. Like most of the ethnic cultural societies, second and third generations lost the language and had very little interest in European culture.

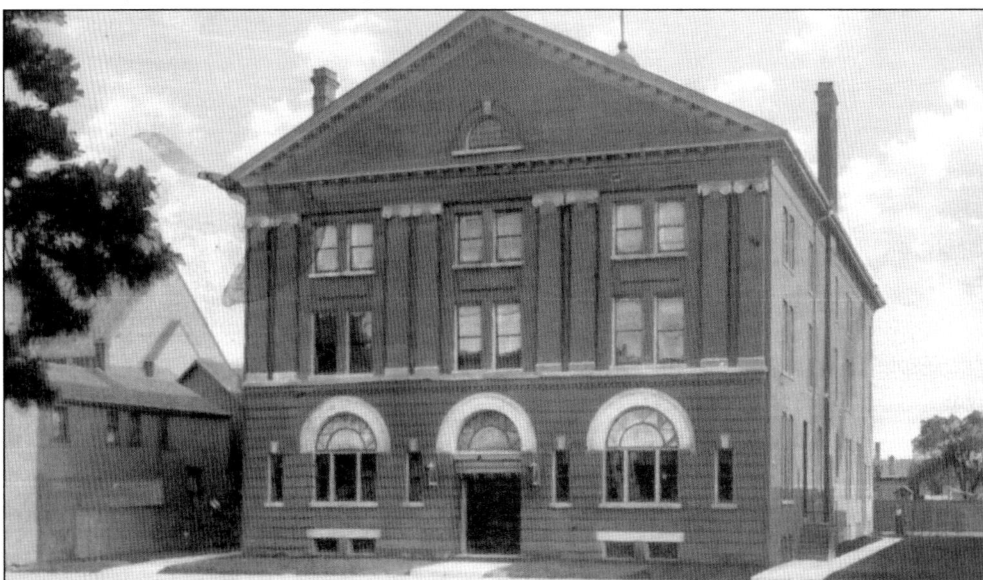

DANIA HALL, *C.* 1910. The Dania Society (a Danish cultural society) was founded in Racine in 1867. It is said that one-third of Racine's population can trace its roots to Denmark. Danish immigrants came to Racine to work in the scores of diverse factories. Dania Hall was built at 1019 State Street in the heart of Racine's large Danish community. The building was designed and built by prominent local architects Chandler and Park in 1904, and still stands to remind one of the strong Danish presence in Racine.

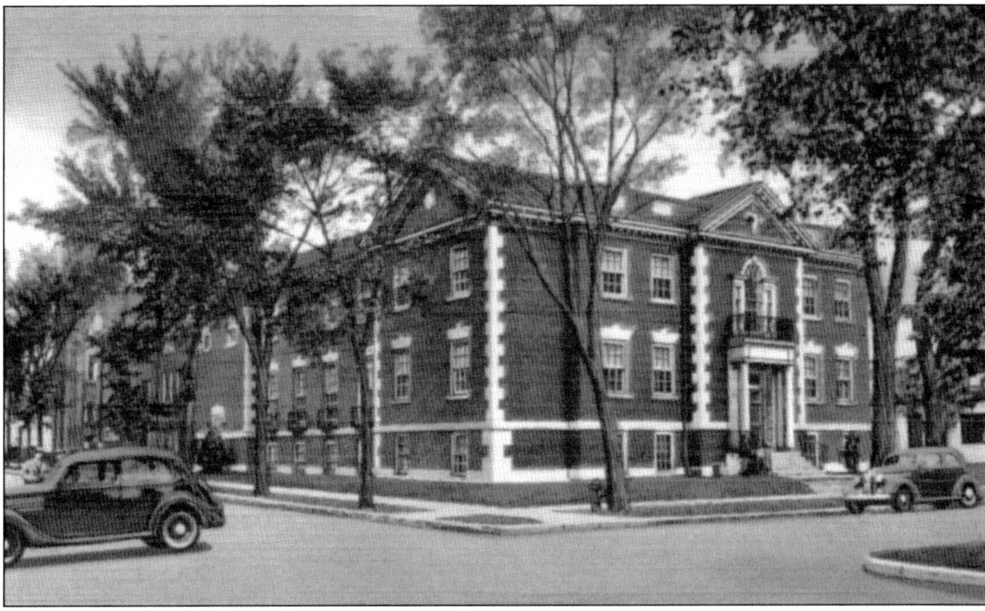

WOMEN'S CLUB. The Women's Club of Racine was organized on October 7, 1896. For decades, the members met at halls, meeting rooms, and churches around the city. In 1929, the club decided to build a beautiful Georgian revival-style clubhouse on the northwest corner of Eighth Street and Lake Avenue. The Women's Club of Racine was clearly in the mainstream of conservative taste of its time. The building was dedicated in 1930 and the mortgage was burned in 1946.

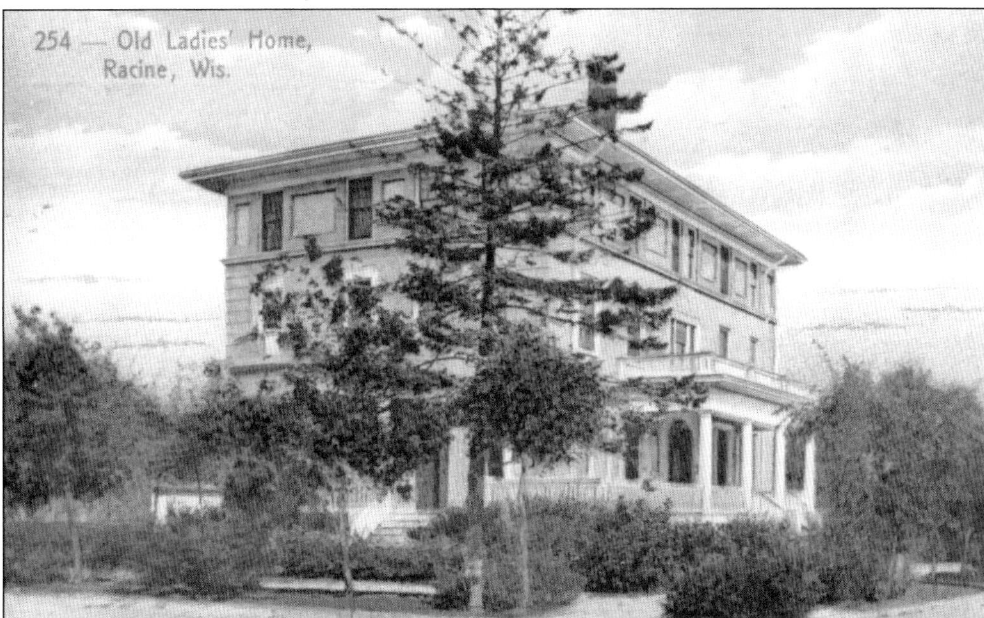

OLD LADIES HOME. The institution known as the Palmeter House for Old Ladies was founded by John and Eliza Palmeter. They were a childless couple who felt their property should be left so an assisted living home for older ladies could be built. In 1905, this building was completed. The Palmeter home was the only Racine social service institution specifically dedicated to the care of elderly ladies. The building is still standing at 1547 College Avenue.

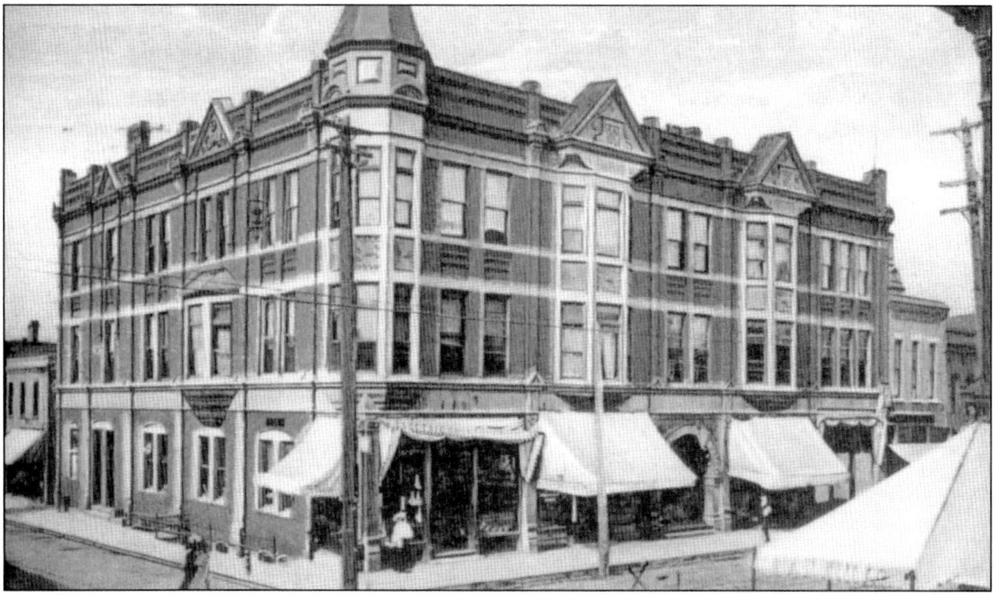

YMCA BUILDING. This monumental Queen Anne–style structure of cream brick with red sandstone trim was the first building constructed by the Racine YMCA. It was built in 1886 at the corner of Sixth Street and College Avenue on the former site of the 1,250-seat Blake Opera House that had been destroyed by fire in 1884. On the College Avenue side of the building tucked up by the roofline is a carved sandstone panel reading simply YMCA. For years, the lower level housed the main store of the Red Cross Drug Company.

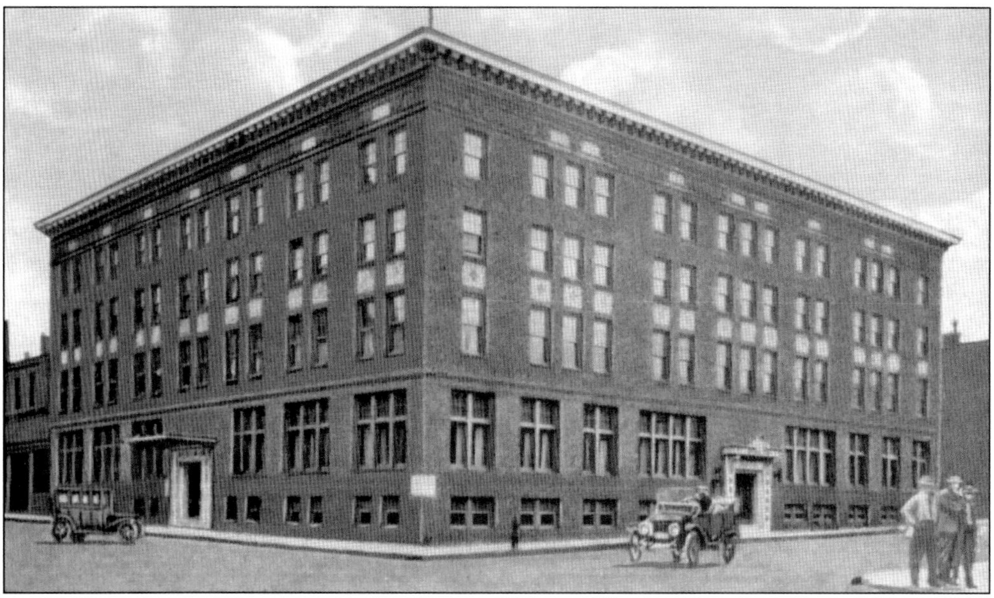

RACINE, YMCA. The second building to house the Racine YMCA was constructed at the corner of Wisconsin Avenue and Sixth Street in 1915. The massive building was designed by Guilbert and Funston, local architects whose buildings still dot Racine's streetscapes with many listed as local landmarks. The construction of this building is rather unique because it is one of a handful of buildings in Racine constructed of heavy, red, street paving brick. The Sixth Street building was eventually sold to the Knights of Pythias to be used as their castle.

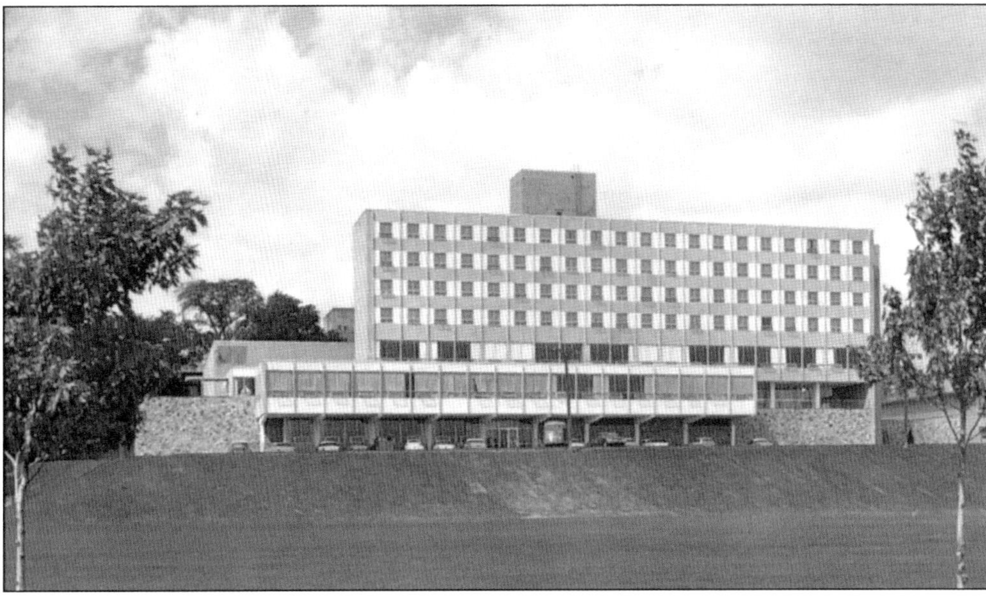

LAKE FRONT, YMCA. Racine's modern styled seven-story lakefront YMCA was completed in 1960. Built on the lake bluff, the upper stories have a stunning view of lakeshore activities and Lake Michigan. The $3 million raised for construction was said to be the largest sum ever raised for a semi-public organization then in Racine. The exterior construction gives the impression of a liberal use of glass. The appearance stems from the use of pale green enamel panels and grey brick walls.

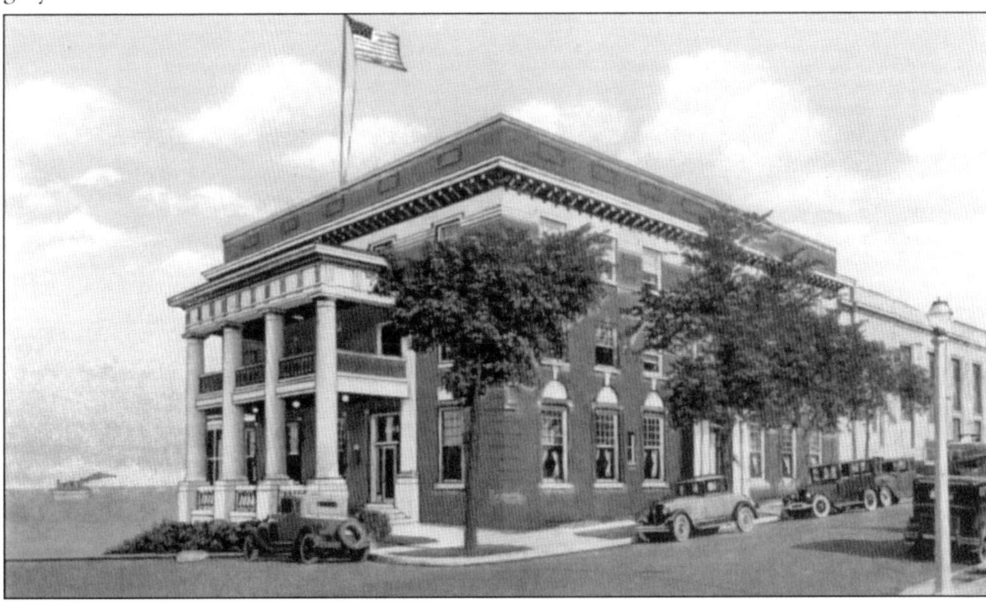

RACINE ELK'S CLUB. The Racine Elk's lodge No. 252 was organized on January 6, 1893. In 1912, this spacious clubhouse was built on the lakeshore at the foot of Sixth Street. During torrential storms, waves from Lake Michigan would crash against its lower levels. Designed by local architect A. Arthur Guilbert, the building combines the classical elements of the portico with the horizontal emphasis and decorative tile motifs of the prairie style. The composition has changed very little and the building was later converted into office space.

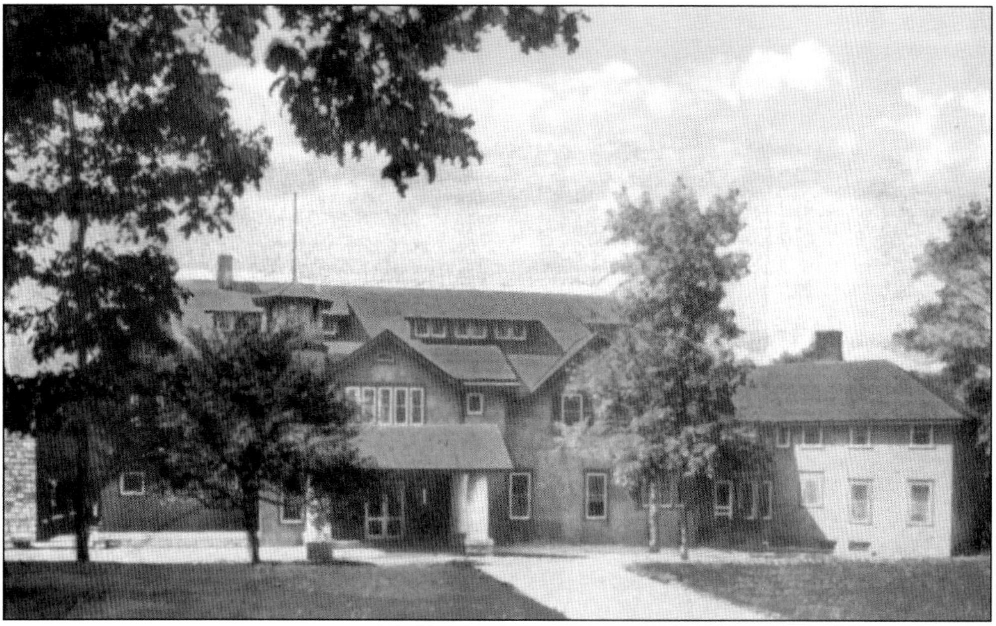

Country Club, *c.* 1910. By 1909, Racine's wealthy needed a place to play. A large parcel of land was purchased on Northwestern Avenue and this fine country clubhouse was built. The area was known as Idlewild at the time. The clubhouse, with a spectacular view, was built on a bluff overlooking Root River. The river lowlands were turned into golf links. The grounds were designed by Jens Jensen, a well known landscape architect of the time.

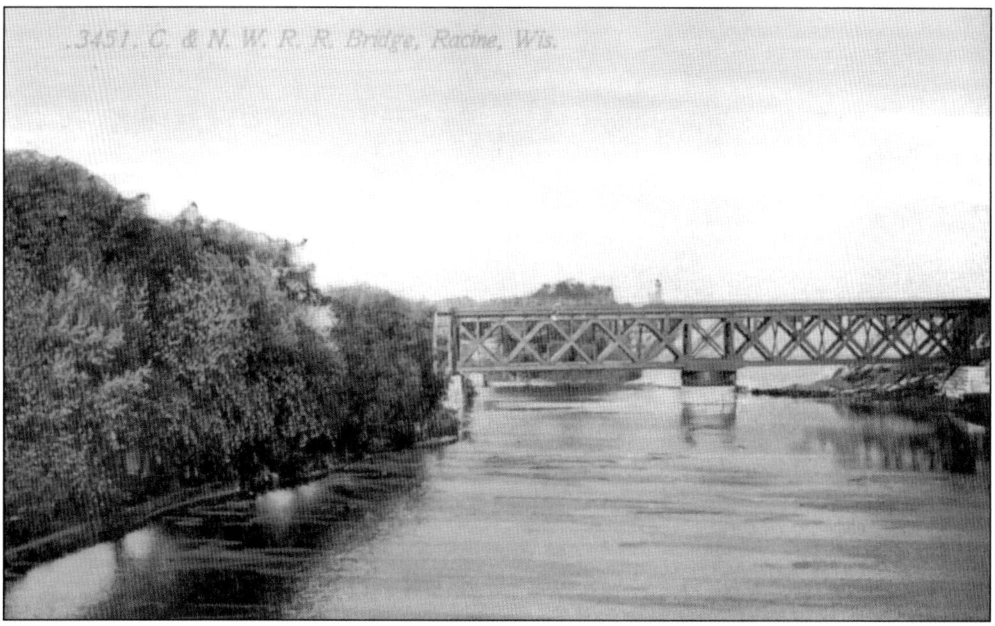

Chicago and Northwestern Bridge. Throughout the years, this massive trestle, known as the "High Bridge," also had other nicknames such as "Cat Walk." The bridge was constructed in 1909 and had a turn mechanism in the center pier. It replaced a smaller structure that was the only single-track bridge between Chicago and Milwaukee.

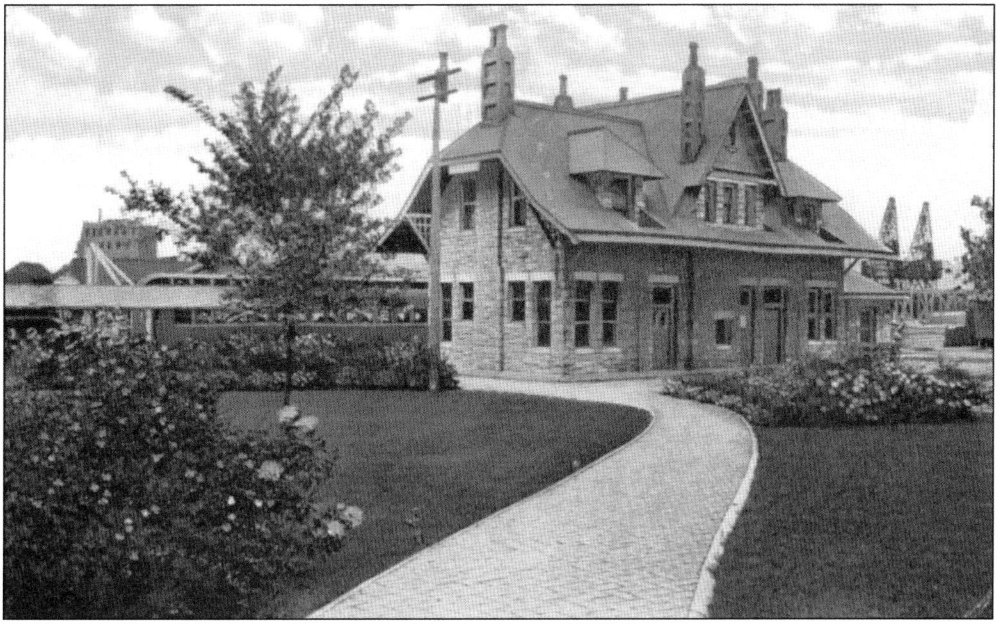

CHICAGO, MILWAUKEE AND ST. PAUL DEPOT. The Chicago, Milwaukee and St. Paul Railroad Station was considered a beauty spot in the 1900s. Flower beds and shrubbery flanked the winding brick walk. Built of stone, the building was located on the east side of Main Street between Second Street and the Root River. The tracks have long been gone and very little survives to remind one that trains stopped daily in the heart of the city.

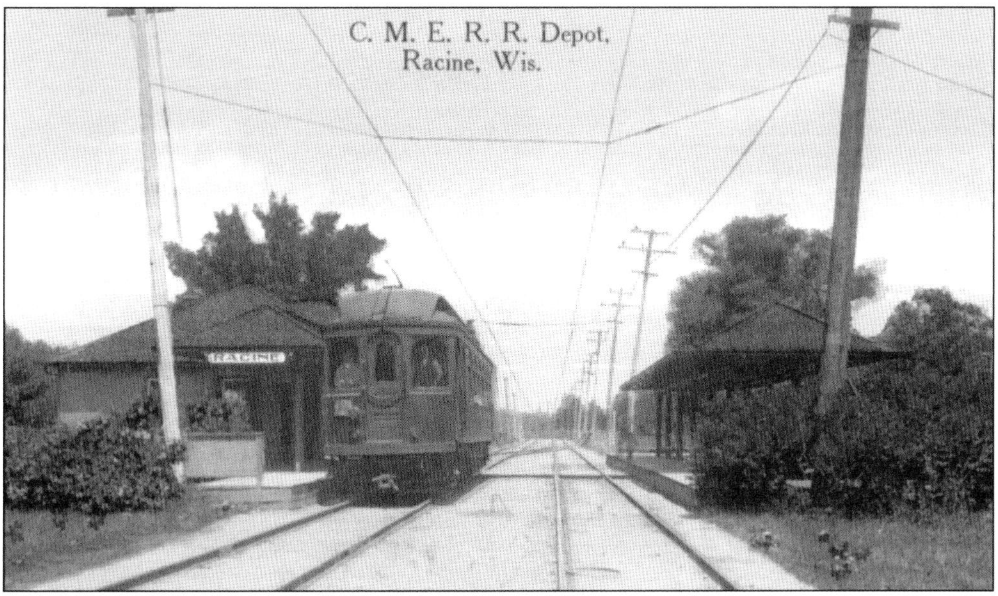

CHICAGO-MILWAUKEE ELECTRIC RAILROAD DEPOT. In 1906, the Chicago-Milwaukee Electric Railroad was completed into Racine. The depot was located on the east edge of the West Racine business district across from the main gate of Mound Cemetery. The first depot on the site burned down in 1908 and was replaced by the depot in this view. Later the railroad was renamed the Chicago North Shore and Milwaukee Railroad, locally called the "North Shore." The last North Shore train made its final run out of Racine on January 21, 1963.

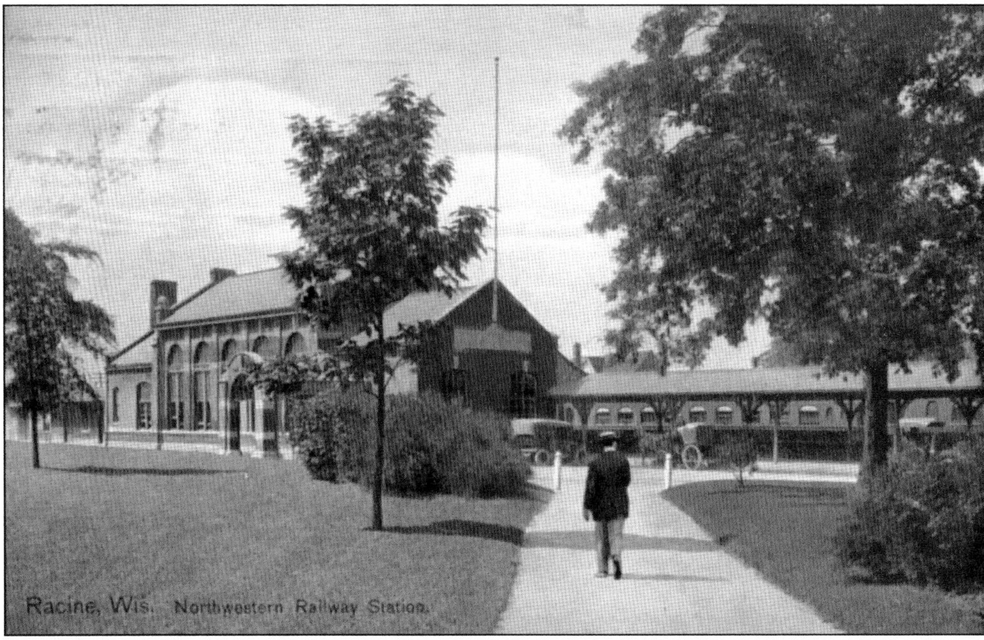

CHICAGO AND NORTHWESTERN DEPOT. Racine's Chicago and Northwestern Depot was built in 1902 of red brick with stone trim. A tunnel walkway allowed people to walk under the double tracks to reach the second waiting station on the opposite side. It was at this station that Pres. Woodrow Wilson's special train stopped on January 31, 1916, to address citizens of Racine on his program of national preparedness for the war. When the Chicago and Northwestern Railroad ended rail service in Racine, the depot was sold and stood vacant. The design of the depot was the work of the highly successful Chicago firm of Frost and Granger. When the brick depot was completed, the old small frame depot was moved to the side of the road. St. Stephen's Episcopal Church at 1769 State Street took notice of the old abandoned depot and sent a message to the president of the railroad asking him for a gift of the old depot. "Go right ahead," the president replied. The building was then moved to church property and is still being used by the church today.

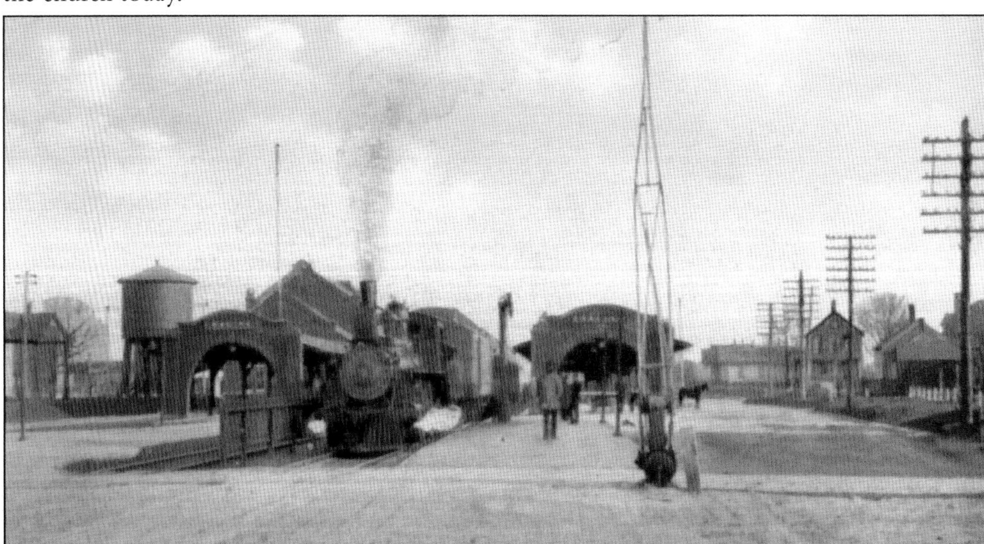

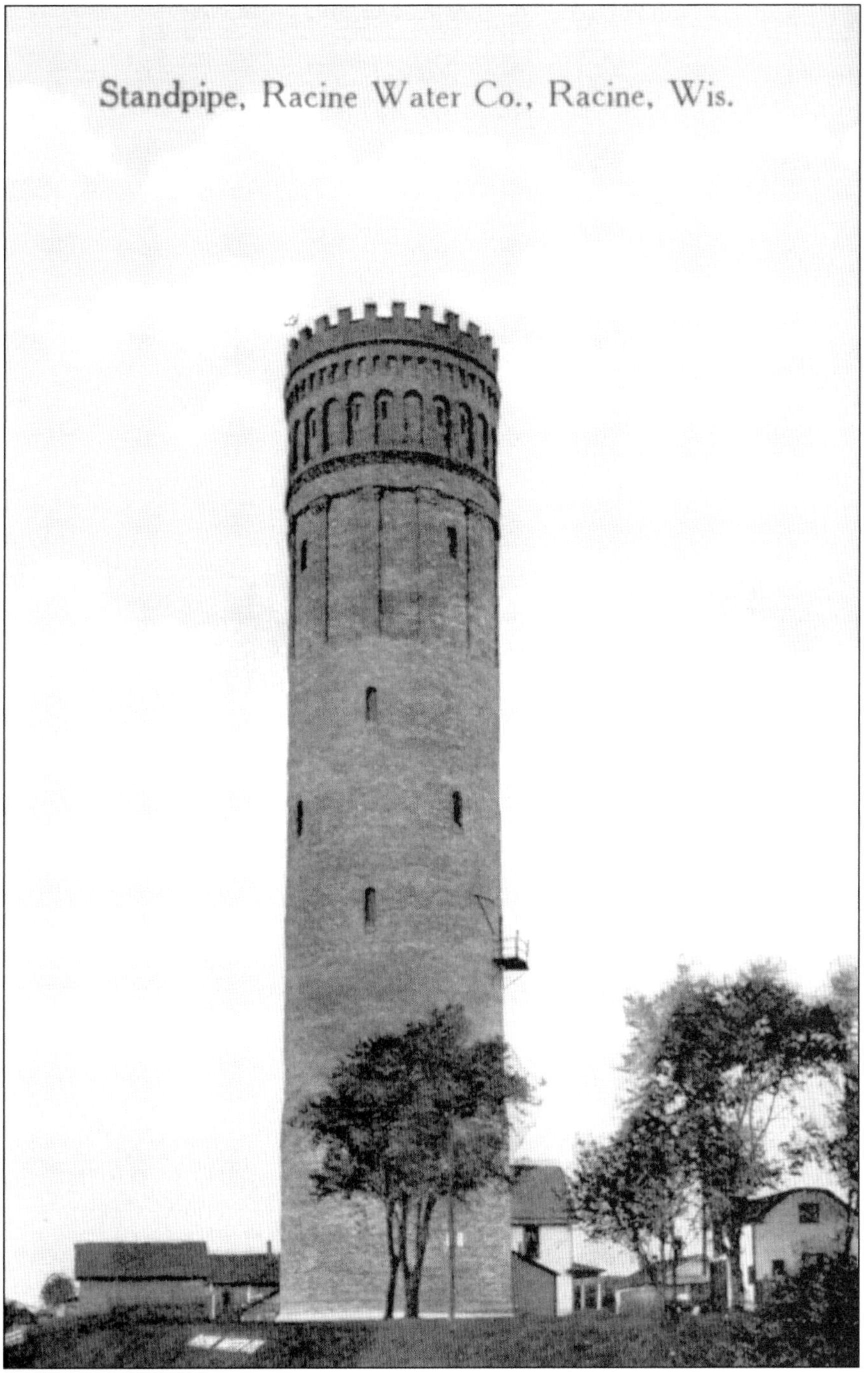

RACINE WATER TOWER. In 1886, the Racine Water Company was incorporated. A pumping station was built near the mouth of the Root River. Also constructed was a standpipe water tower at Tenth Street and the Chicago and Northwestern Railroad tracks. The original construction was a tall, metal tank on a limestone base designed to add additional water pressure to the system. In 1897, a castle-like cream brick veneer was added. The tower, also known as "Solomon's Temple," stood as a local landmark until 1953 when it was razed.

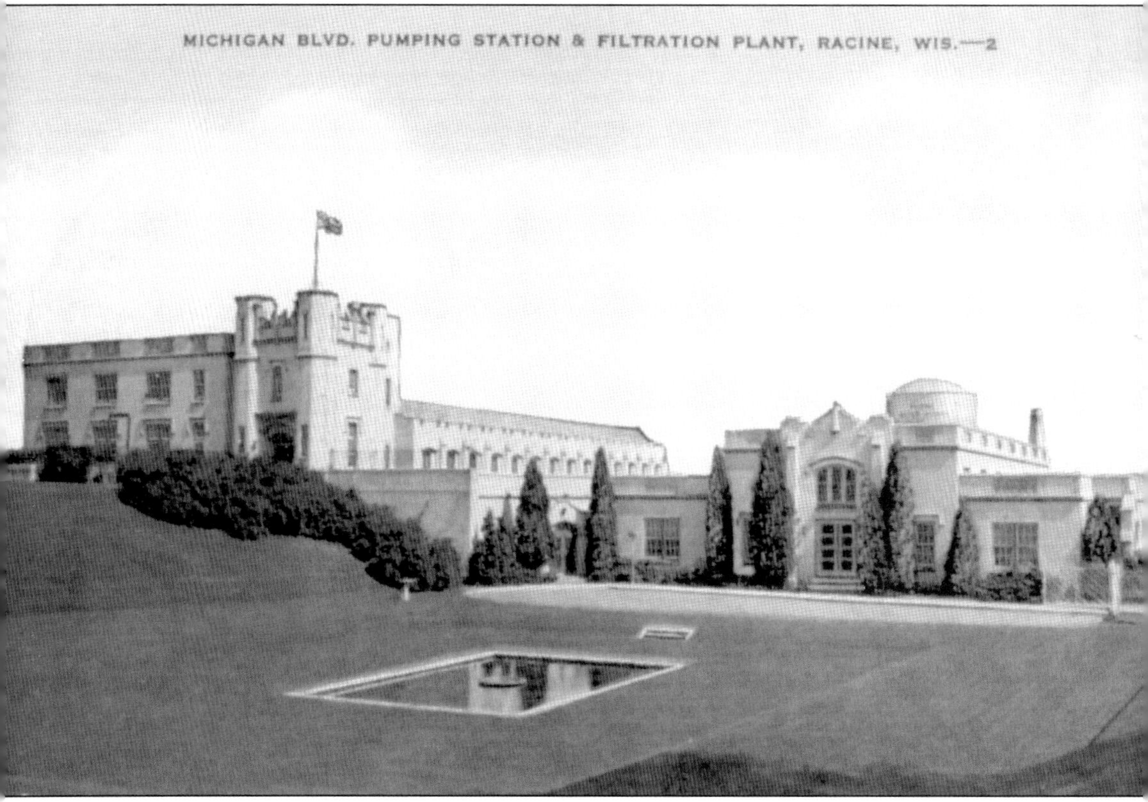

WATER DEPARTMENT. In 1924, Racine industries were making major requests for more and larger water mains. The problem was resolved in 1925 when the city purchased land and built a new plant with a two million-gallon coagulation basin at Michigan Boulevard and Hubbard Street. In 1928 a storage reservoir, holding two-and-one-third-million gallons, was built, giving Racine one of the first totally modern treatment plants in the world. The Gothic fortress–styled buildings provided a romantic charm for a building constructed for such a utilitarian purpose. Built of glazed brick and stone, its main entry suggests the gate of a medieval fortress.

Four

MONUMENTS AND PUBLIC PARKS

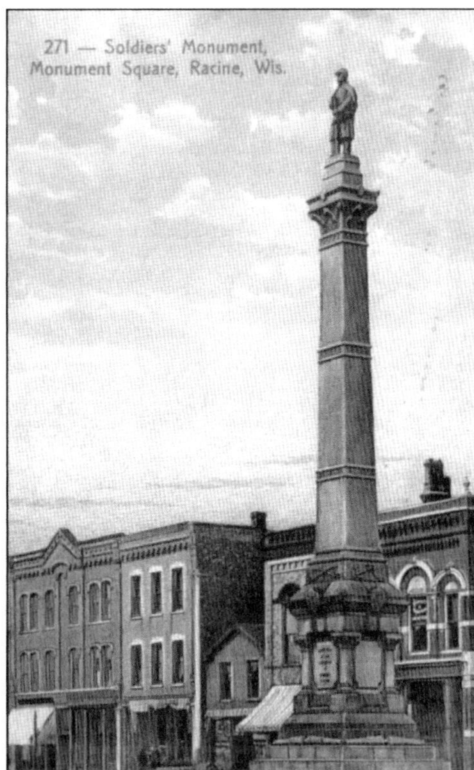

SOLDIER'S MONUMENT. On July 4, 1884, a Civil War soldier's monument was dedicated in the center of Racine's public square and from that point on it has been known as Monument Square. The entire monument stands 61.5 feet high with an 8-foot-9-inch Civil War soldier in full uniform representing a sentry on duty. Constructed of Vermont granite, the landmark weighs 140 tons. On the east face of the shaft is the simple inscription "Erected by the Citizens of Racine, 1884." The west face reads "In memory of Racine's loyal and noble sons who enlisted to defend and perpetuate the union of these United States in the War of 1861–1865."

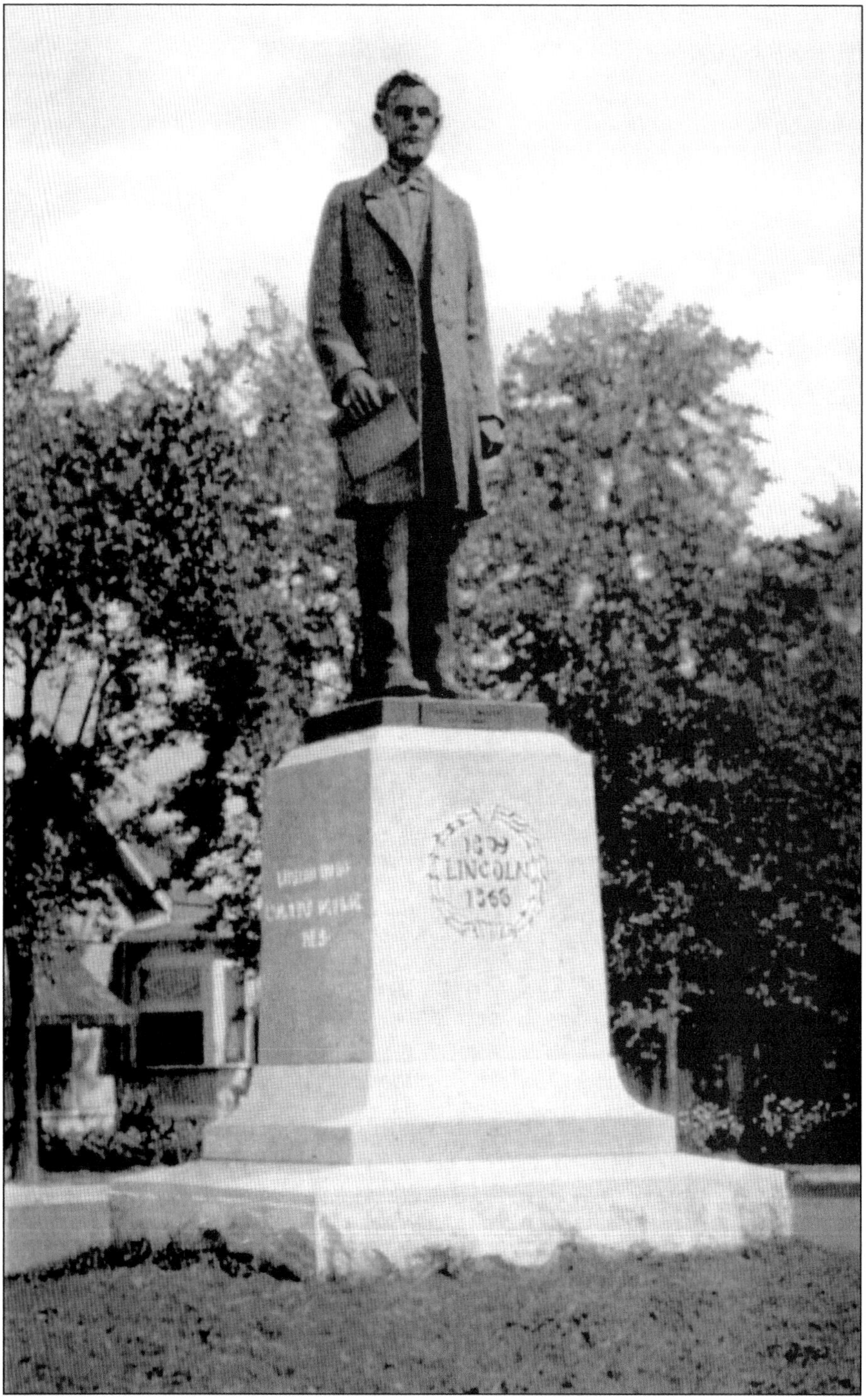

LINCOLN MONUMENT. This wonderful statue of Abraham Lincoln was erected on a small triangle near the old Lincoln School, where Hamilton Street, Summit Avenue and State Street intersect. The statue of heroic proportions is one foot taller than Lincoln's actual six-foot-four-inch frame. It was erected in 1924 with money raised by Racine's Ninth Street Boosters Club.

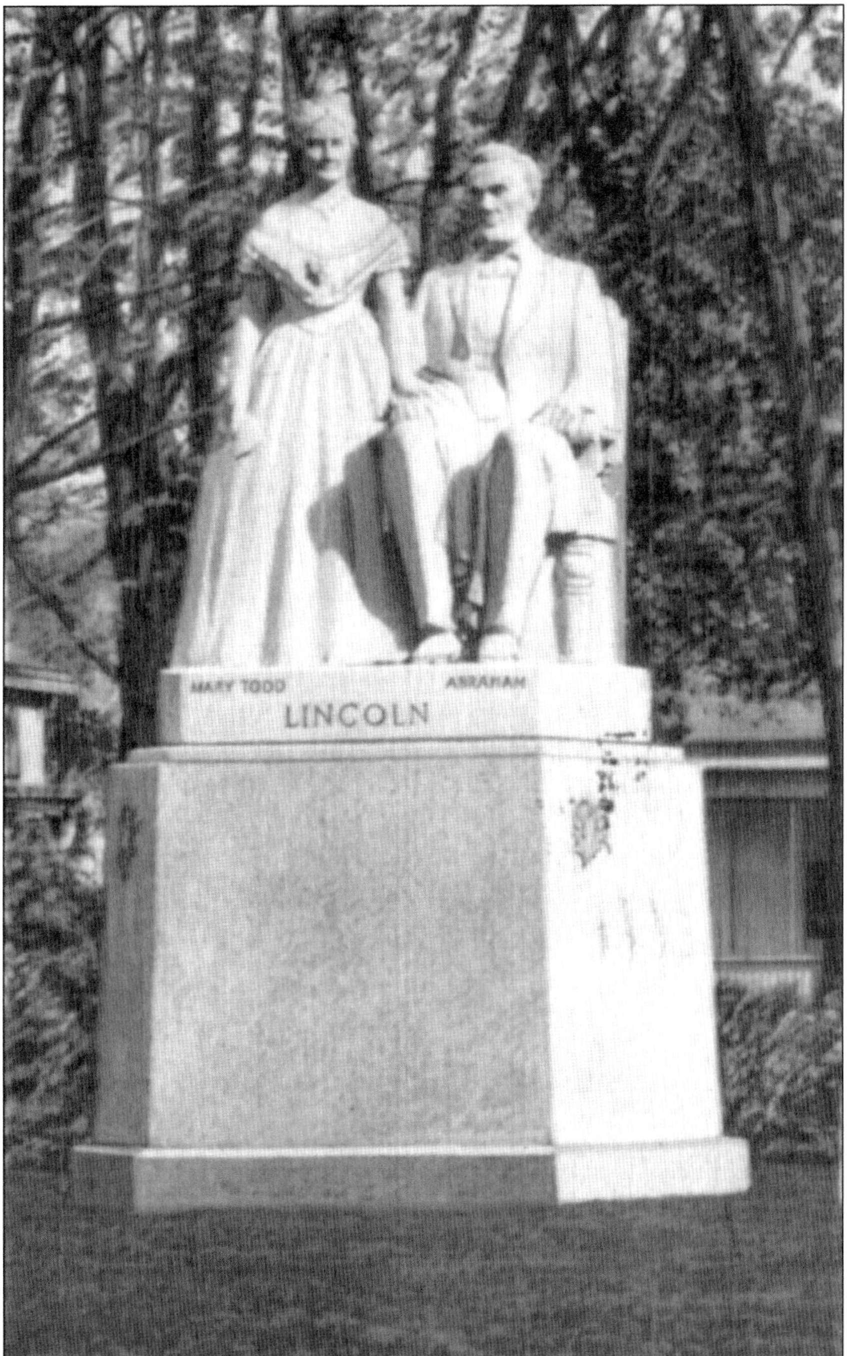

ABRAHAM AND MARY TODD LINCOLN. When this monument was unveiled on July 4, 1943, it was the first of its kind in the United States to honor both a president and his wife. The statue was a gift of Miss Lena Rose Wall, a resident on Racine's north side. The sculptor was Frederick C. Hibbard of Chicago. The monument is located in East Park at Tenth and Main Streets, where Mary Todd Lincoln was known to take morning strolls and spend quiet time during her visits to Racine.

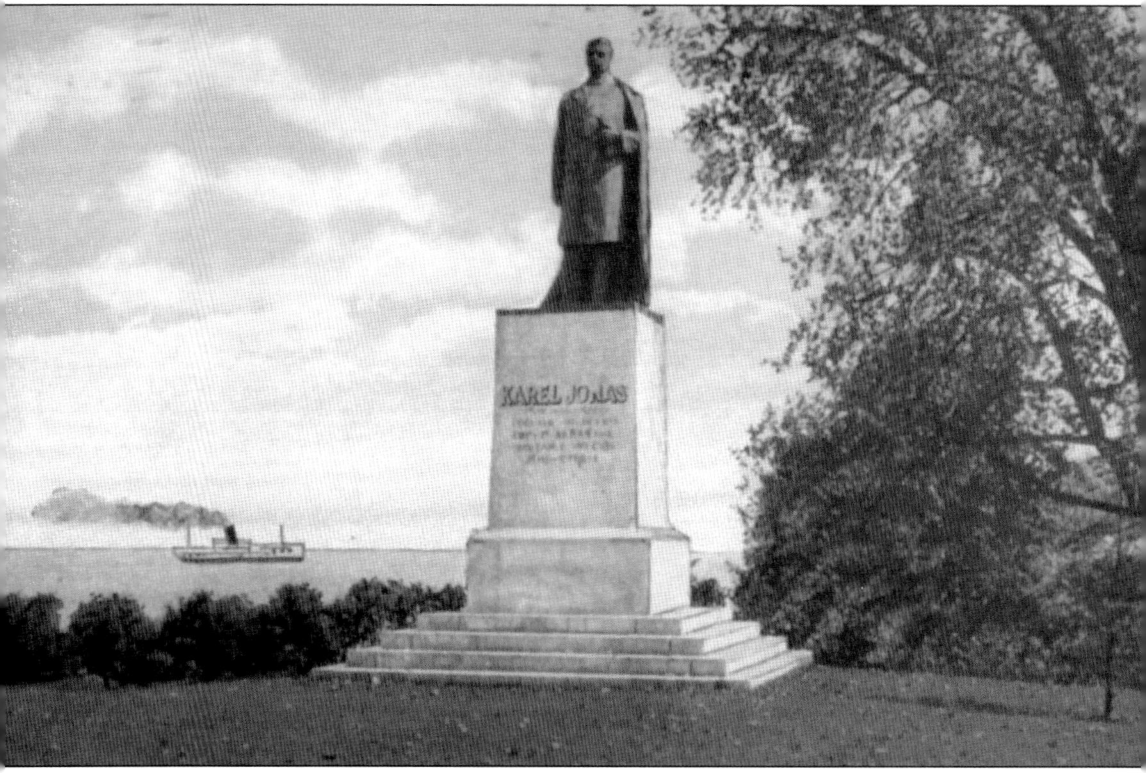

KAREL JONAS. When the Karel Jonas monument, a tribute to Racine's nationally famous Bohemian-American statesman, was originally dedicated in 1912, it was located on the lakefront in a small park at the corner of Barker Street and Michigan Boulevard. Erected by his grateful countrymen, the bronze statue, by sculptor Mario Korbel, is set on a 38-ton granite base. The statue was later moved to its present site called "Flat Iron Square," where Douglas Avenue and High Street intersect.

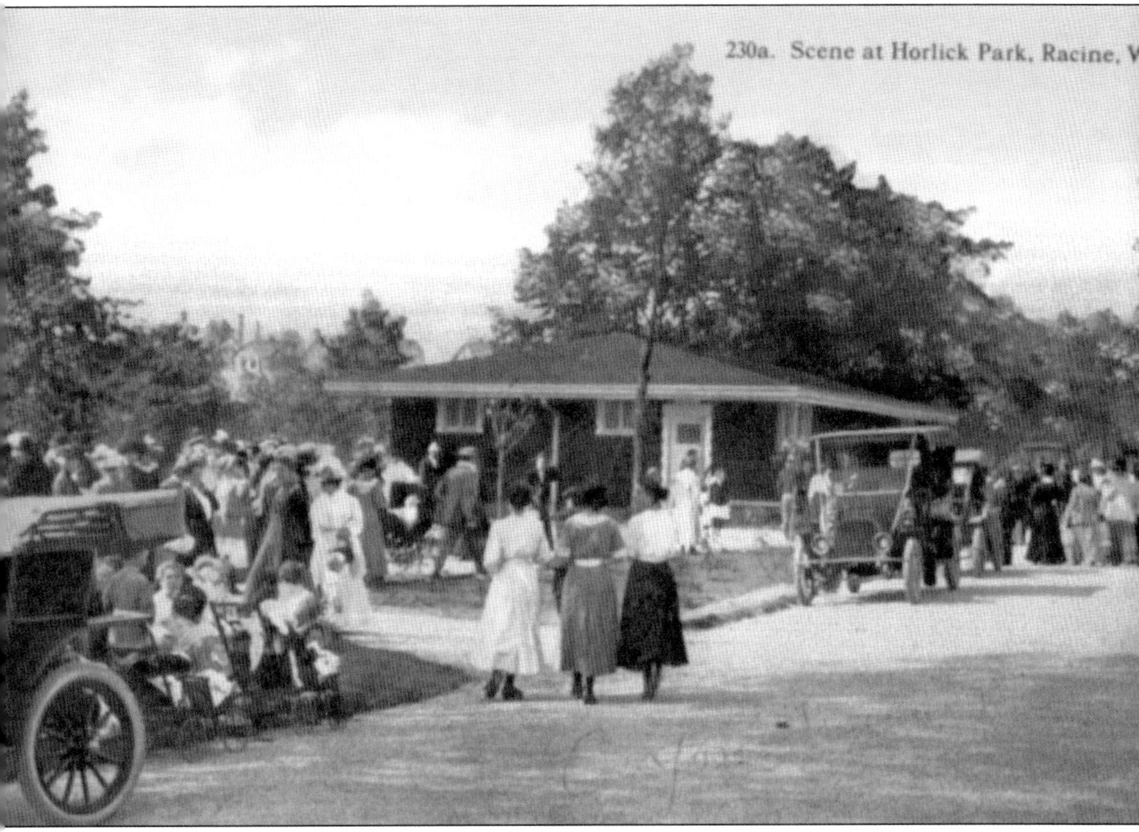

HORLICK PARK. In an effort to beautify and create picnic areas and playgrounds, the city began laying out an extensive park system around 1900. One of the finest parks was added when William Horlick purchased and donated an odd parcel of lowland that was surrounded by the Root River. Its legal name is Horlick Park but locals have always known it as Island Park. In January 1908, the Racine park board decided to add a refectory (pavilion), and $3,000 was allocated for its construction. The refectory, completed in 1910, is still being used.

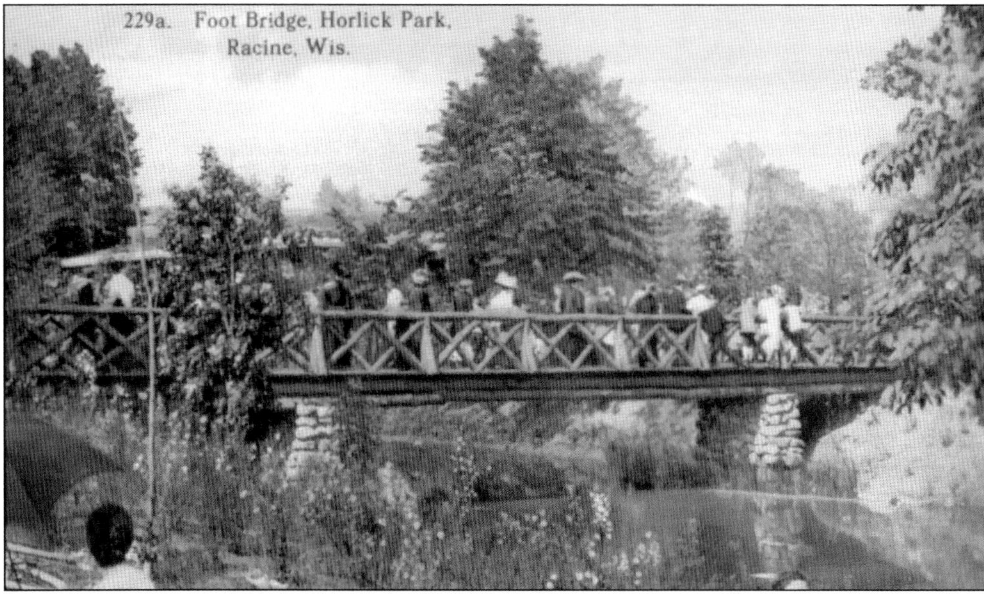

RUSTIC BRIDGE. Horlick Park, or Island Park, has changed through the years. The river once flowed behind the refectory (pavilion), dividing Horlick Park from Lewis Field where the ball diamonds and tennis courts are located. In 1910, the Racine parks department built this rustic walk bridge across the river to connect the two parks. During improvements to the park and river shorelines, a portion of the river was filled in to make a parking area behind the pavilion that exists there now. The bridge is no longer in existence.

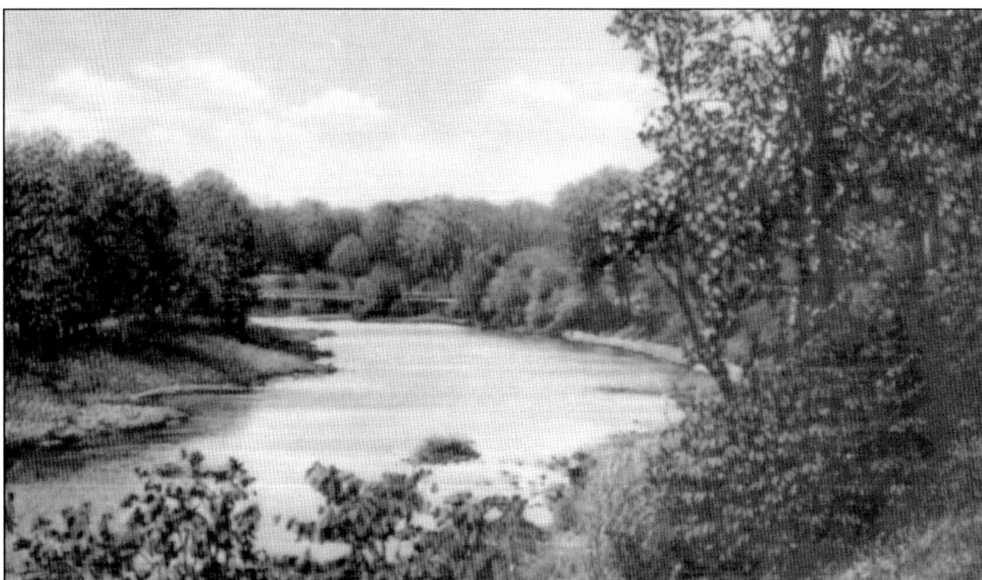

RIVERSIDE PARK. Prior to 1905, Racine had a number of small parks, but no major public parks. In his annual message to the city council that year, mayor Peter B. Nelson called attention to the need for public park land. To begin a major park system, the Racine Park Commission petitioned the council to set aside a strip of land along the Root River between West Sixth Street and Twelfth Street. This action created Riverside Park and heralded the beginning of a wonderful city park system. This view is looking south at the Washington Park footbridge.

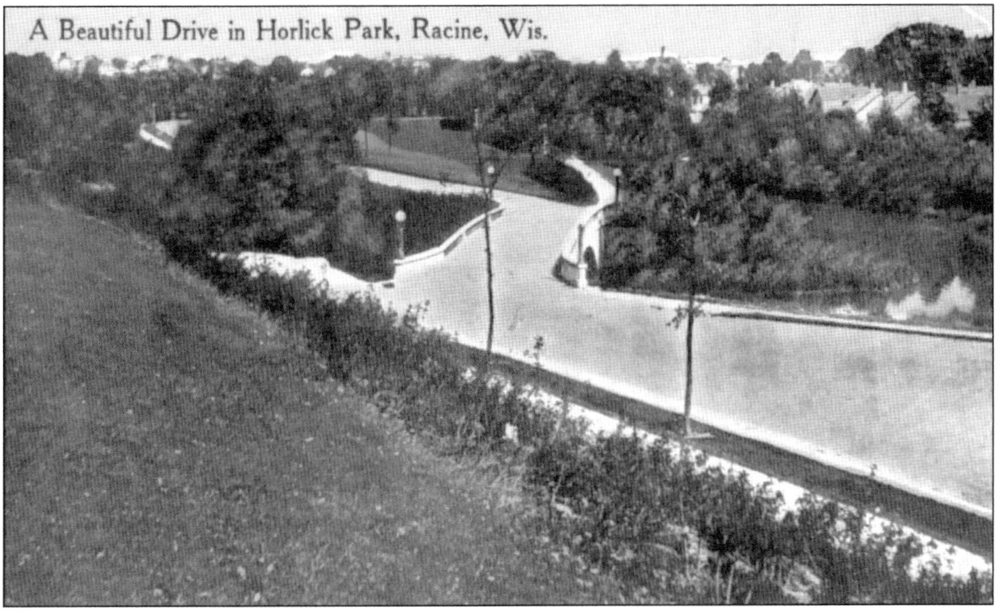

A BEAUTIFUL DRIVE IN HORLICK PARK. Looking down from a bluff where West Sixth Street and Kinzie Avenue meet is the west entrance to Horlick Park. The west entrance bridge was built in 1907. Unlike the methods of bridge building today, a portable cement mixing machine was set up at the site and workmen would mix batches of concrete and then wheel them by hand over to the workers.

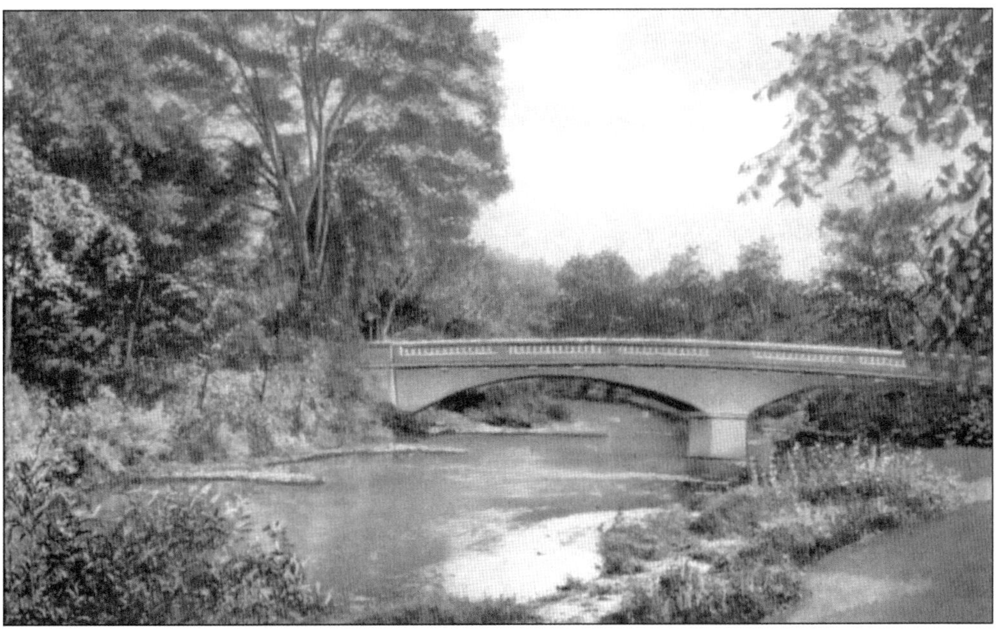

EAST ENTRANCE TO HORLICK PARK. Two bridges were built in Horlick Park in the early 1900s—one at the foot of Liberty Street on the east end and the other on the west end. The roadway twists and turns as it makes its way through a splendidly landscaped park. Later two walk bridges were added so that the people from the surrounding residential areas would have easy access to the park and playgrounds.

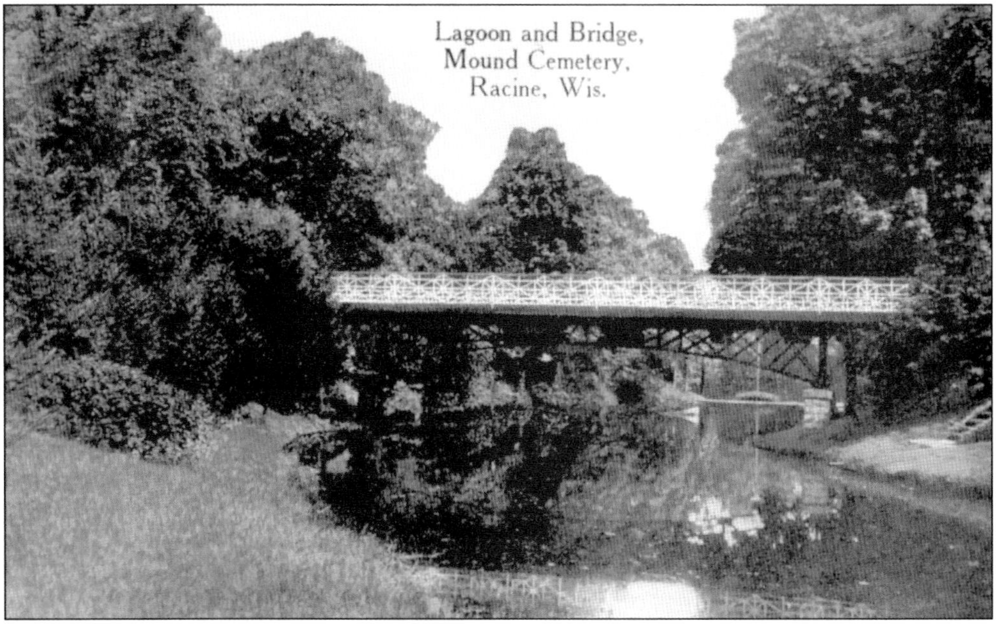

MOUND CEMETERY. Mound Cemetery has always been considered a beautiful spot. Before Racine had its public park system, many residents would spend a day picnicking there and in surrounding areas. Mound Cemetery derived its name from the prehistoric Native American burial mounds that once dotted the area. Today only 14 mounds still exist on the cemetery grounds. Although the old bridge in this view was replaced years ago, the spot is still beautiful today.

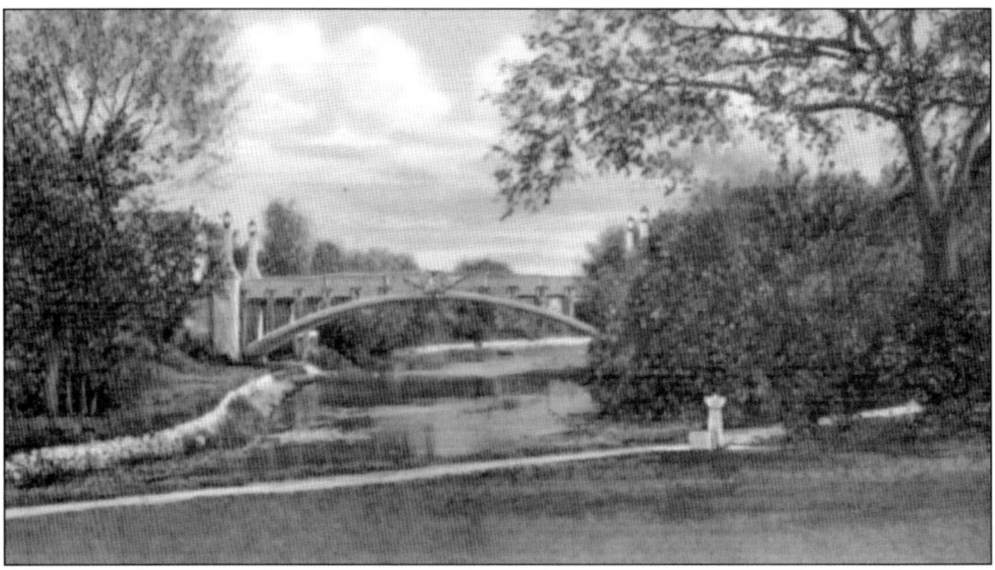

RIVER VIEW, HORLICK PARK. In 1928, the old iron bridge on West Sixth Street was replaced by this spectacular span. The sides of the bridge have interesting terra-cotta art panels that are embedded in the poured concrete construction. When the bridge was under construction, Mayor William Armstrong was criticized by those who considered the ornate extras as a waste of taxpayers' money and began calling the bridge "Armstrong's Folly." The columns and lights were stripped off in the 1960s and two of the lights now illuminate the steps at the main entrance of the Racine Heritage Museum building.

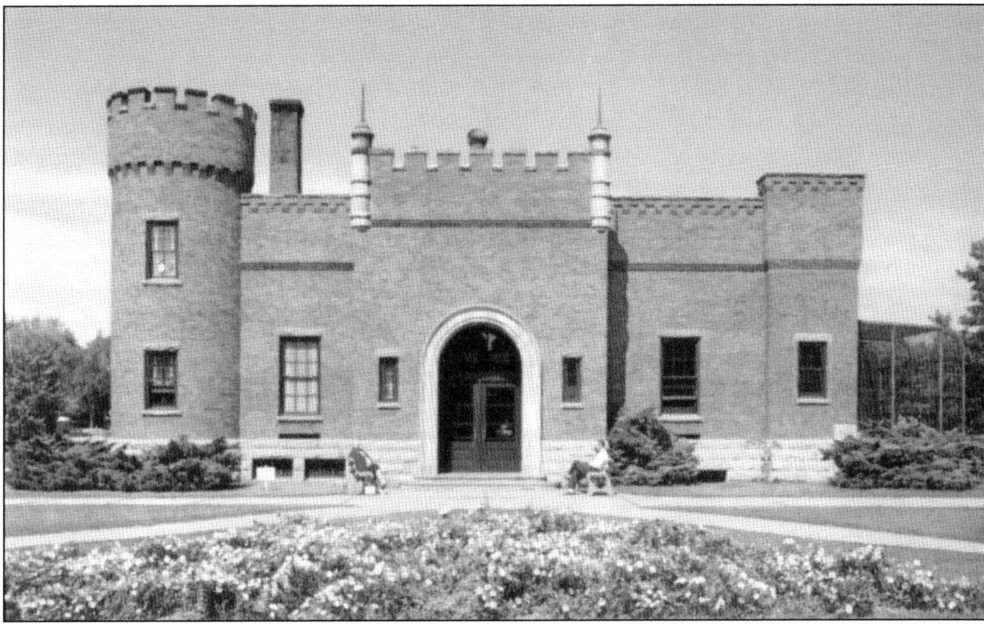

RACINE ZOO. The Racine Zoo got its start in 1923, when Jacob Stoffel Jr., president of the park board, donated three monkeys to the city that were housed at Island Park. In 1925, the zoo was moved to its present location on North Main Street. The Racine Zoo occupies a 28-acre site on the lakeshore, where the Bauman and Haumerson brickyards were once located. The clay pits were landscaped and became ponds and lagoons. The castle-like administration building was added in 1936. The Racine Zoo has always been a free zoo relying on government funding, personal donations, and fund-raisers, but in 2007, the zoo began charging a fee to view and enjoy the animals.

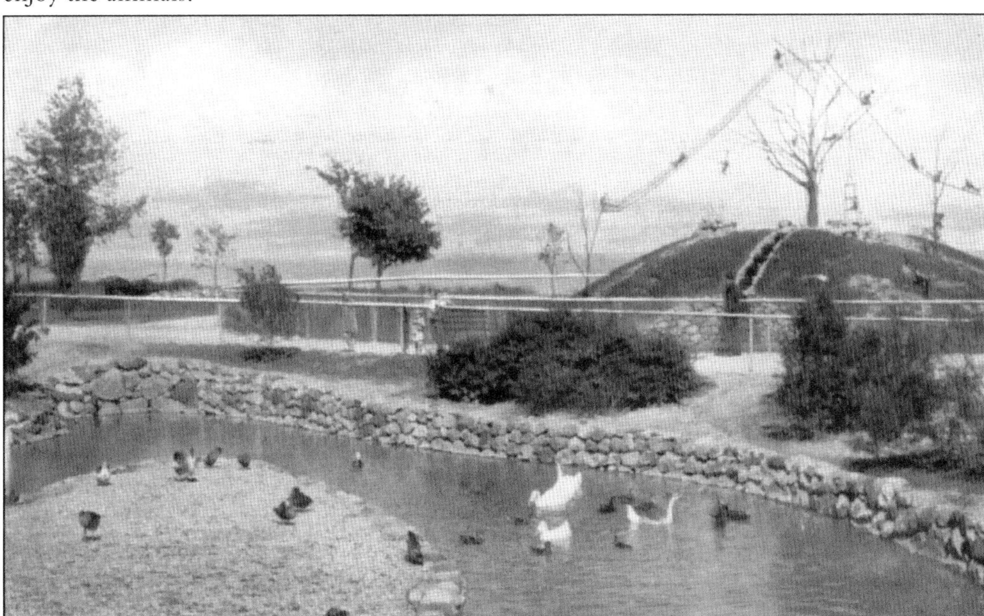

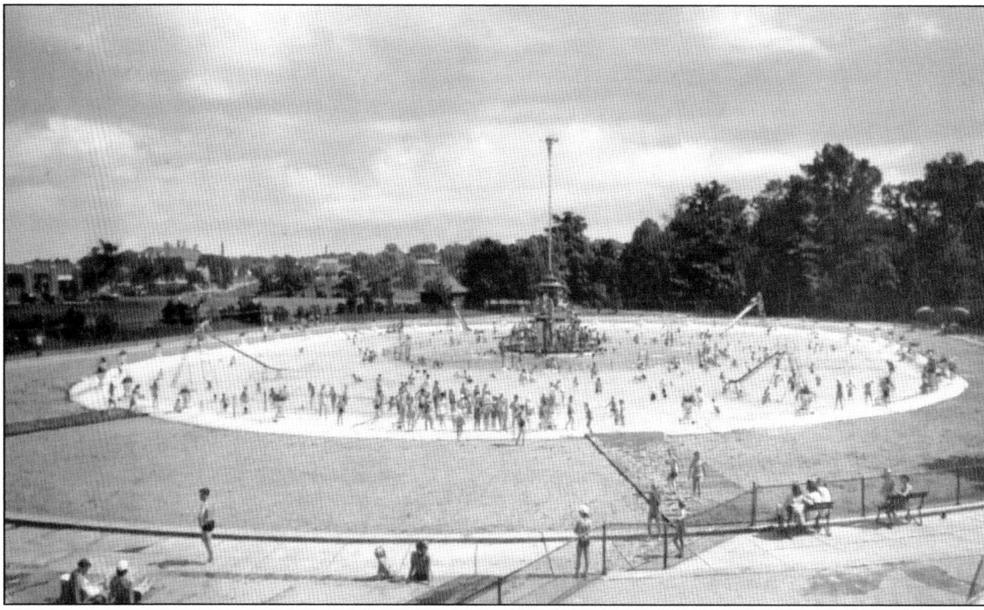

WASHINGTON PARK POOL. Built as a Works Progress Administration project in 1939, the Washington Park recreation center and swimming pool was a favorite summer activity for close to 30 years. The pool cost $150,000 to construct and was considered state-of-the-art. The only one of its kind in Wisconsin, it was built with the idea of providing a seashore atmosphere in the heart of the city. The pool was closed in 1968 and later removed. The recreation building (below) included a gym and showers. The pool's changing rooms were located in two open air areas with benches and changing stalls. The boys were located on the east side of the building and the girls on the west side. Street clothes were placed in baskets and each patron got a rubberized ankle band with a medal tag with the basket number on it. There was also a concession window that sold goodies for the long walk home.

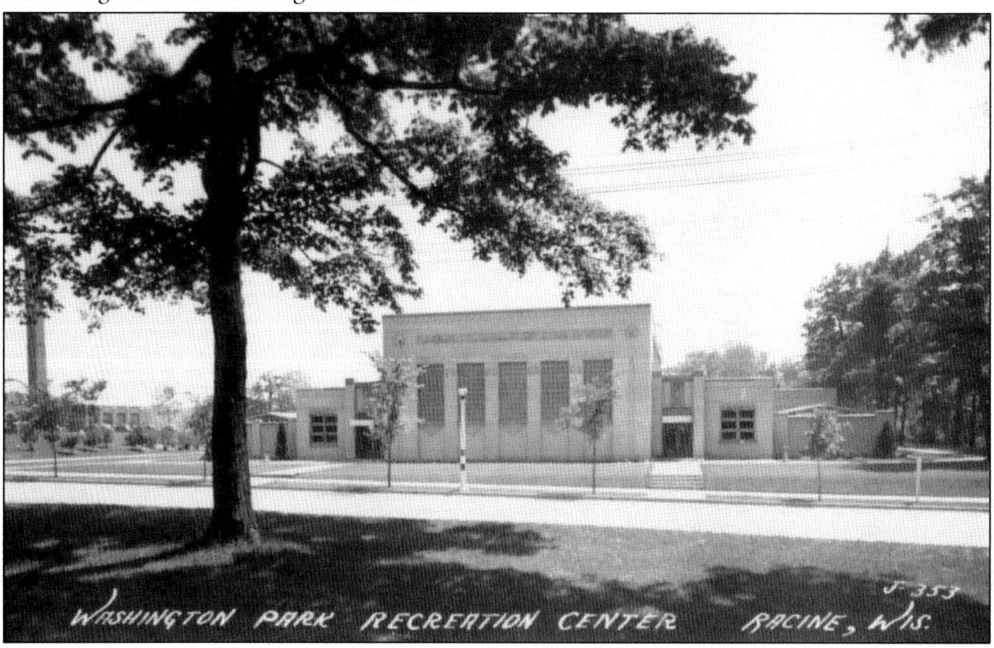

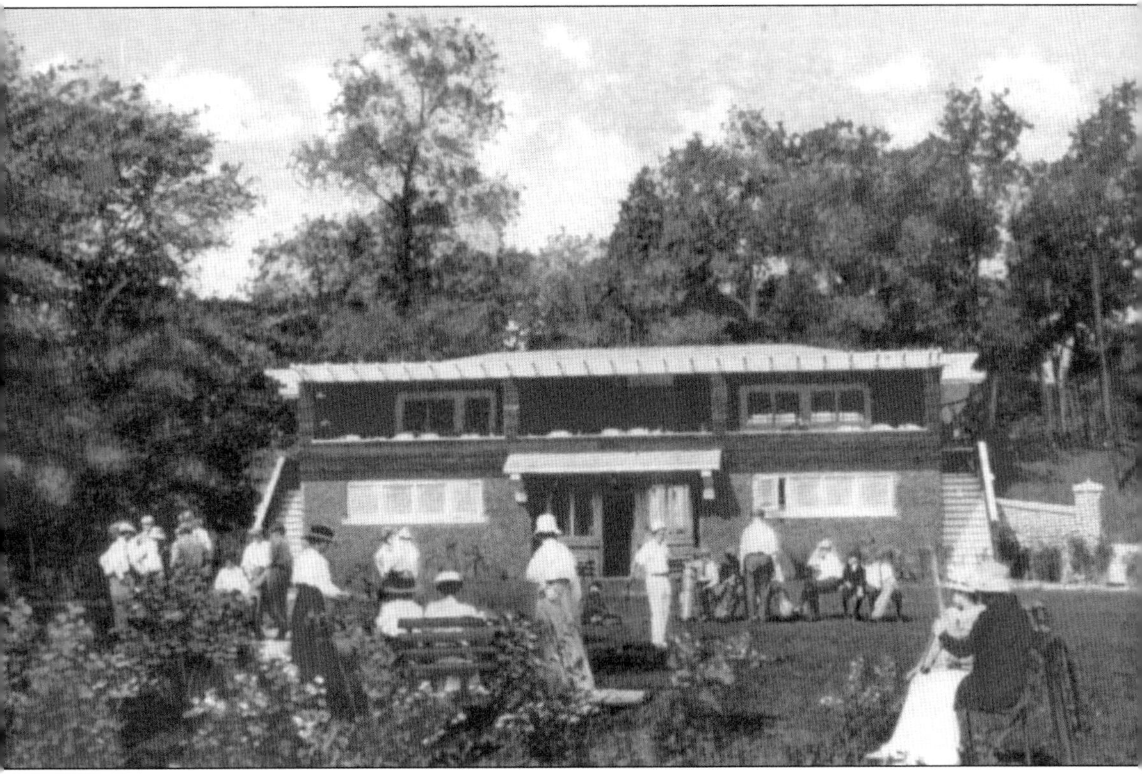

MUNICIPAL GOLF COURSE. In 1905, Mayor Peter B. Nelson asked landowner Charles Erskine if he would sell 47 acres of lowland to the city for park purposes. Within a few months, the deal was finalized and the city paid $20,487.50 for the land. This park had a natural flowing landscape and was popular because of its beautiful, mature wooded areas. Later, parts of Washington Park, Riverside Park, and Cedar Bend were developed into the Washington Park Municipal Golf Course.

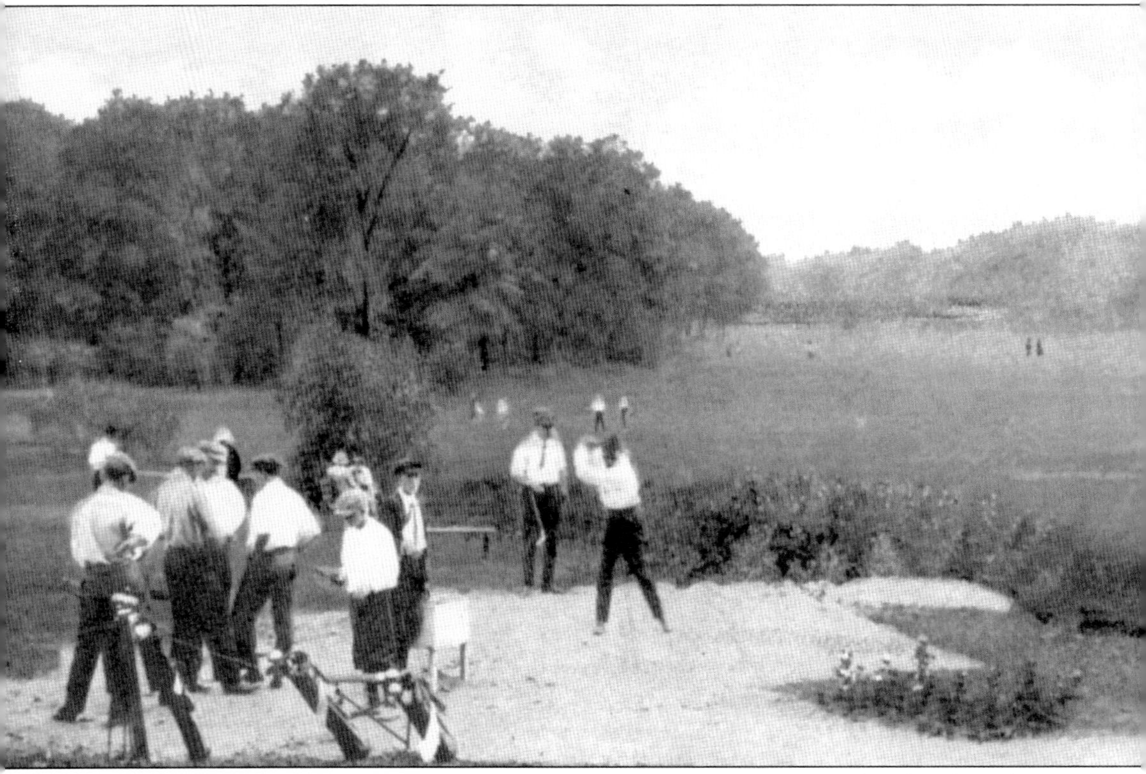

WASHINGTON PARK GOLF LINKS. Soon after Riverside Park was completed and Washington Park was improved, the city began to develop the area known as Cedar Bend, a big turn in the Root River and the lowlands, to create Washington Park and the Washington Park Golf Course. A footbridge was constructed across the river for golfers. Here a group of early golf enthusiasts spend a day at Washington Park Golf Course. The course is still a popular golfing site.

Five

Lighthouses and Lakefront Scenery

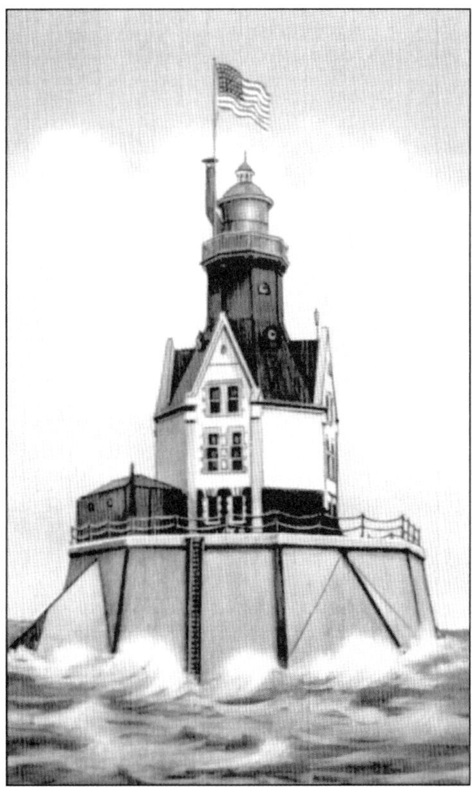

Reef Lighthouse. About two miles east of Racine's lakeshore is a shallow reef that is a hazard for vessels passing or entering Racine's harbor. A buoy with a ringing bell helped to protect sailors from the treacherous limestone formation during pioneer years. A number of warning devices were placed there to mark the danger. In 1906, the Reef Lighthouse was finished. Octagonal in shape, it was constructed of brown and white brick with an iron skeleton. Somewhat artistic in design, the structure incorporated four gables in its roof lines. It stood on an octagonal concrete base 75 feet across and 17 feet above the water. It was built at a cost of $80,000. This beautiful landmark was razed in 1961 and replaced by a mechanical beacon.

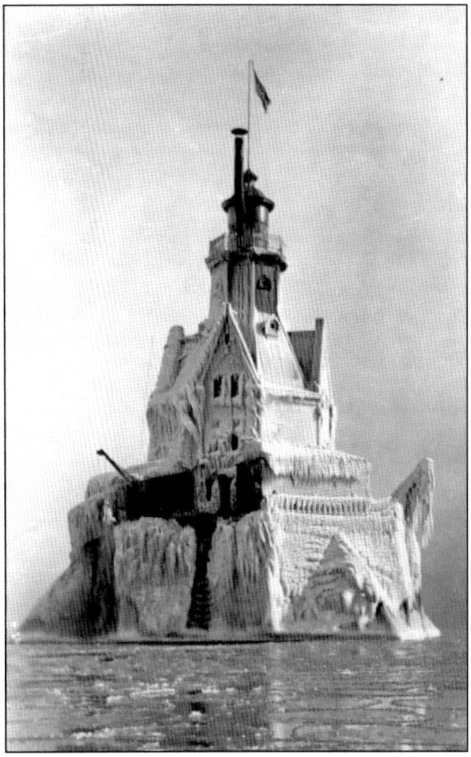

RACINE REEF LIGHTHOUSE. Showing the lighthouse frosted like a wedding cake, a note on the back of the card states that the winter ice covering the structure was from one to four feet thick. The Victorianesque structure was laid out in a cruciform plan with four main decks. The building stood 66 feet from the upper surface of the crib where it was constructed to the top of the lantern. The beautiful landmark was dismantled in 1961.

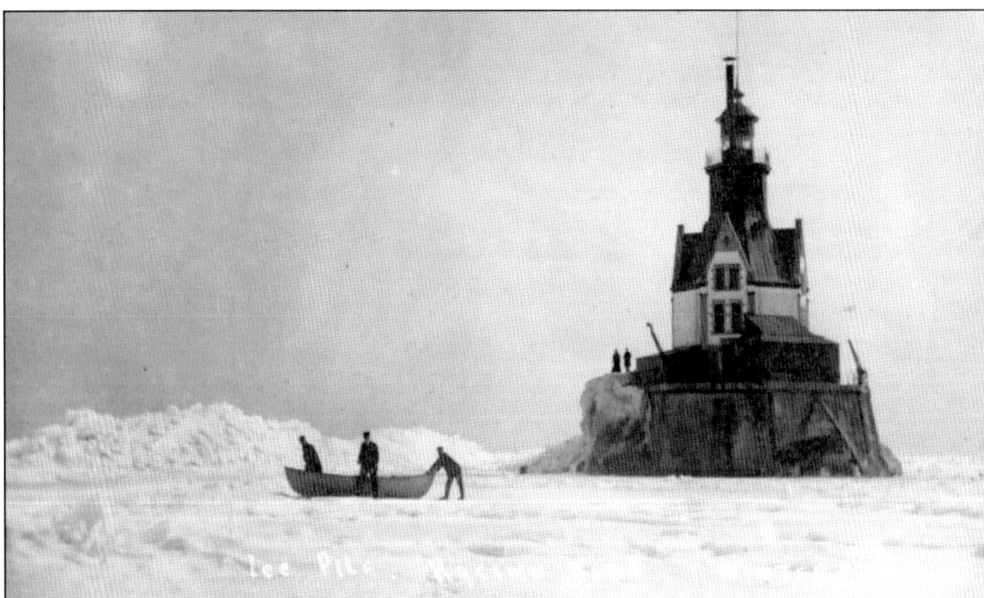

ICE PILES RACINE REEF, WINTER 1912. The winter weather was so bitter in early March 1912 that it was said that Lake Michigan froze over. It is unknown if that truly happened; however, photographs document the lake frozen out past the Reef Lighthouse that year. In April 1949, the Coast Guard men stationed at the Reef Lighthouse were the envy of television fans when their new television set went into operation. The Racine Coast Guard station was one of the first along the lakeshore to receive a television set.

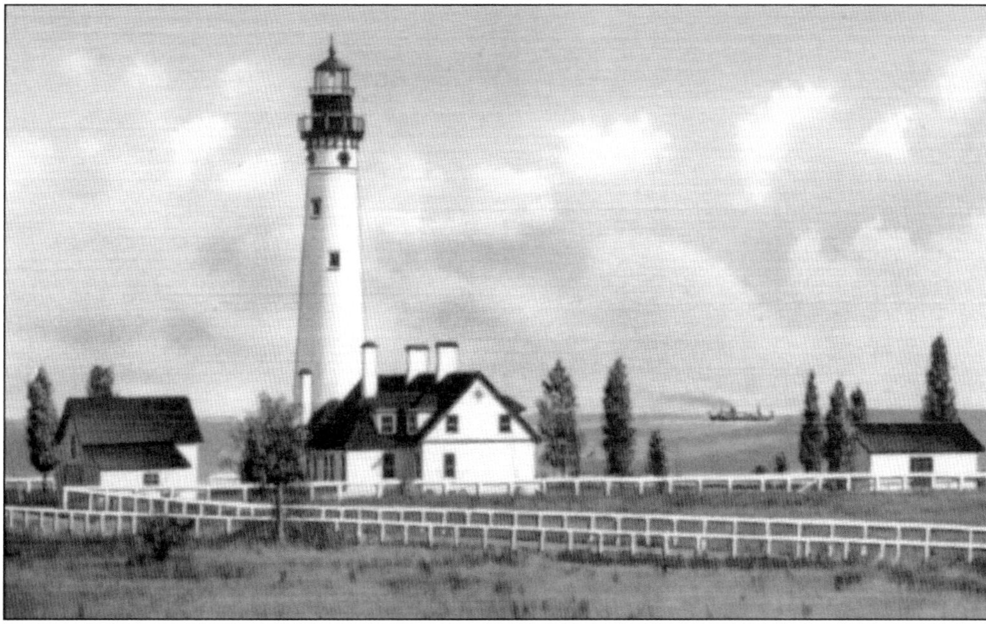

WIND POINT LIGHTHOUSE. One of the finest examples of a Great Lakes lighthouse still stands on the Racine shore of Lake Michigan. Wind Point Lighthouse is one of the most popular subjects for artists and photographers. Originally known as North Point lighthouse, its protecting light reaches about 18 miles out on the lake to warn vessels of the treacherous Racine reef. The stately slender brick lighthouse standing 112 feet above the lake was built in 1880. The tower has a diameter of 22 feet at the base where the walls are seven feet thick and is capped with a 10-sided cast iron lantern house. The lantern house is reached by 144 iron grate steps that spiral up though the center of the tower. The light, originally an Aladdin's lamp fueled by kerosene, was electrified in 1924. The village of Wind Point has used the buildings as a village hall and police headquarters since 1964. Over the years, the weather and other elements have taken their toll on the 127-year-old structure. Many restoration and preservation projects have been done to help keep its majestic historical presence. In 2007 a major window restoration project was started.

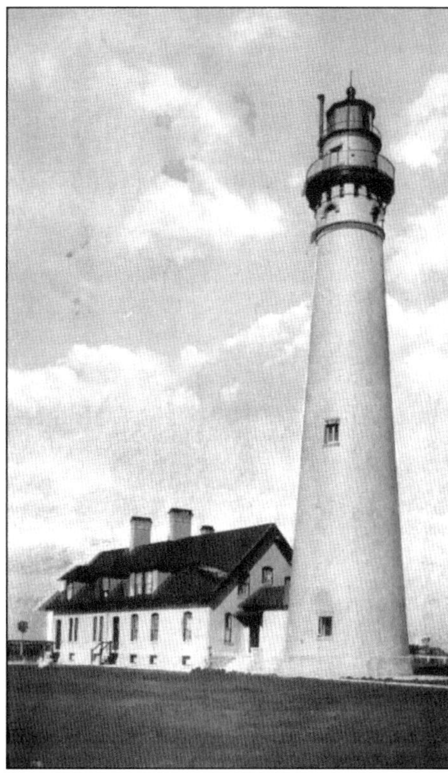

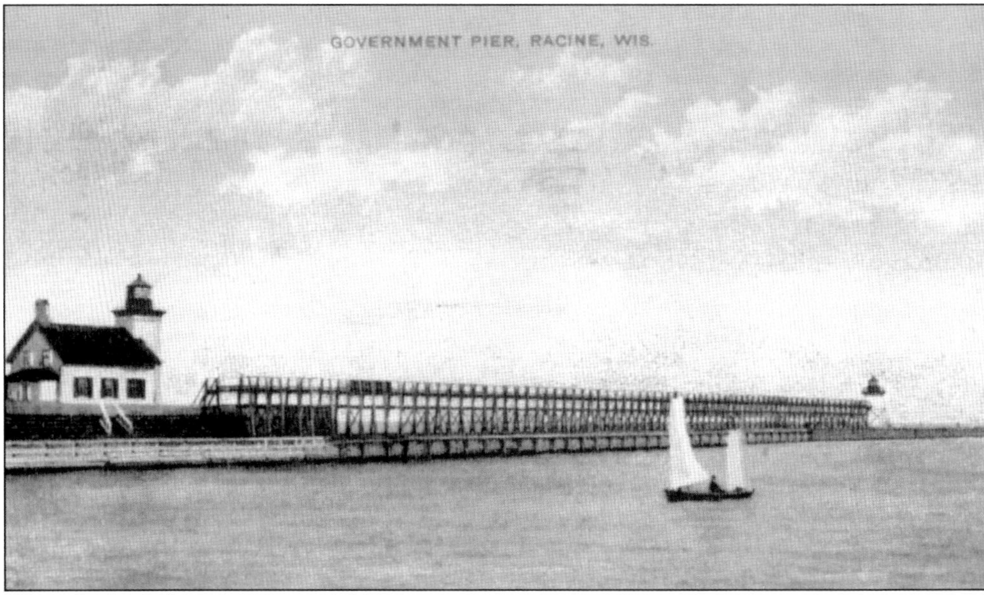

GOVERNMENT PIER AND LIGHTHOUSE. When the 1866 Harbor Lighthouse was built, it was on a stone-filled wooden crib far out in the lake. Through the years, the shore was back filled and the lighthouse became part of the Root River's north shoreline. Later the pier was extended and the catwalk was added to aid the lighthouse keepers who had to tend the light when waves were crashing over the pier. This landmark lighthouse still stands on the north side of the Root River.

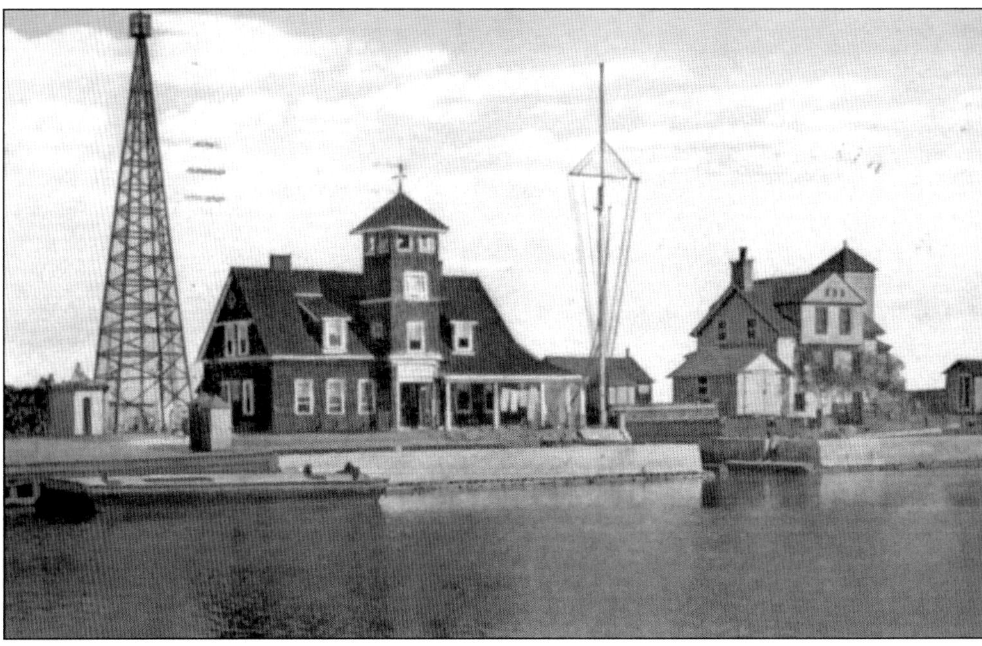

LIFE SAVING STATION. The Coast Guard life saving station (left) was built at the mouth of the Root River in 1903 next to the old 1866 Harbor Lighthouse. It replaced an older structure that was located on the river at the foot of Michigan Boulevard closer to the Main Street Bridge. The Coast Guard discontinued service in Racine in 1973.

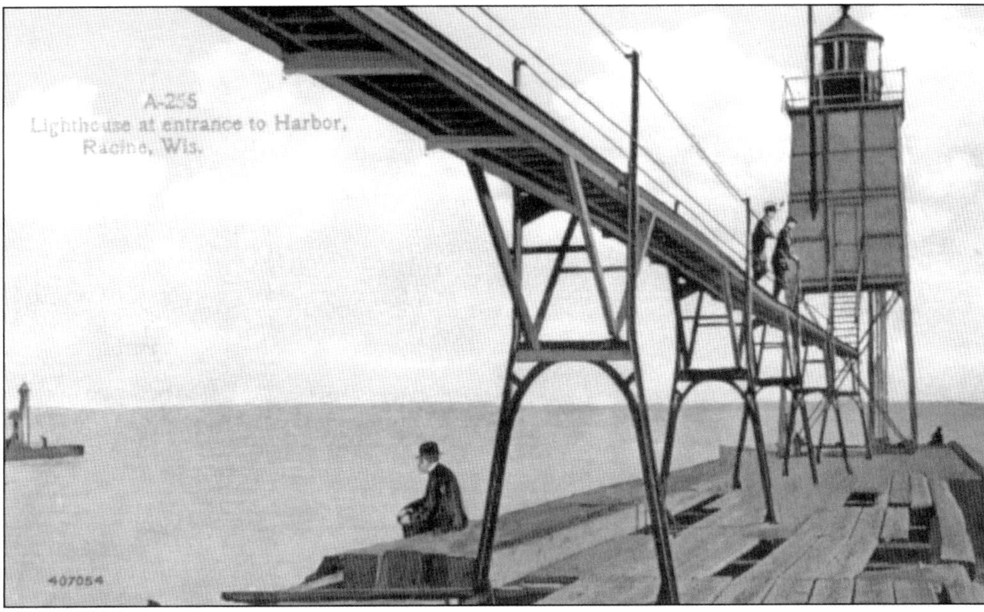

LIGHTHOUSE AT ENTRANCE TO HARBOR. Today the old landmark Red Lighthouse stands proudly on the edge of Reef Point Marina. When this view was photographed, the massive steel structure was located on the original wooden North Pier that jutted straight out from the Root River. When the concrete arrowhead breakwaters were built creating an outer harbor, the lighthouse was moved to the new North Pier. The lighthouse appeared to be painted white during its early years but was later painted red.

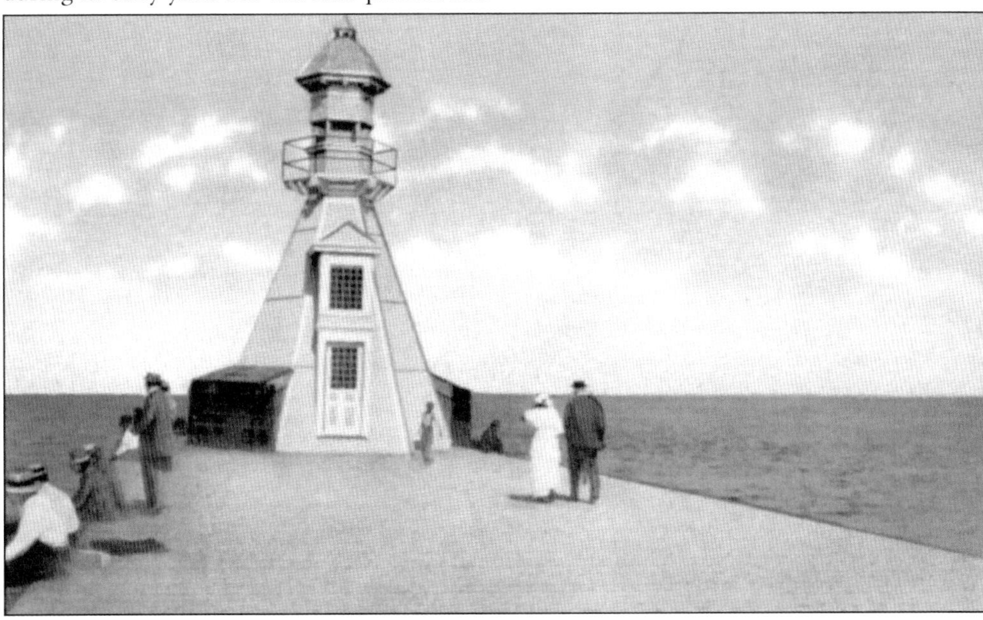

LIGHTHOUSE AT END OF NORTH PIER. This small beacon was built to mark the entrance of Racine's outer harbor after the new concrete arrowhead piers were constructed. Later the large Red Lighthouse was moved from the mouth of the river to replace it. During the summer, hundreds of people took strolls out on the pier to enjoy the cool Lake Michigan breezes. Also it was a favorite spot for fisherman to catch a stringer of fresh lake perch.

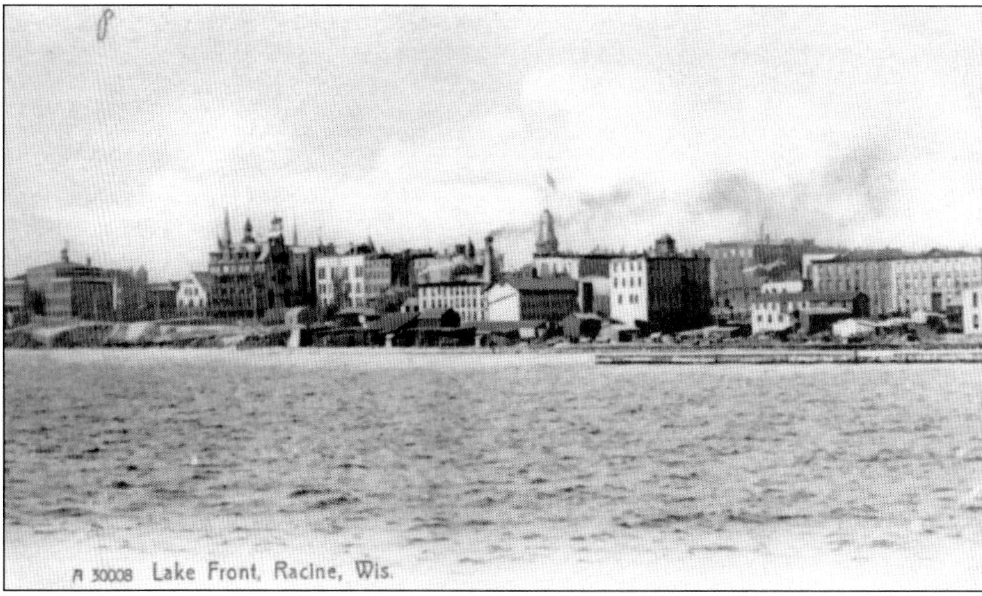

CITY SHORELINE LAKE FRONT. The city of Racine is pictured from out in Lake Michigan about 1906. In just one lifetime the little pioneer village on the banks of a muddy root-filled river was transformed into a city with fine public buildings, schools, churches, business blocks, and large factories. Companies like J. I. Case Threshing Machine Company, Horlick's Malted Milk, and Johnson's Wax were putting the city on world maps. Today Festival Hall and Reef Point Marina fill the water's edge.

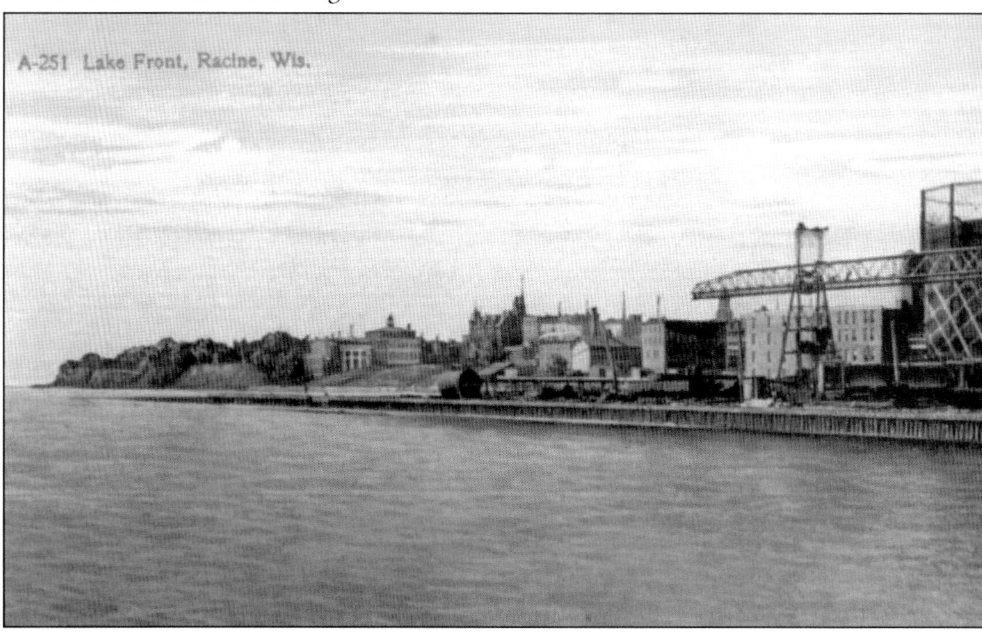

LAKE FRONT. Racine's lakefront has changed completely through the years. The center of this 1916 view is where Festival Hall and the Reef Point Marina were constructed. The south pier was not built yet and Pershing Park had not even been started. In fact, the only building in this view that is still standing is the Elks lodge at Lake Avenue and Sixth Street; however, many of the buildings in the photograph were still standing as late as 1980.

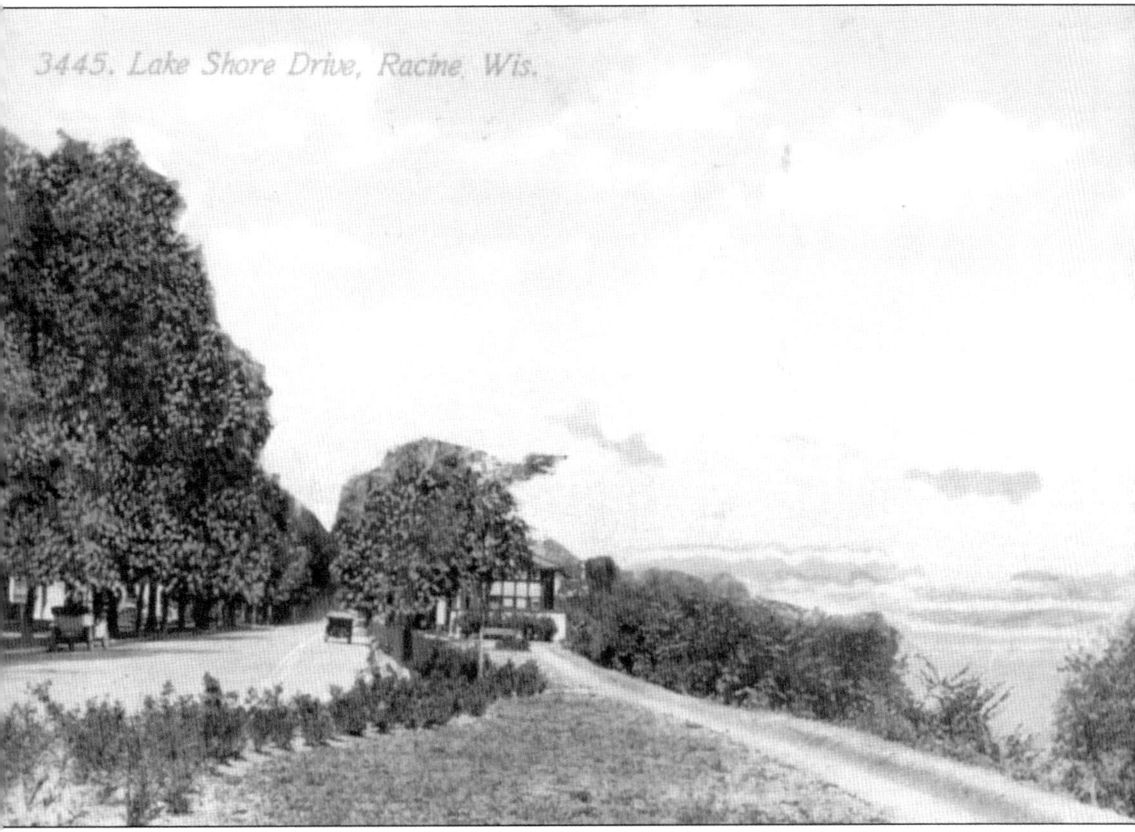

LAKE SHORE DRIVE. This view looks north along South Main Street from the intersection of Fourteenth and Main Streets about 1914. Because Main Street came so close to the bluff, no homes were built on the lakeshore lots. The first house seen to the right is the Hardy house built in 1905. The three-story prairie-style lake bluff home was designed by world famous architect Frank Lloyd Wright. In 1905, South Main Street was lined with classical revival, Greek Revival, and Italianate houses. The Hardy house with its symmetrical, rectangular shape with stucco looked out of place among the neighboring houses. The house was often mistaken for a bathhouse because of its double entry design and it has been said that, more than once, the owners found bewildered bathers standing just inside the doorway. The Hardy house still stands there today.

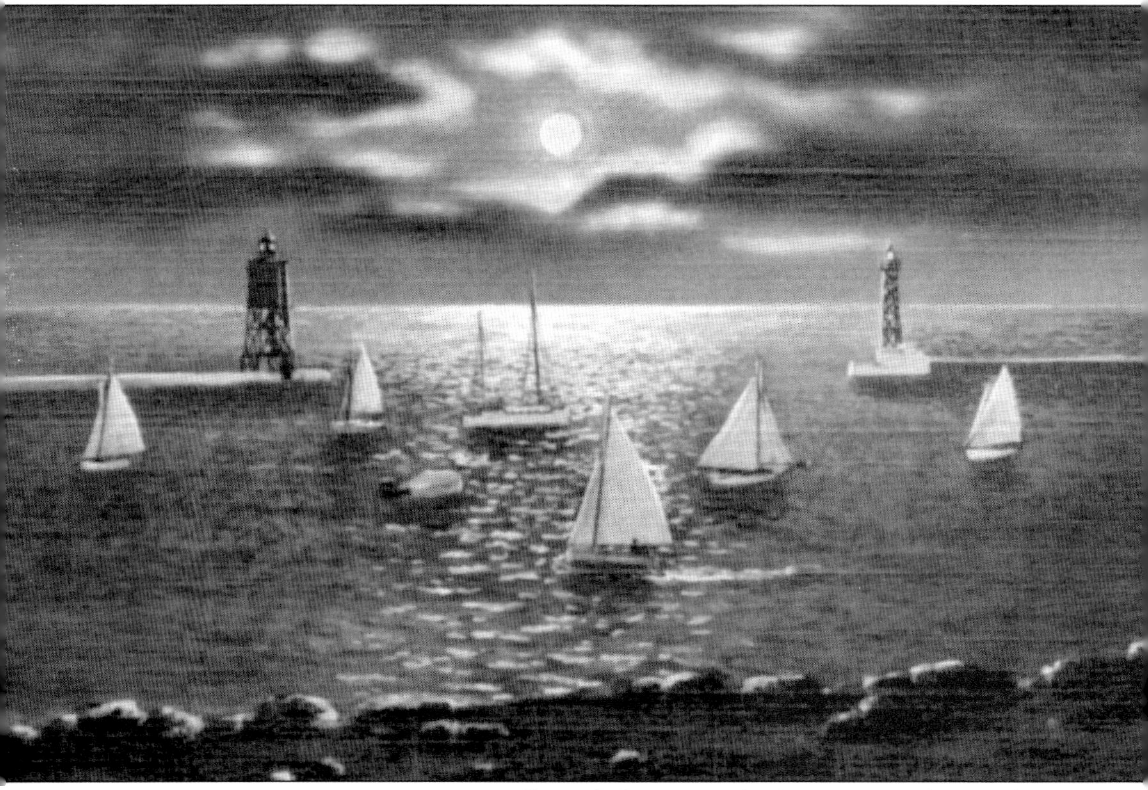

MOONLIGHT ON LAKE MICHIGAN. Sailboats frolic just inside the entrance of Racine's outer harbor. The Racine Yacht Club and its members have always sponsored and participated in annual boat races and regattas. At times during the boating season, hundreds of sails can be seen dotting the blue waters off the shore of Racine. This view shows the old arrowhead outer harbor piers with the Red Lighthouse to the left. In November 1982, a Racine lakefront development plan was drafted to create a spectacular harbor and marina. The plan was adopted and soon thousands of loads of stone were trucked to the project from the quarry north of Racine. New breakwaters and a peninsula were created. The peninsula was backfilled with sand and sediment dredged from the new docking areas.

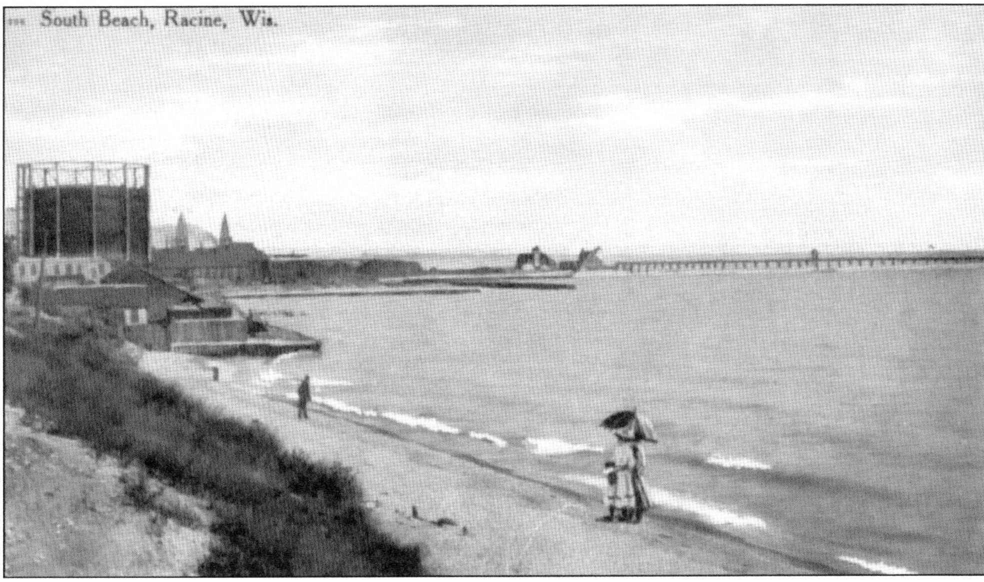

SOUTH BEACH. For decades the lots on Lake Avenue between Fifth and Sixth Streets were open, unsightly weed lots where ashes and trash were being dumped. The beach was narrow and consisted of more gravel than sand. In 1910, the city purchased the property from the Dietrich Brothers for $15,000 for use as a lakeshore park. In the distance, along the shoreline at the foot of Fourth Street, was one of the first large natural gas storage tanks for the Racine Gas Light Company (now Wisconsin Gas and Electric Company).

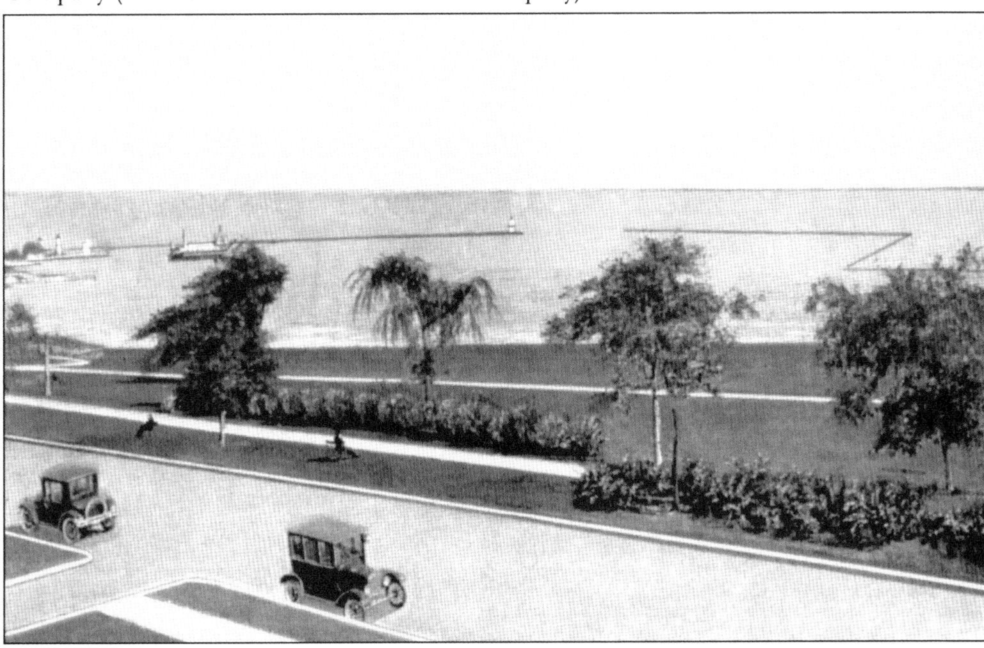

LAKE MICHIGAN FROM HOTEL RACINE. When visitors gazed out over the lakeshore from Hotel Racine after about 1915, they saw a carefully manicured parklike setting with grass, shrubs, and trees. Just a few years before, the area was a trashy weed lot. Needing more open space and park land along the lakeshore, the city started filling in the shoreline out to the stone rubble breakwater and created what is now Pershing Park.

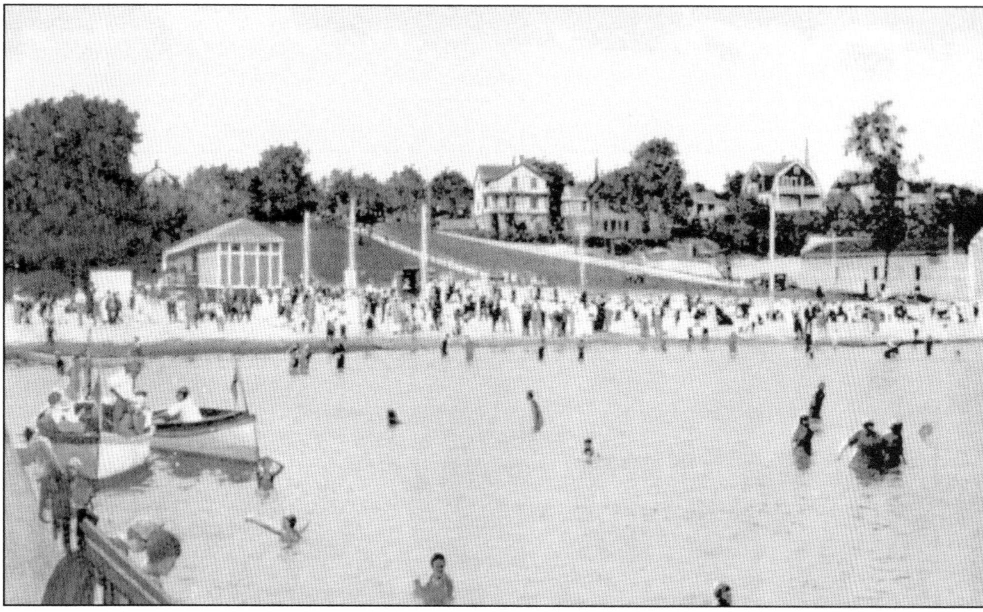

SANDY NORTH BEACH. This 1919 view was taken from the North Pier showing people enjoying a day at the beach. From the day the bathing beach was opened in 1908, it has been a popular spot to spend summer days. The bathhouse has been gone for decades and was replaced by one a few thousand feet to the north. In recent years, a magnificent children's playground has been built in the dune area for all to enjoy.

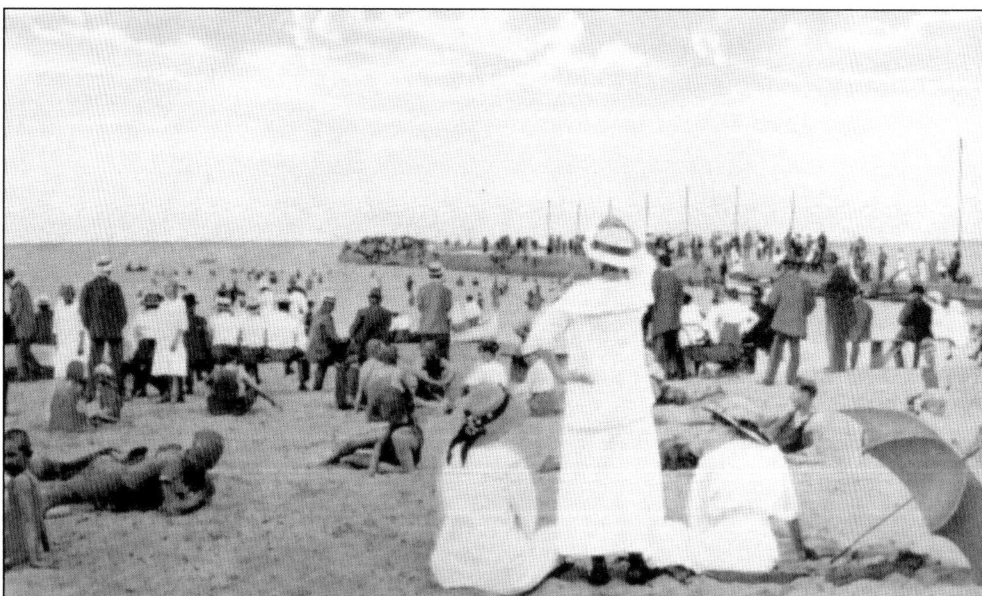

SCENE AT NORTH BEACH. After a long week at work, hundreds of people flocked to the beach to socialize and relax. This may be a Sunday afternoon because so many men are still in suit coats. Fashion was quite conservative at the time. Note the three ladies in full dress, shoes, and hats sitting with their umbrella to shade them from the sun. Many in the picture appear as if they could be at church instead of a beautiful beach.

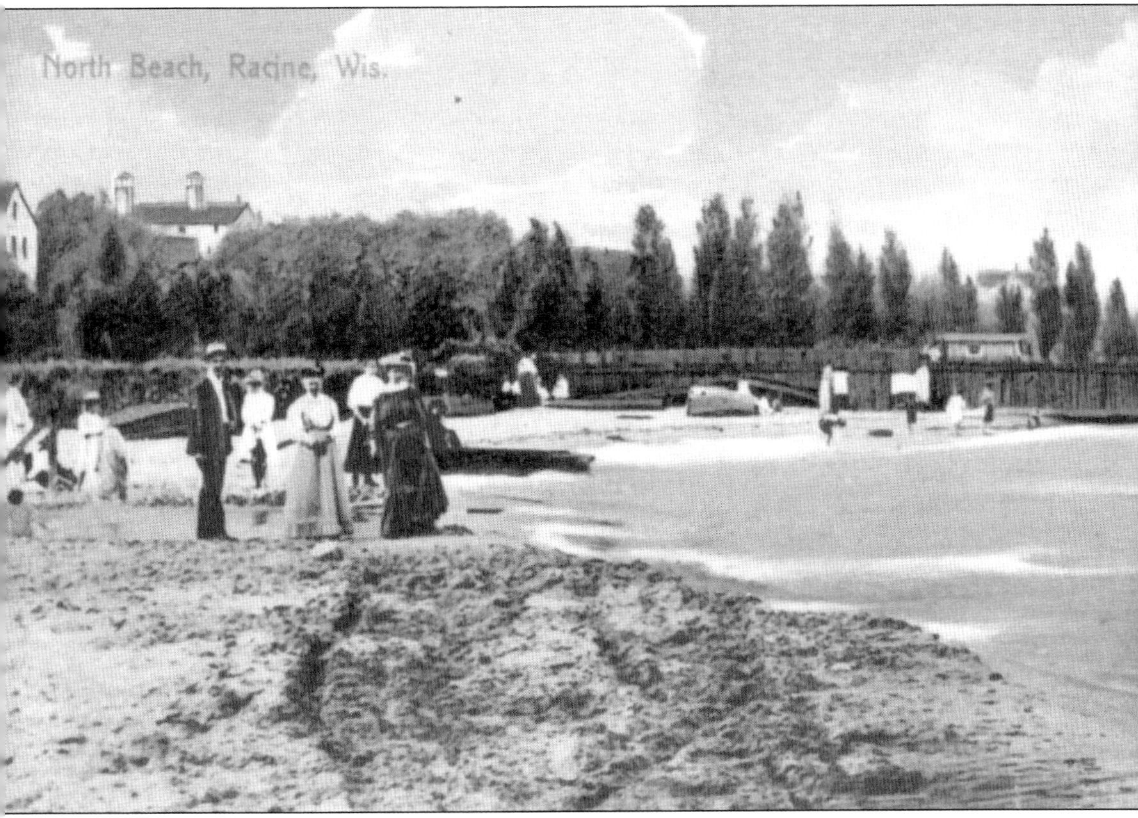

North Beach. This 1908 view shows North Beach at the foot of Kewaunee Street and Lake Michigan. At the time the shoreline was still privately owned with many groups owning summer cottages built on the beach to enjoy the cool lake breezes. In the upper left corner the Weber brewery and malt house can be seen. William H. Weber founded the brewery on the site in 1878 because there was a natural spring that continuously flowed out of the bluff. Weber manufactured Weiss Beer. The beer was an effervescent light-colored beer usually made from wheat. The second stage of fermentation was allowed to take place in the bottles, so heavy bottles were needed. Early bottles were made of pottery and were marked "W. Weber Racine, Wis."

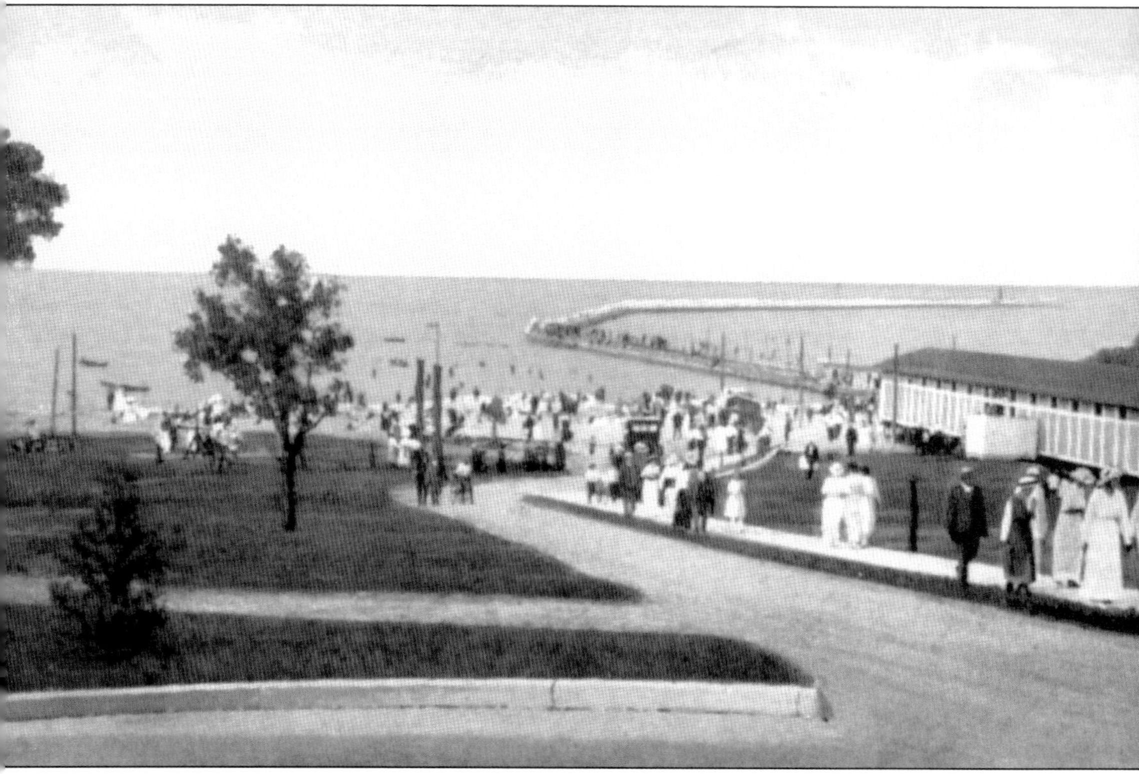

NORTH SIDE BATHING BEACH. When the pioneers settled in Racine, there was a natural sand bar at the mouth of the Root River. The lakeshore north of the river was a low, sandy, flat area just a few feet higher than the lake. As the city grew, the area was filled in and developed. One of the buildings still on the flats is the Racine Water Company on Michigan Boulevard and Hubbard Street. A small public beach area was created at the foot of Barker Street and it became a very popular bathing spot. In 1908, the first city-owned bathhouse was built on the site. During the following decades, all the homes and private properties on the lakeshore side north from Barker Street to Gould Street were purchased and became city park land. North Beach is one of the largest natural sand beaches on the Great Lakes.

Six

BUSINESS

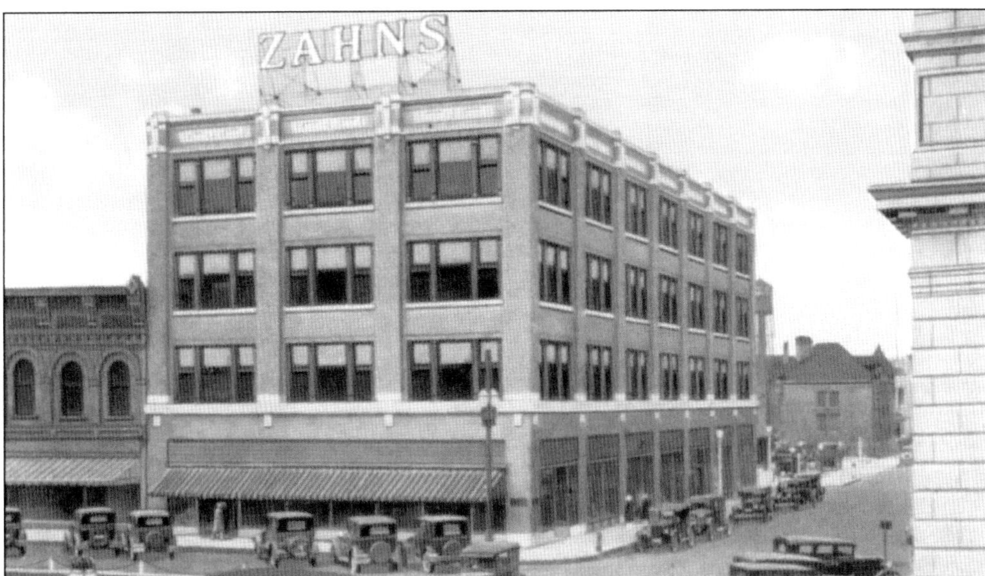

ZAHN'S DEPARTMENT STORE. One of the best known stores in Racine's history was Zahn's Department Store. Originally at 528 Main Street, the store moved to a Monument Square building at Fifth and Main Streets in 1927. A true department store, Zahn's had a manned elevator that would take a shopper to four floors and a basement area full of top of the line merchandise. The store closed in 1981 in the midst of a gripping recession when Racine's unemployment rate reached nearly 16 percent.

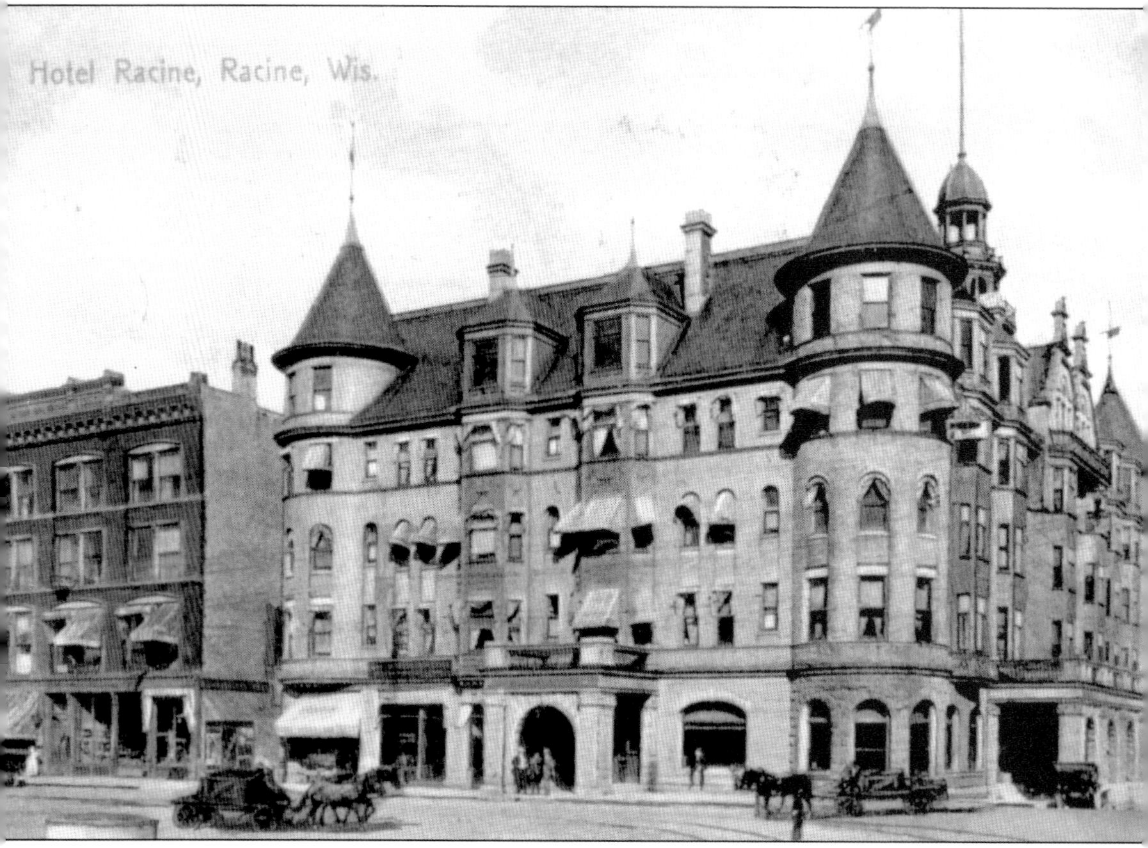

HOTEL RACINE. The 1890s, Hotel Racine was clearly one of the most picturesque commercial buildings ever constructed in Racine. Its architecture gave it the appearance of a European castle with massive towers and turrets. Construction began in 1892 on the elegant five-story structure at the corner of Sixth and Main Streets overlooking Monument Square. When it was completed in 1894, it boasted 125 rooms complete with electricity and modern steam heat. Guests could enjoy a meal in the spacious dinning room with a lake view or just relax on one of the four full-length verandas at the rear overlooking the lake. By the 1920s, the hotel was completely out of date. It was lacking proper bathrooms and was also considered a fire trap by fire standards of the day. It was replaced by an up-to-date, modern, reinforced concrete and brick hotel in 1926.

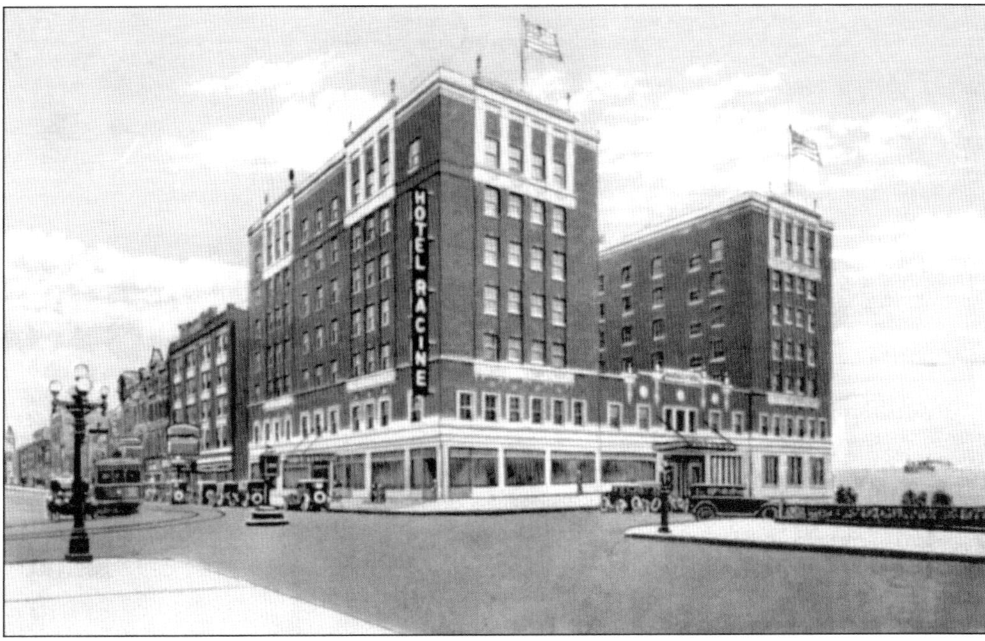

SECOND HOTEL RACINE. The second Hotel Racine, completed in 1926, was seven stories tall with an 11-lane bowling alley in the basement. There were businesses located at street level and a six-chair barbershop. The structure was built of reinforced concrete and red brick with terra-cotta trim. It was designed in an Adamesque style of architecture. Both the lobby and main dining room were decorated with plaster art decor much like the classic theaters being built in the 1920s. In 1965, the hotel was closed and the new owners stripped it to bare bones and rebuilt both the interior and exterior in a modern style. The hotel was called the Inn On The Lake when it was razed in 1992.

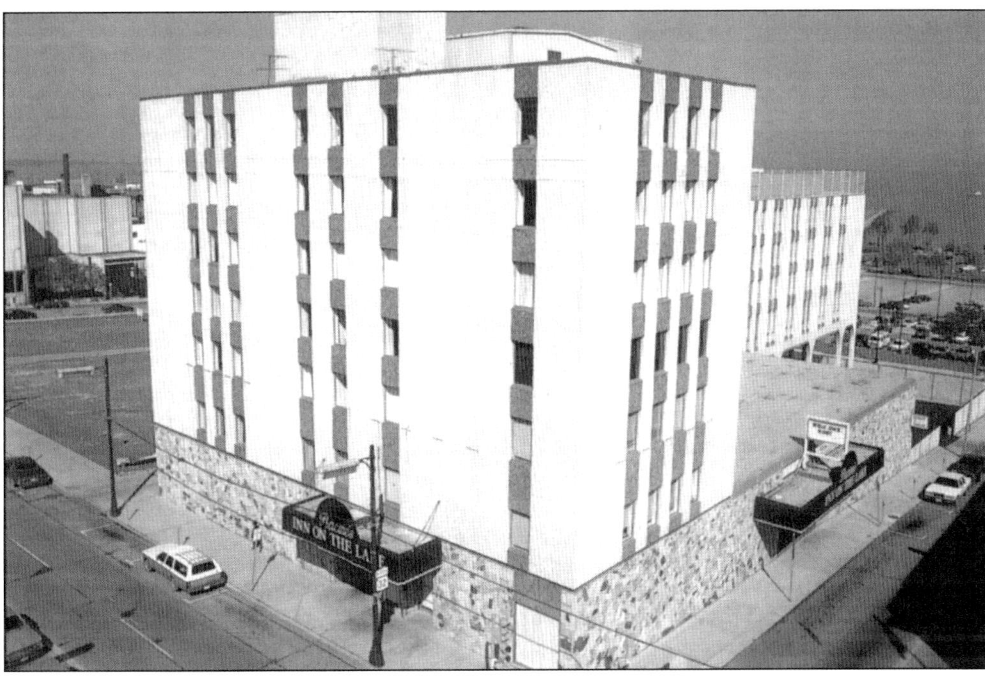

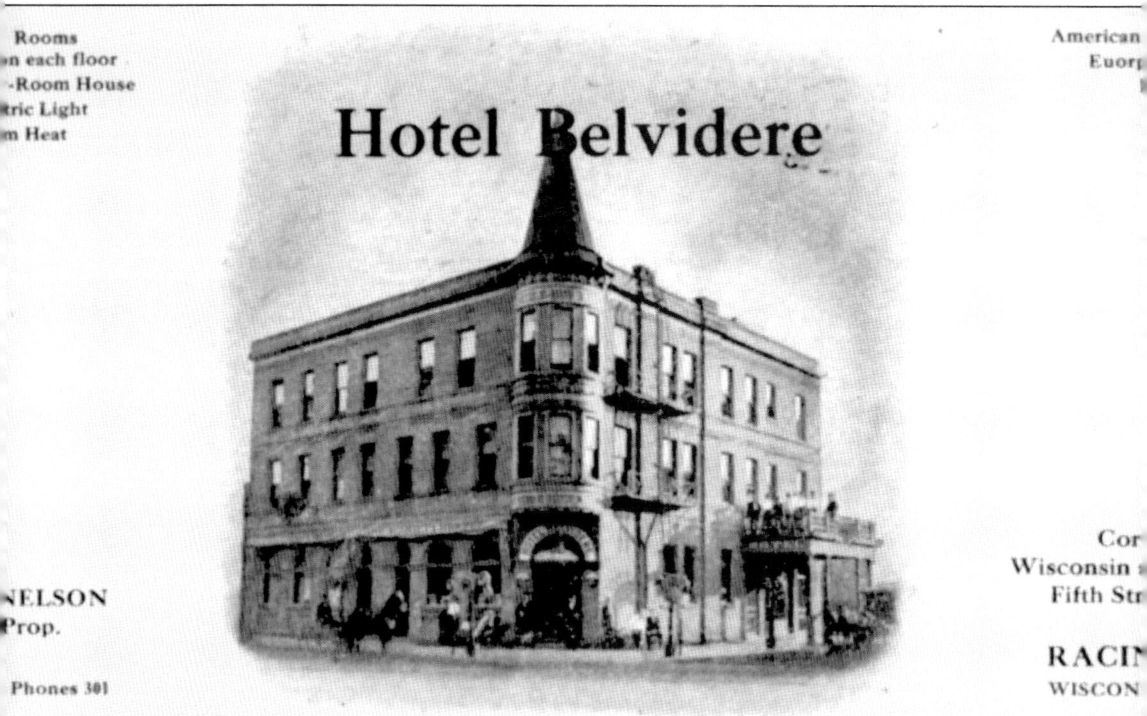

HOTEL BELVIDERE. This interesting advertising postcard shows the Hotel Belvidere, which was located at Fifth Street and Wisconsin Avenue. According to the card there were bathrooms on each floor, electric lights, and steam heat. The hotel also offered the American and European plans. Racine was dotted with small hotels. Being in an industrial city, many of them offered sleeping rooms by the week where newly hired employees could stay until they found a home.

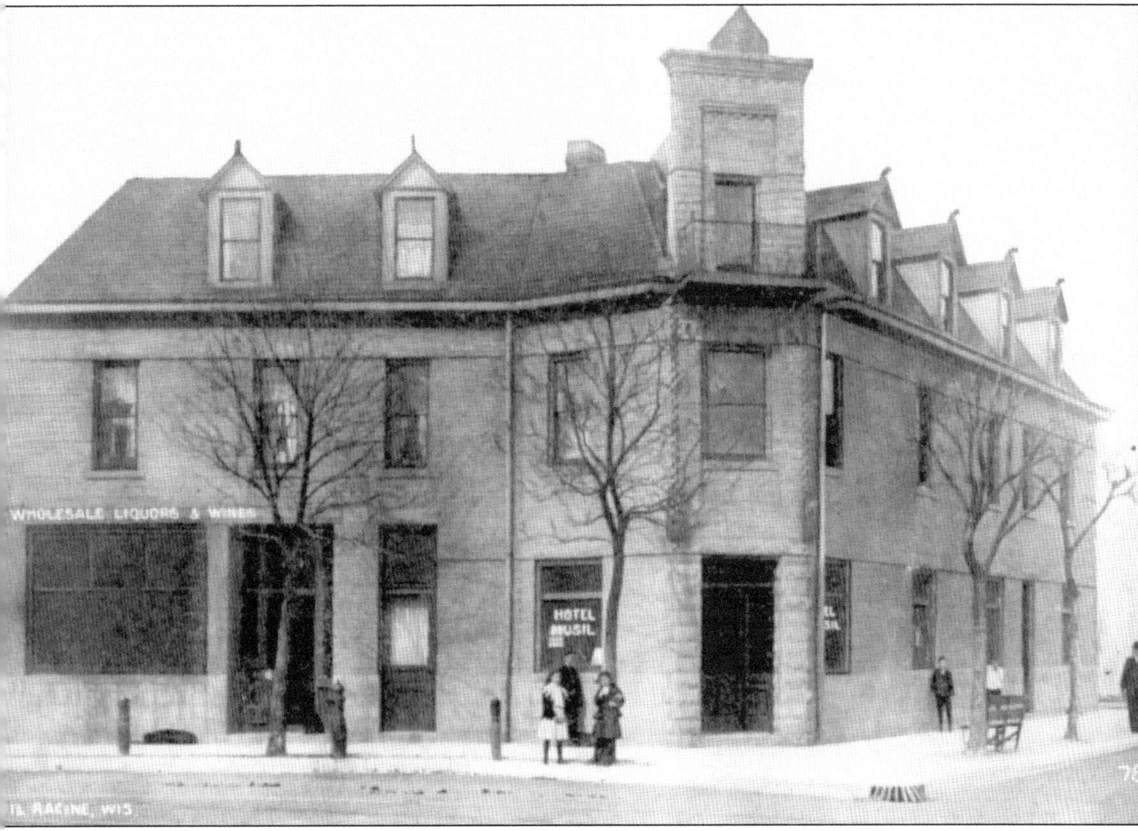

HOTEL MUSIL. This small hostelry was located on Douglas Avenue and Hamilton Street on Racine's near north side. Louis Musil also operated a bar in the building and a wholesale liquor and wine business. The upper floors were hotel rooms, many of which had just enough room for a small bed and dresser. One of the liquor brands Musil sold was Root River whiskey. In later years, the building had a popular restaurant called Little Bohemia. The building housed numerous bars and restaurants until it was totally destroyed by fire on January 1, 1979.

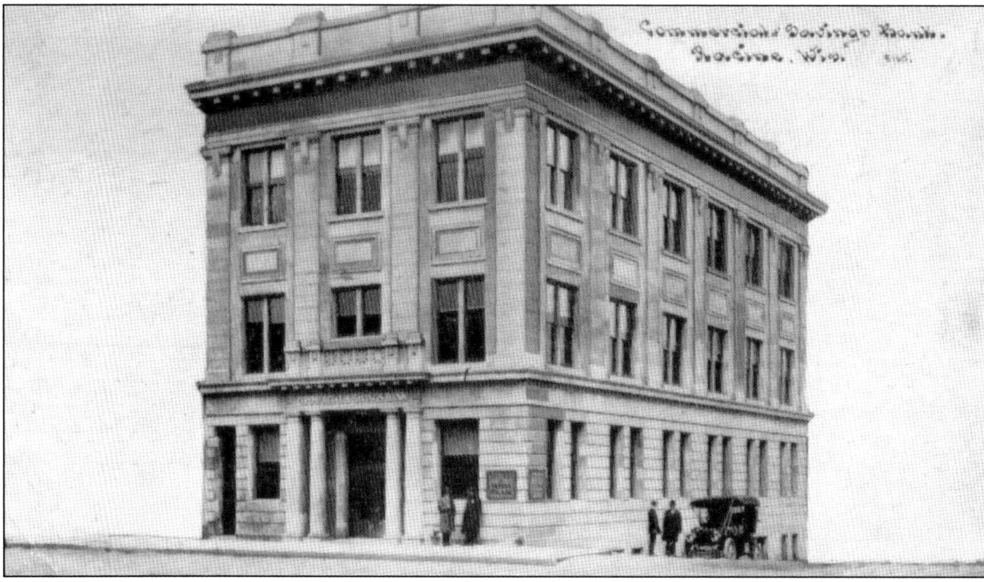

COMMERCIAL SAVINGS BANK. The Commercial Savings Bank purchased the old Gorton Block at Fifth and Main Streets and remodeled it with a classic design in grey stone seen in this view. In later years, it housed the American Trades and Savings Bank. In the 1930s, it was known as the American Bank and Trust Company and became an interesting part of Racine history when famous bank robber John Dillinger robbed it in 1933. For decades the building continued to house banks. Today it houses the Racine Art Museum (RAM).

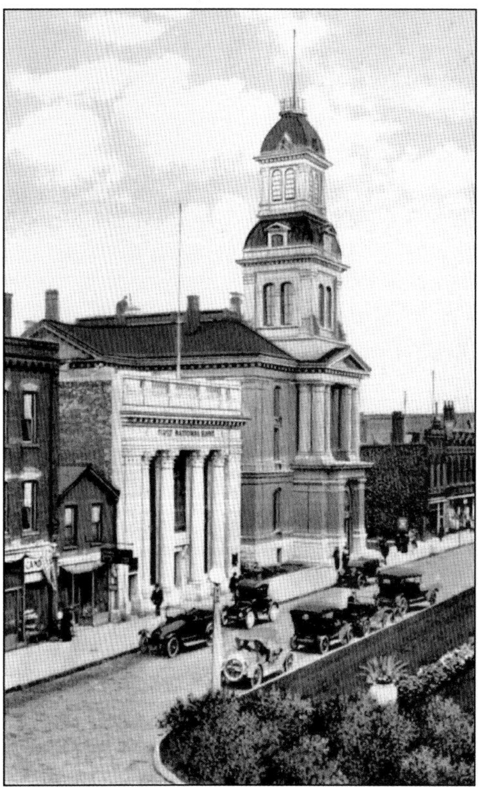

FIRST NATIONAL BANK. In 1913, the First National Bank of Racine rebuilt its older structure into a new stately classic bank building on Monument Square. Founded in 1853, it was Racine's largest bank. When the First National Bank built its new building on Wisconsin Avenue and Fifth Street in 1958, the old building was sold. Gutted and remodeled, the beautiful columns were hauled to the lakeshore and dumped over the bank just south of Eighth Street. They remained on the shoreline until the area was filled in for parkland.

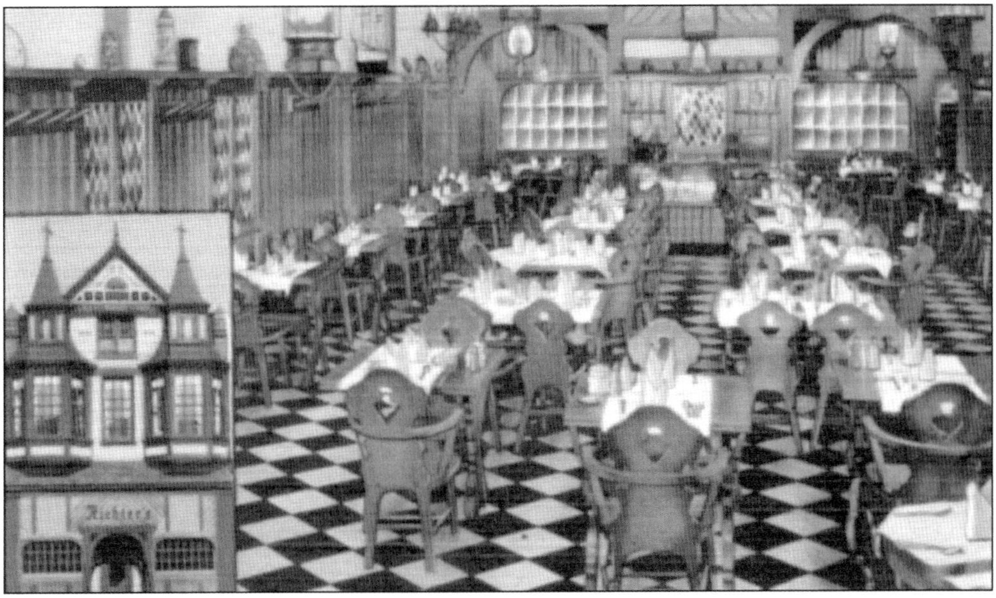

RICHTER'S RESTAURANT. Built in the 1890s as a saloon, this picturesque landmark building at 231 Main Street was designed in the German style. In 1921, Barney Richter opened Hotel Badger in the building and years later added what was to become the famous Richter's German restaurant on the lower floor. By 1957, the restaurant was known as Ivanhoe. During the mid-1960s, the building housed a teenage dance hall called Ivanhoe. In recent years, it was opened as a restaurant and bar and again called the Ivanhoe Pub and Eatery.

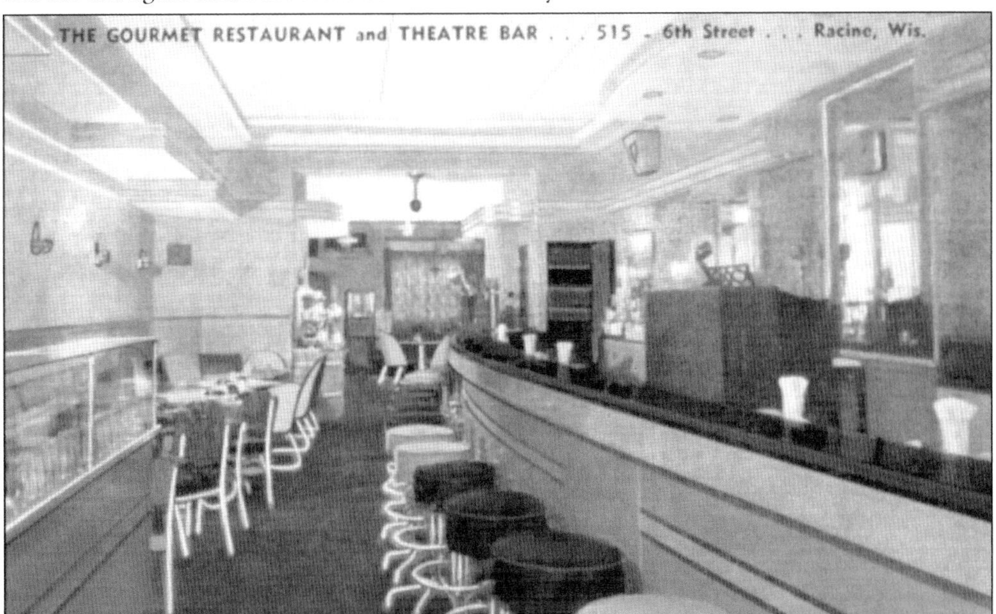

GOURMET RESTAURANT AND THEATRE BAR. With Sixth Street being a main route into and out of downtown, it was always dotted with taverns and restaurants that came and went. Even today a number of taverns still operate there. The back of this postcard stated, "The Gourmet Restaurant and Theatre Bar—'Famous for Food'—515 Sixth Street, Racine, Wisconsin—A restaurant and bar that lives up to its name—Air Conditioned."

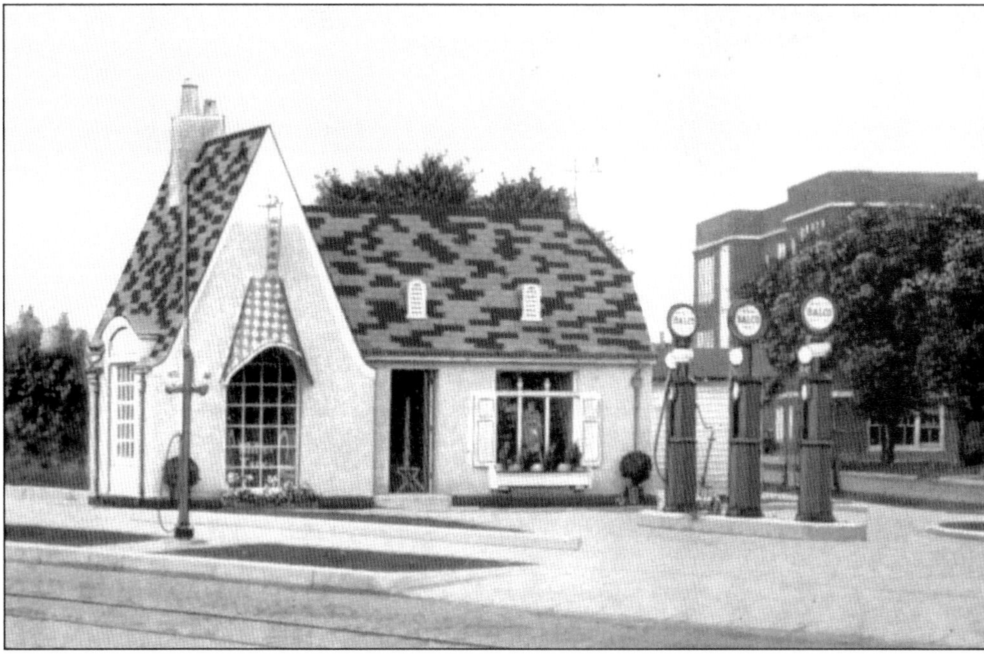

RACINE'S MOST BEAUTIFUL SERVICE STATION. The stylish Douglas Avenue Service Station at 1501 Douglas Avenue, built in the late 1920s, was positioned on a triangle lot at the intersections of Douglas Avenue, La Salle Street, and Kewanuee Street. When this view was taken the station was selling Balco Gas. In the background is the old Washington Junior High School.

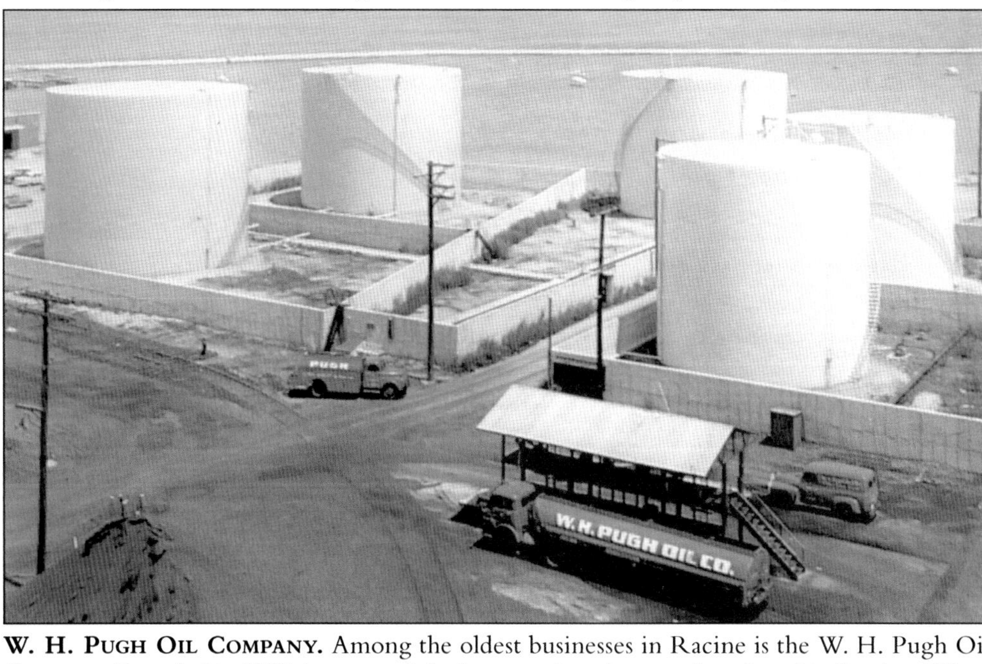

W. H. PUGH OIL COMPANY. Among the oldest businesses in Racine is the W. H. Pugh Oil Company. Founded in 1850, it operated the largest privately owned coal yard in Racine. When fuel oil became popular, it invested heavily in giant storage tanks on its property near the mouth of the Root River. When demands for fuel oil dropped, the tanks were removed. This bird's-eye view shows the tanks and the Racine harbor in the background.

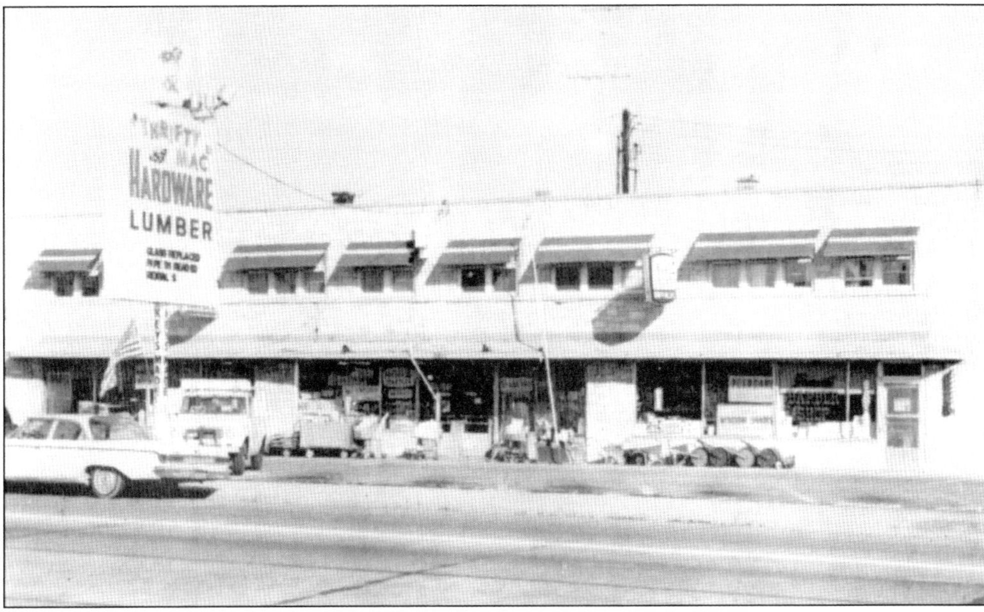

THRIFTY MAC HARDWARE STORE. For decades, the Thrifty Mac Hardware Store at 2011 Lathrop Avenue was a household name throughout the city. The store carried a legendary inventory of hard to find and even obsolete hardware. Through its early years, the store specialized in building, plumbing materials, lumber, millwork, and paint.

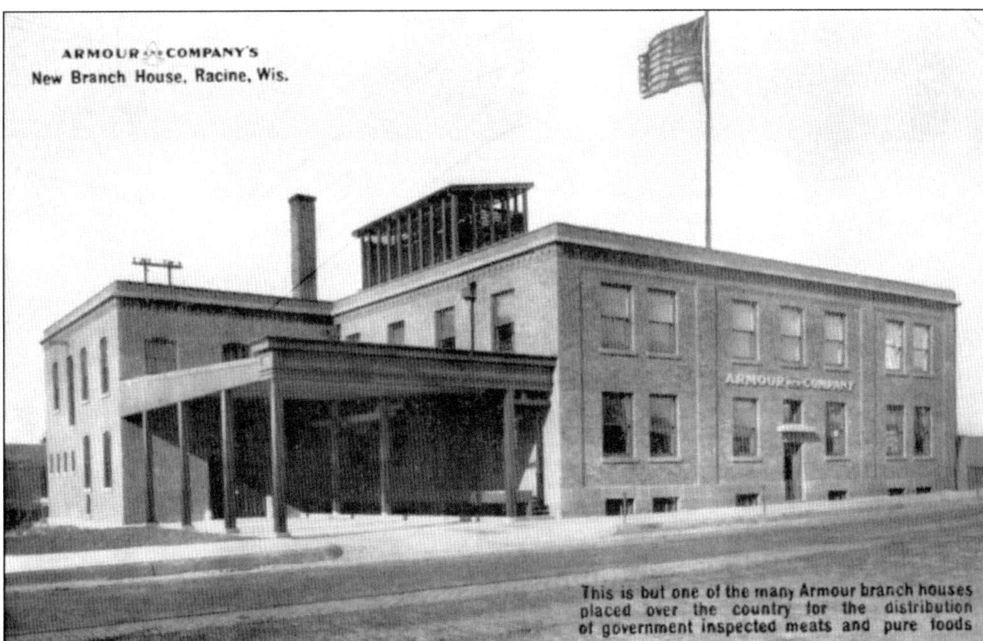

ARMOUR COMPANY'S NEW BRANCH HOUSE. In October 1910, the meat packing firm Armour and Company razed its old building on the west side of South Main Street next to the Root River. In the same month, the foundations for a new $75,000 brick, fireproof meat processing plant were being laid. It was razed in the 1980s to make room for a small marina development.

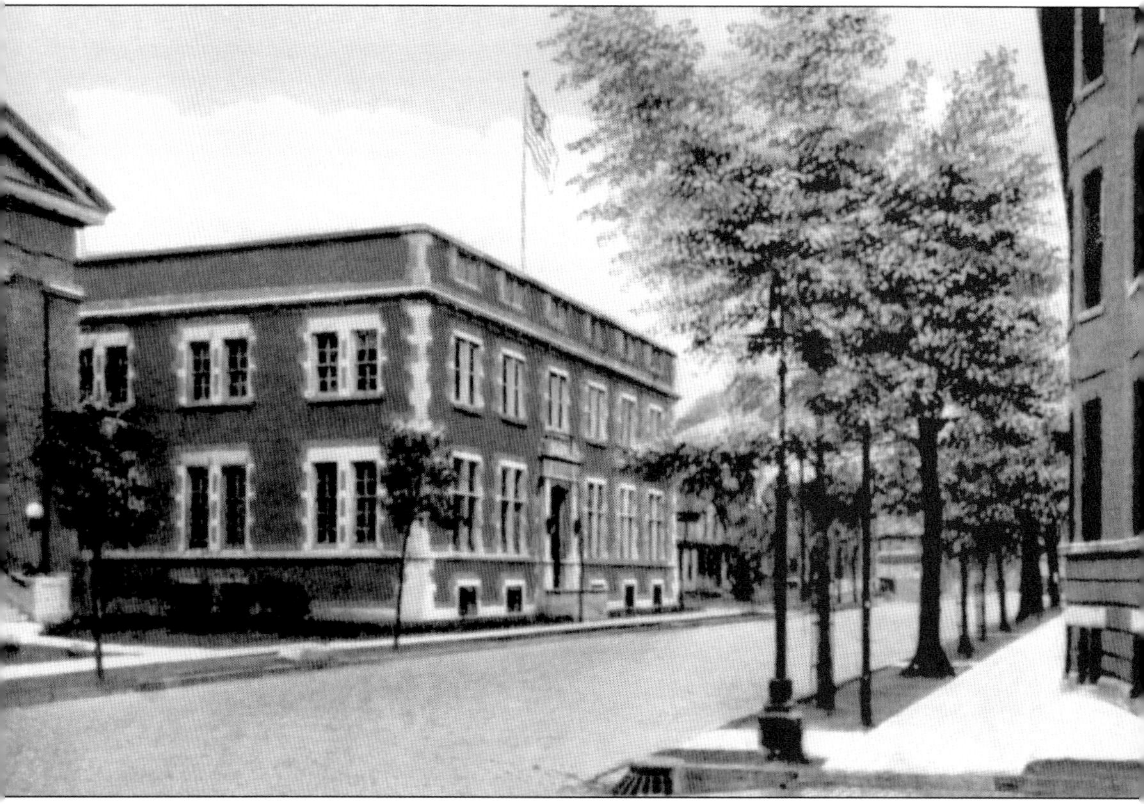

SEVENTH STREET, SHOWING WISCONSIN TELEPHONE BUILDING. Like most cities in the United States, Racine had telephone service soon after its invention in 1879. Later two separate telephone companies operated in Racine. The 1908 Racine City Directory listed Citizens Telephone Company at 300 Fifth Street and the Wisconsin Telephone Company at 627–631 Main Street. In 1911, the Wisconsin Telephone Company had 5,493 operating phones on its lines and by 1923 the number grew to 10,000. This view shows the Wisconsin Telephone Company building at 411 Seventh Street as it looked in the 1940s.

Seven

INDUSTRY

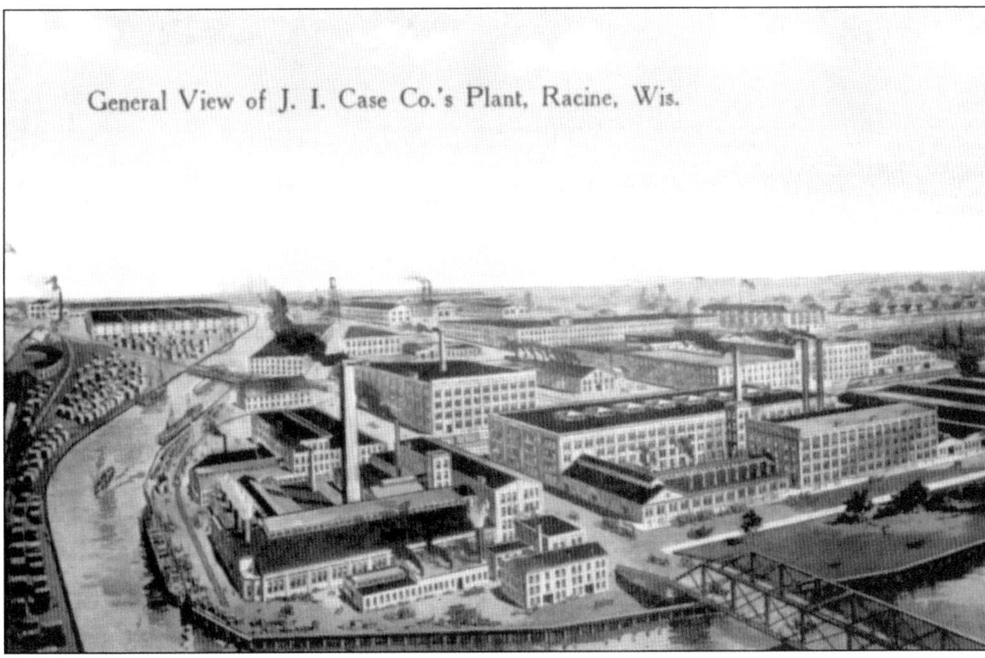

GENERAL VIEW OF J. I. CASE COMPANY. This bird's-eye view shows the J. I. Case Threshing Machine Company complex in the heart of Racine. Jerome Increase Case moved his business to Racine from Rochester in 1844, and rented a small shop where he built his threshing machines. By 1849, Case had built a three-story factory building on Bridge Street where he continued building quality machines. Case soon became Racine's largest employer with thousands of men and a few women working in his shops. The company grew to become one of the largest manufacturers of farm machinery in the world. The Fourth Street Bridge seen in the foreground is gone and all of the company's buildings north of the Root River have been razed except for the main office at 700 State Street.

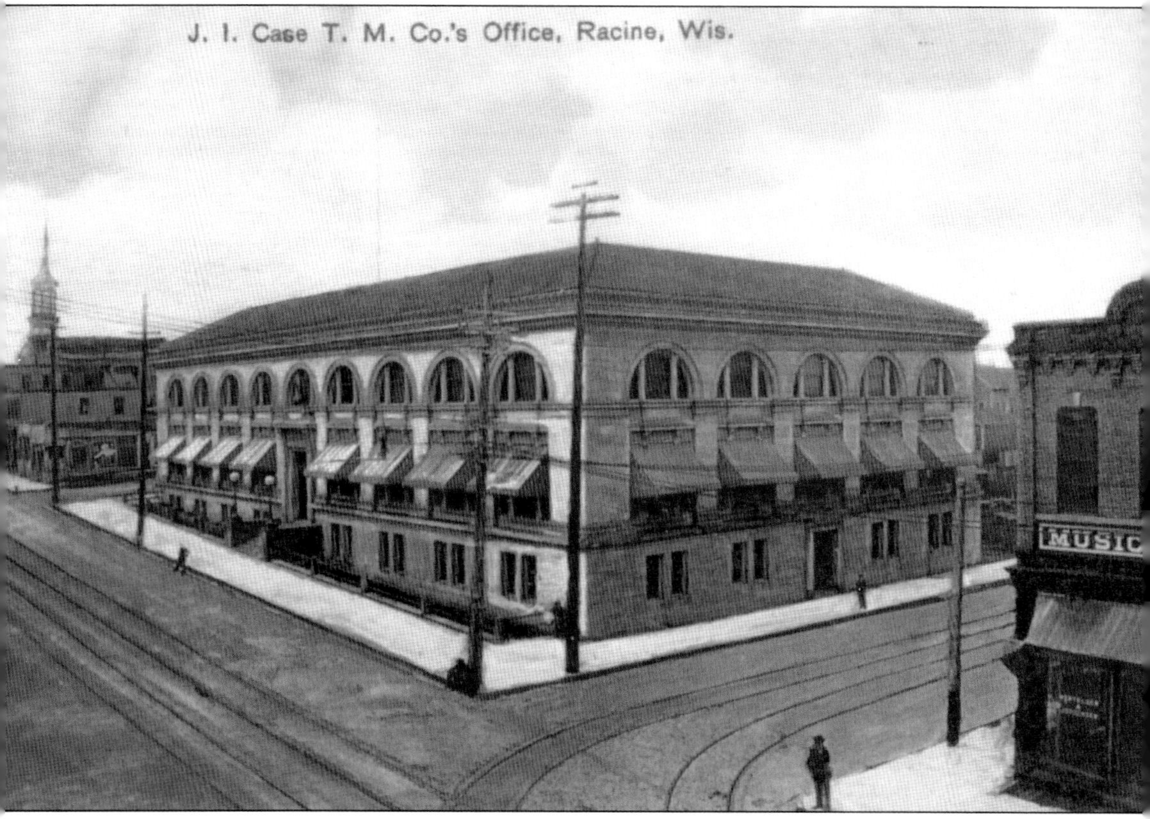

J. I. Case Threshing Machine Company's Office. When constructed in 1904 and 1905, the main office building at 700 State Street was the pride of the J. I. Case Threshing Machine Company. Built of gray stone in a Renaissance design, its appearance was unique. The interior was built of the finest tile, mahogany, and marble and had a tinted skylight about 50 feet above the main floor. In 1957, the interior was extensively remodeled but the exterior has remained basically the same. The original Old Abe Eagle statue is still on guard above the main entrance.

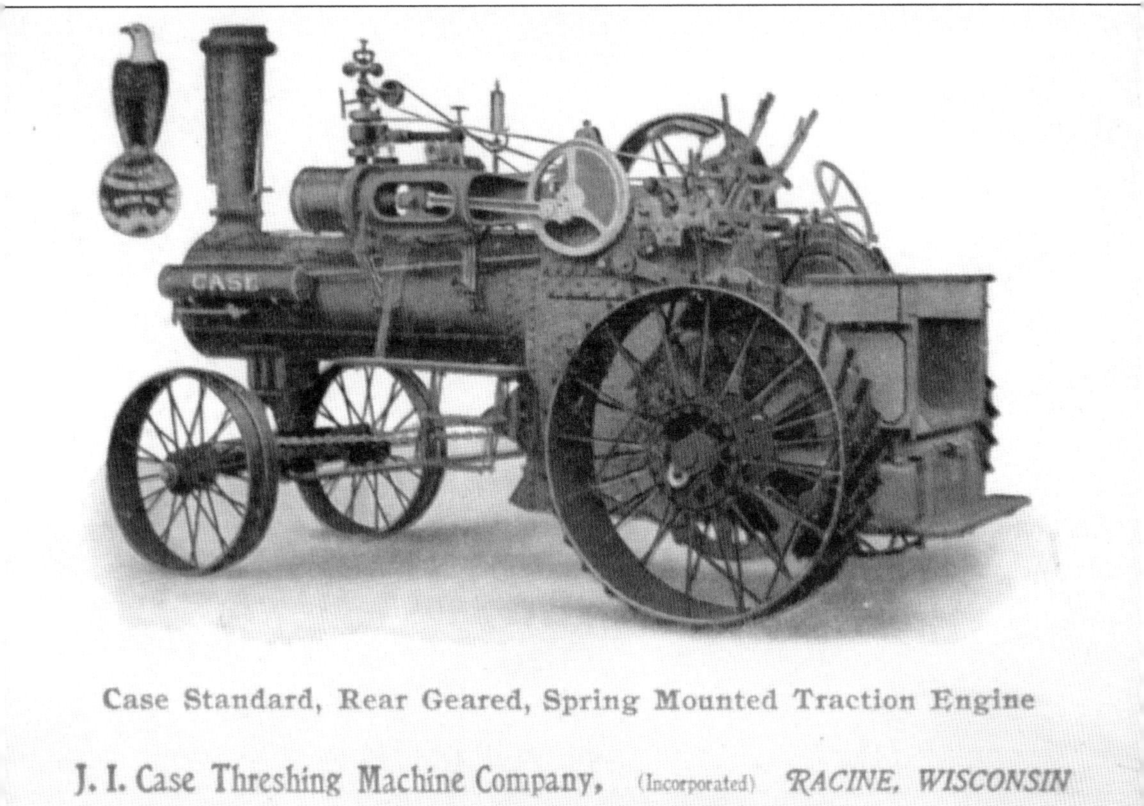

J. I. Case Threshing Machine Company. In 1869, J. I. Case began manufacturing steam engines for agricultural use. The early engines were pulled from site to site by horses. Later traction engines were built that traveled under their own power and were used for pulling or plowing. Special trains, almost like circus trains, left Racine with loads of these engines and threshing machines headed to markets in the west and Canada. The cars were decorated with banners and flags and many had a calliope that played as they traveled through small towns and villages. The company stopped building steam engines in 1928. Up to that time, Case had been the largest steam engine manufacturer in the world building 36,000 engines. Many of these still operate and often run at tractor shows.

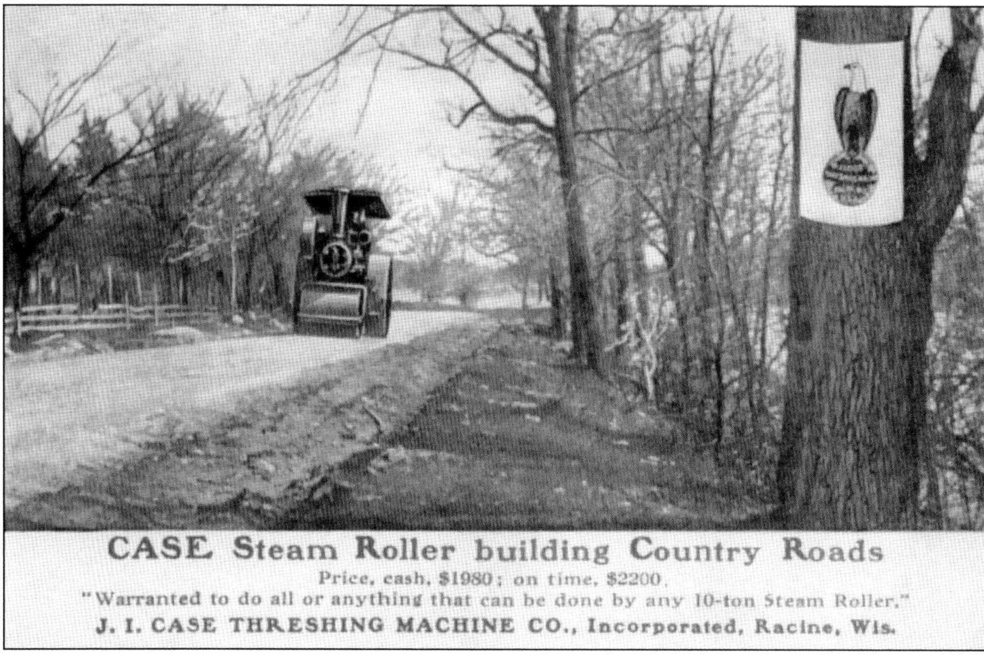

CASE STEAMROLLER BUILDING COUNTY ROADS. Along with its full line of steam traction engines and threshing machines, the J. I. Case Threshing Machine Company also built steamrollers, road graders, and other equipment used in construction. The card above advertises steamrollers. These large machines were seen throughout the world building roads and highways. The largest steam engines built by the company were gigantic 150-horsepower road engines. The Ringling Brothers Circus used one called "Hercules." Built in 1892, the massive road locomotive was a star performer during the circus's opening show. Other company engines were performers, too, traveling around the country doing hill climbing and other contests, as seen below.

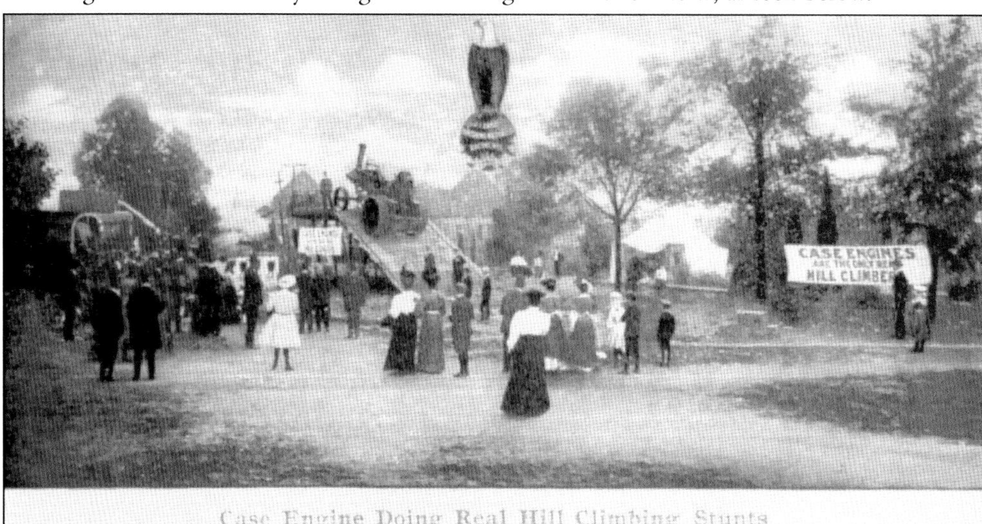

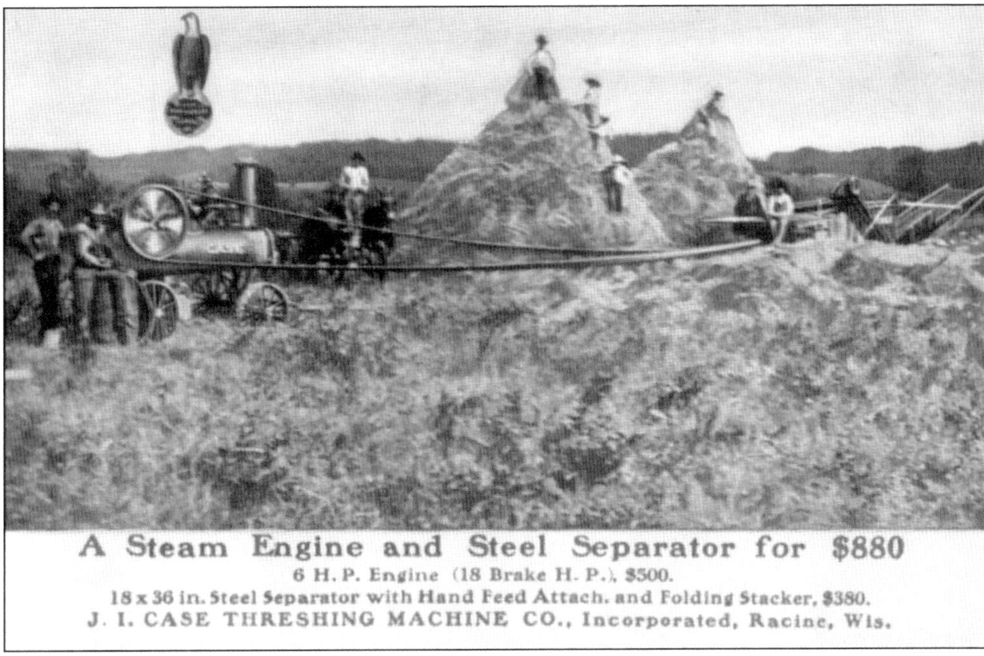

STEAM ENGINE AND SEPARATOR. This series of cards promoted the J. I. Case Threshing Machine Company outfits farmers could buy. In its time, the company was the largest steam traction engine manufacturer in the world. Other engine manufacturers built engines by orders received, whereas Case continually built engines and stored them in large warehouses ready to be shipped. These threshing packages were often sent out by train loads, which was a very impressive sight. By 1923, Case had built over 100,000 threshing machines. The company became a household name to farmers in many countries around the world. Today these old machines can still be seen at tractor and engine shows operating as they did a century ago.

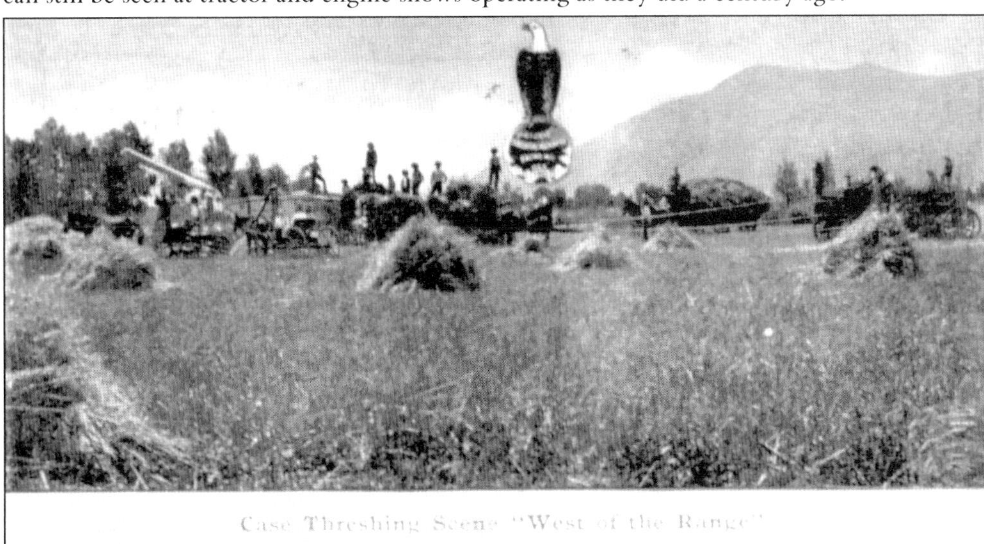

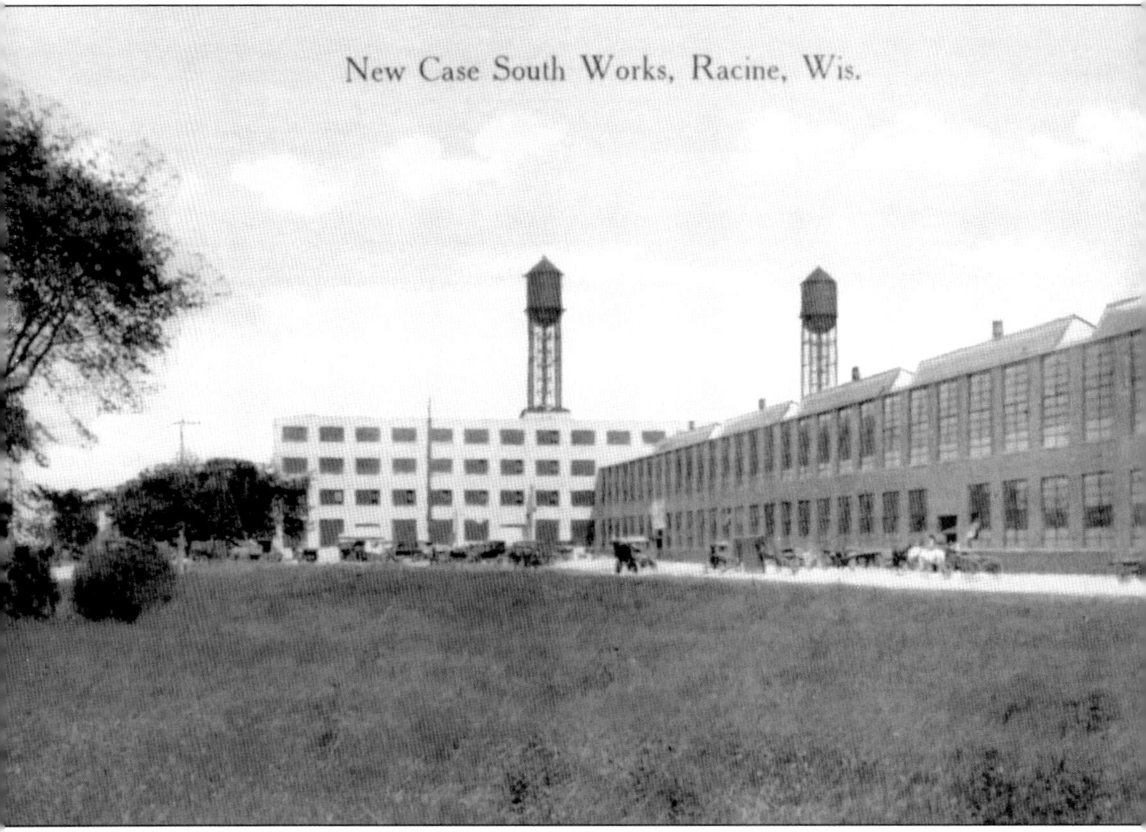

NEW CASE SOUTH WORKS. By 1910, the massive J. I. Case Threshing Machine Company needed more manufacturing space. Plans were made to build a new plant south of Racine. The first building constructed on that site was the foundry and, by 1913, a gigantic machine shop and power plant were finished. Through the years, the plant was called a number of names including South Works, Clausen Plant, and Tractor Plant. The complex spread, eventually providing more than one million square feet of manufacturing space. The twin water towers and giant smoke stack were landmarks for decades. In recent years, the entire plant was razed, and the site is now one of the largest parcels of lakefront property waiting to be developed.

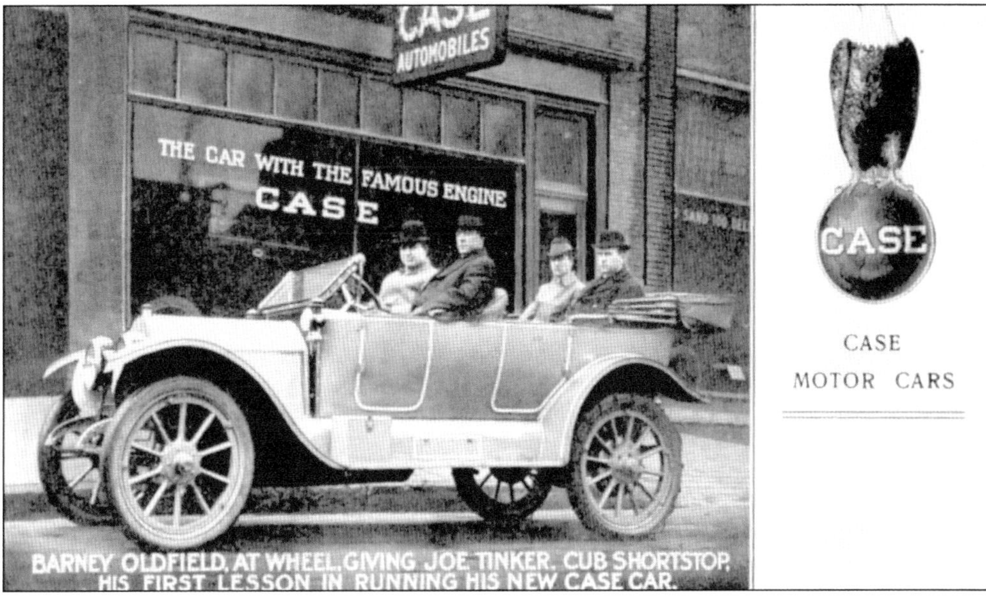

CASE MOTOR CAR. This wonderful old advertising card sent out by the J. I. Case Threshing Machine Company promoted its automobiles. One of the Case slogans was "The car with the famous engine." This card boasts Barney Oldfield at the wheel giving Joe Tinker, a Chicago Cub Shortstop, his first lesson in running his new Case car. In 1925, Case stopped making automobiles. The motor works plant where the automobiles were built still stands at Twenty-second and Clark Streets.

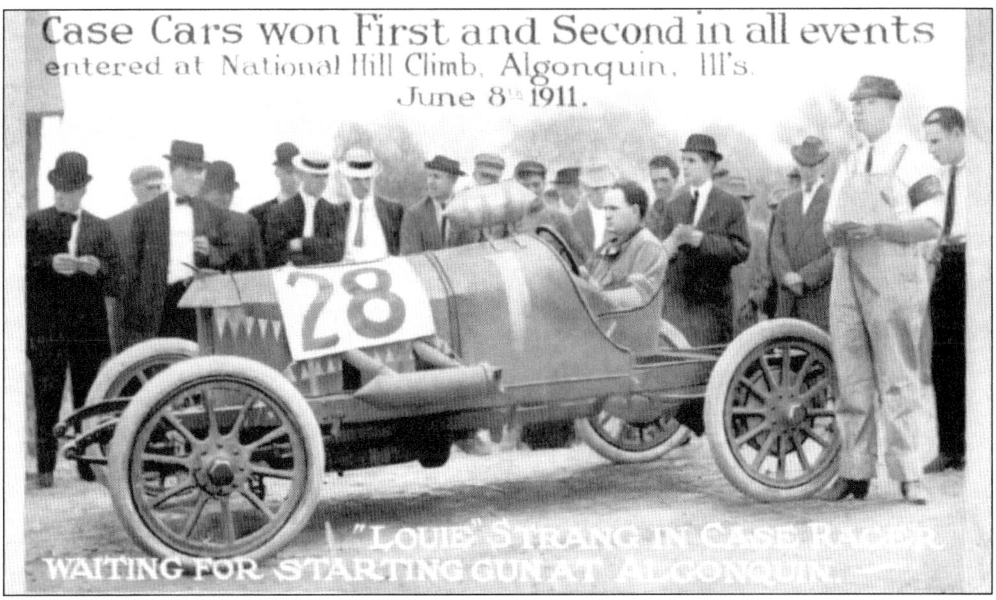

CASE CARS WON FIRST AND SECOND IN ALL EVENTS. In 1910, the J. I. Case Threshing Machine Company bought the Pierce Motor Company of Racine. The car was renamed "Case" and the company hired a racing team as a way to advertise its quality cars. This card advertised that Case automobiles won first and second places in all events entered at the National Hill Climb in Algonquin, Illinois, on June 8, 1911. Also in 1911, three Case racers qualified for the first Indianapolis 500, winning the pole position and two spots in the second row.

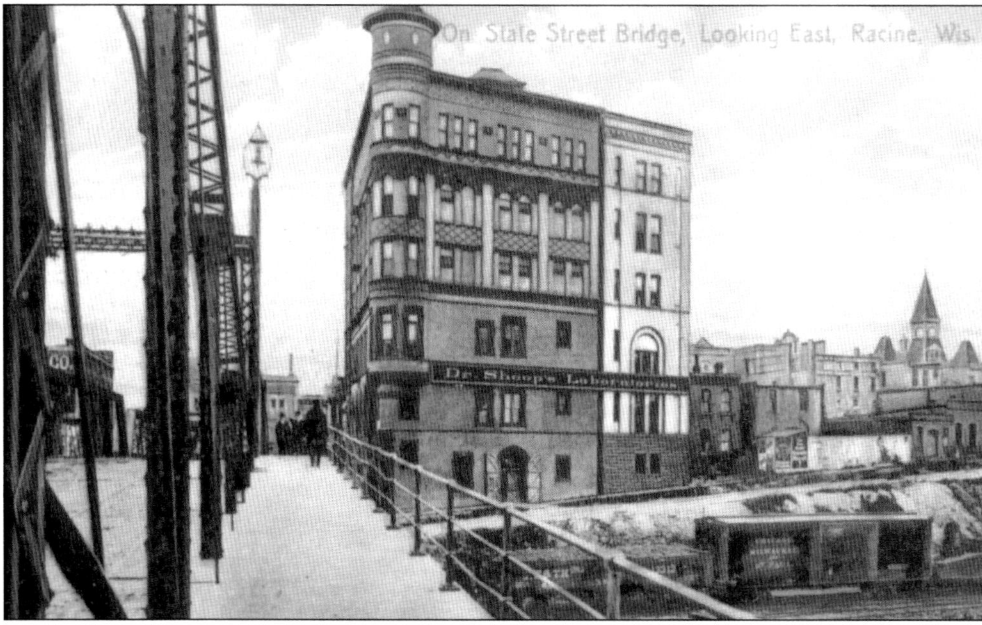

On State Street Bridge Looking East. Dr. Shoops Restorative and other cure-alls were selling so well that it was time to build a building for their manufacture. In 1893, the first three stories of the Dr. Shoop Building at 215 State Street were built with plans to add more stories as needed. The structure, designed by local architects Chandler and Park, was built of cream brick with brown stone trim in the Romanesque Revival style. By 1899, three additional stories had been added making it one of the most pretentious buildings in Racine.

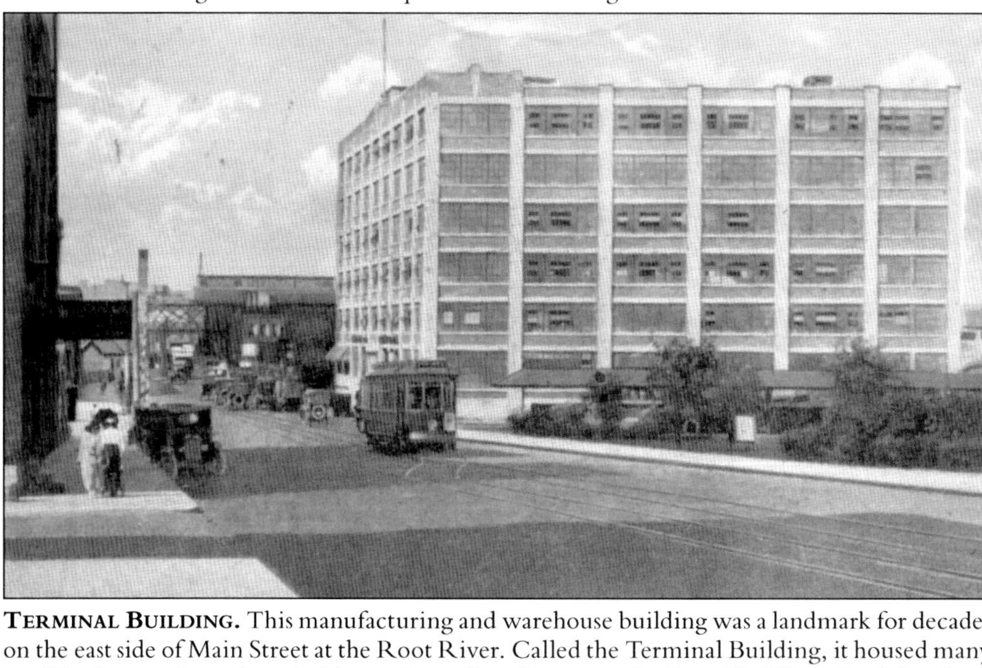

Terminal Building. This manufacturing and warehouse building was a landmark for decades on the east side of Main Street at the Root River. Called the Terminal Building, it housed many small businesses throughout its history. It was later known as the Oster Building after John Oster purchased the Steven's Electric Company in the 1940s and continued manufacturing the famous Osterizer, an electric household blender that helped put Racine manufacturing on the map.

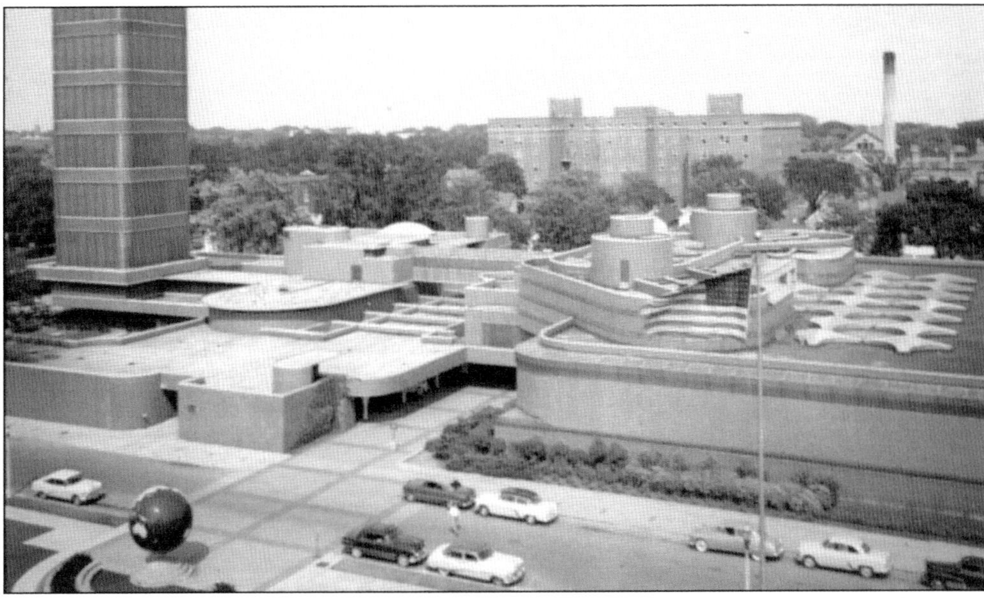

Johnson's Wax Administrative Offices. Over the years, a constant stream of visitors, including many famous people, have come to Racine to see the celebrated home of Johnson's Wax. The world-renowned buildings were the creation of architect Frank Lloyd Wright. The administration building, constructed of red brick and stone in 1939, has 43 miles of glass but no windows. The glass and brick research tower is considered to be one of the seven art wonders of America. It was also designed by Wright and added to the complex in 1950.

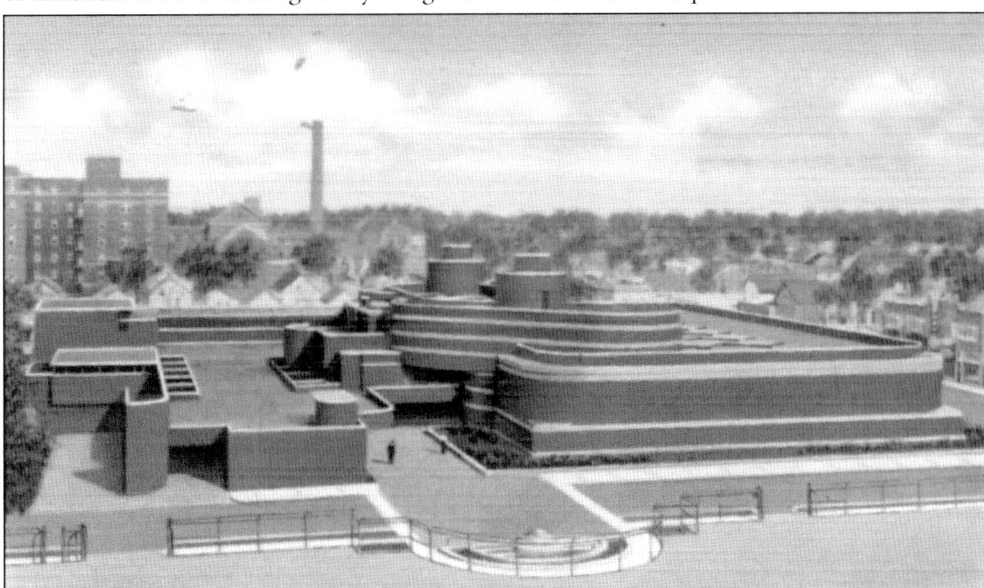

The Office of S. C. Johnson and Son. The Johnson's Wax buildings in Racine have become internationally acclaimed architectural masterpieces and, as national historic landmarks, these buildings are truly unique both in design and construction techniques. Over the past 20 years, the Johnson company has purchased and razed numerous homes and buildings surrounding the complex to create a campus style setting. This view shows the administration building shortly after it was constructed.

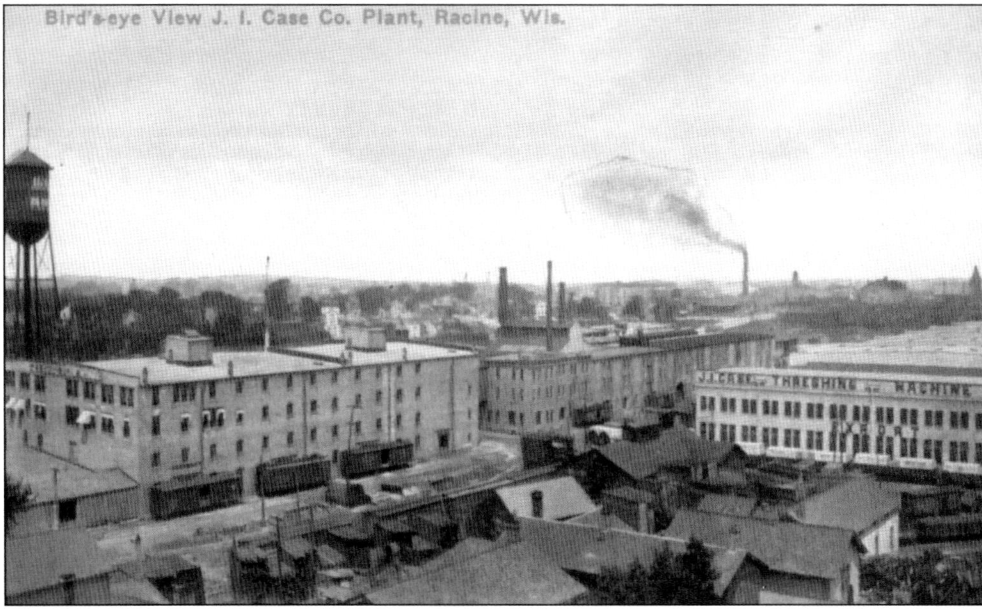

THE J. I. CASE PLANT (PLOW WORKS). Looking from the roof of the Racine Manufacturing Company plant at Sixth and Marquette Streets, this bird's-eye view shows the J. I. Case Plow Works factories just to the north. It is interesting to note that two separate J. I. Case companies operated in adjacent buildings in Racine at the same time. The plow works was founded in 1876 by Jerome Increase Case who had also founded the J. I. Case Threshing Machine Company in 1842. The plow works was inherited by family members while the threshing machine company became a stock corporation. For years, there was confusion at the post office if mail came addressed to "Case." Representatives from both companies would come to the post office to open the mail to try to determine which company it belonged to. This ended in 1928 when Massey-Harris bought the Case plow works and sold all rights to the Case name to the threshing machine company.

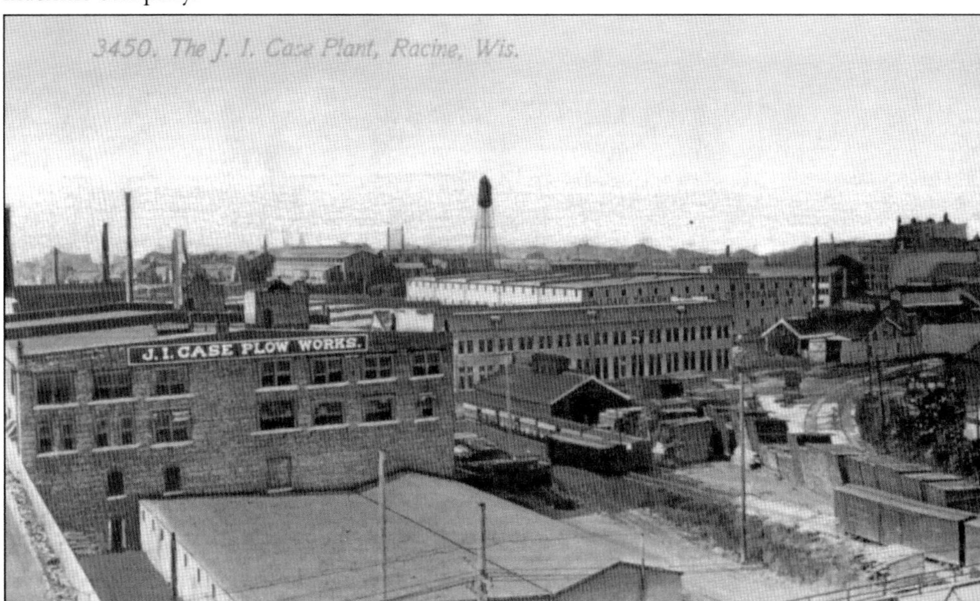

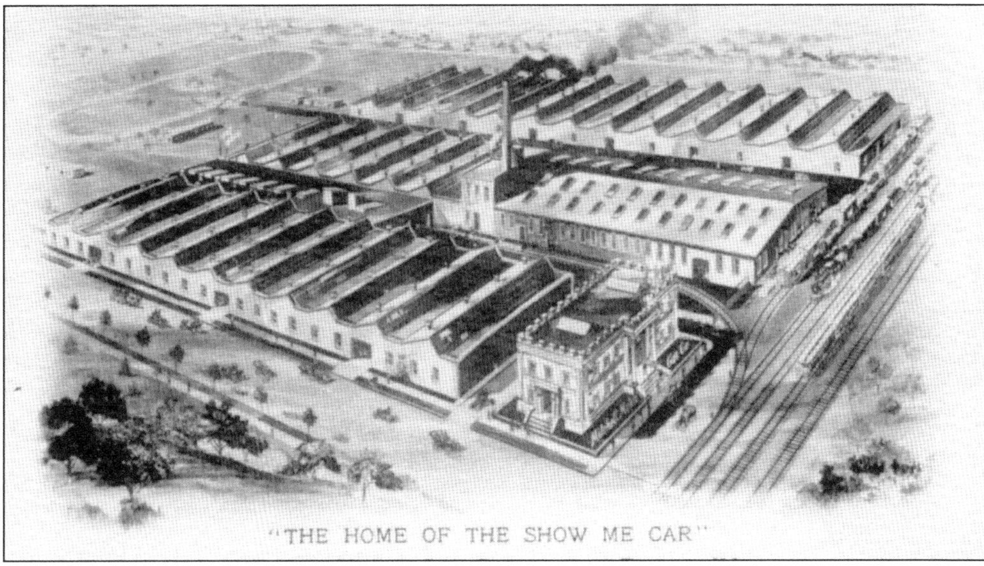

"THE HOME OF THE SHOW ME CAR." Mitchell Motor Car Company was Racine's largest automobile manufacturer. The company's main plant was at 1712 Hamilton Avenue near the Chicago, Milwaukee and St. Paul Railroad tracks on Racine's south side. In 1896, William Turnor Lewis and his son bought the old Beebe Wheel works and manufactured bicycles and then small motorcycles. In 1902, they built their first motor vehicles and continued manufacturing high quality products until 1923. The last company to use the factory complex before the buildings were razed in 2005 was Jacobsen Manufacturing.

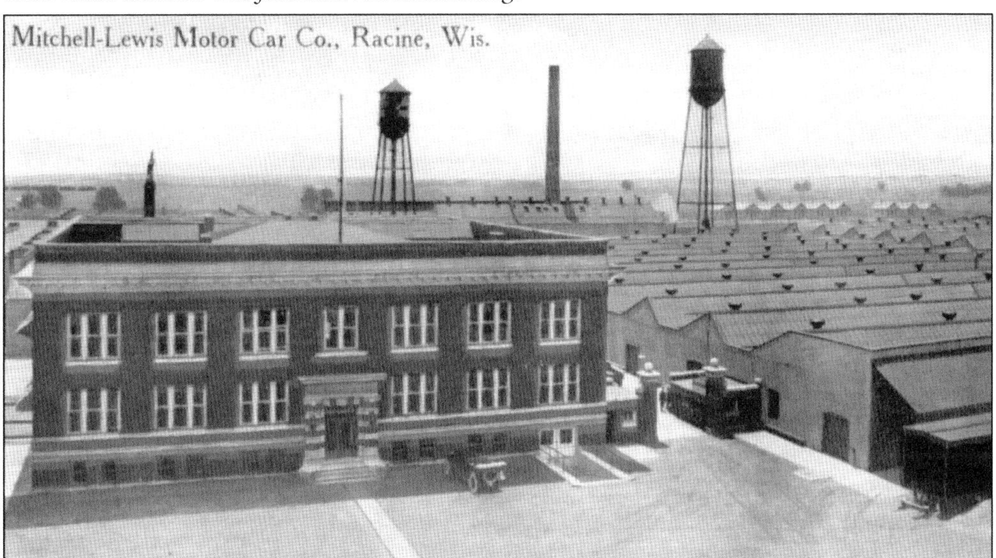

MITCHELL-LEWIS MOTOR CAR COMPANY. In 1909, the Mitchell-Lewis Motor Car Company built a new main office at the factory complex. The building was located at Packard Avenue near the Chicago, Milwaukee and St. Paul Railroad tracks. The red brick classical revival structure was designed by Racine architects Guilbert and Funston. After Mitchell closed in 1923, Nash Motor Car Company bought the complex and built cars there, including the Ajax, in 1925. The manufacturing complex was razed in 2005 to create a new industrial park on Racine's south side.

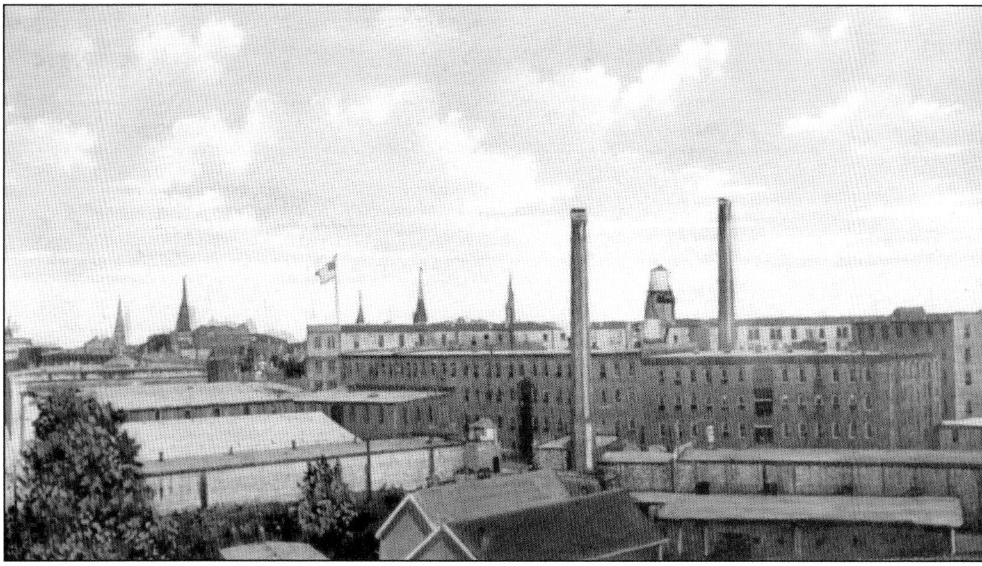

MITCHELL-LEWIS MOTOR CAR COMPANY (DOWNTOWN). In 1910, the Mitchell-Lewis Wagon Company was consolidated with the Mitchell Motor Car Company. The original Mitchell Wagon Company buildings near downtown at Center Street and Washington Avenue became part of the growing Mitchell-Lewis Motor Car Company. Racine's city hall and police station are located where these buildings once stood.

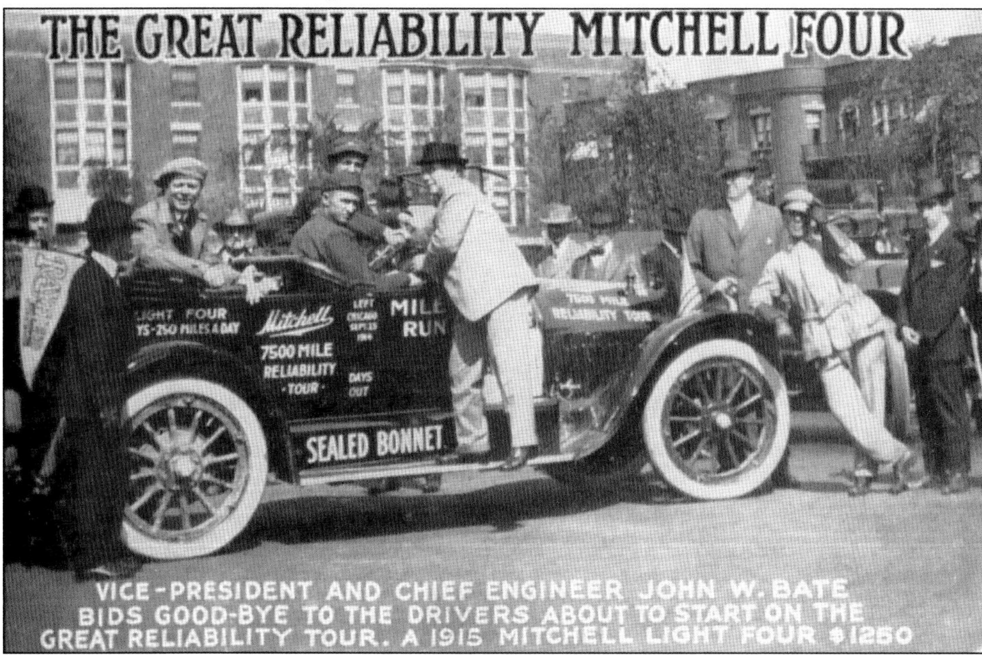

GREAT RELIABILITY MITCHELL FOUR. Every Mitchell automobile motor and chassis was road-tested before the bodies were attached. This view shows Mitchell's vice president and chief engineer, John W. Bate, bidding goodbye to the drivers at the start of one of many reliability tours made with Mitchell cars. The hoods were sealed and the vehicles were driven throughout the nation for publicity. At the time, a 1915 Mitchell Light Four sold for $1,250, a big piece of change in 1915.

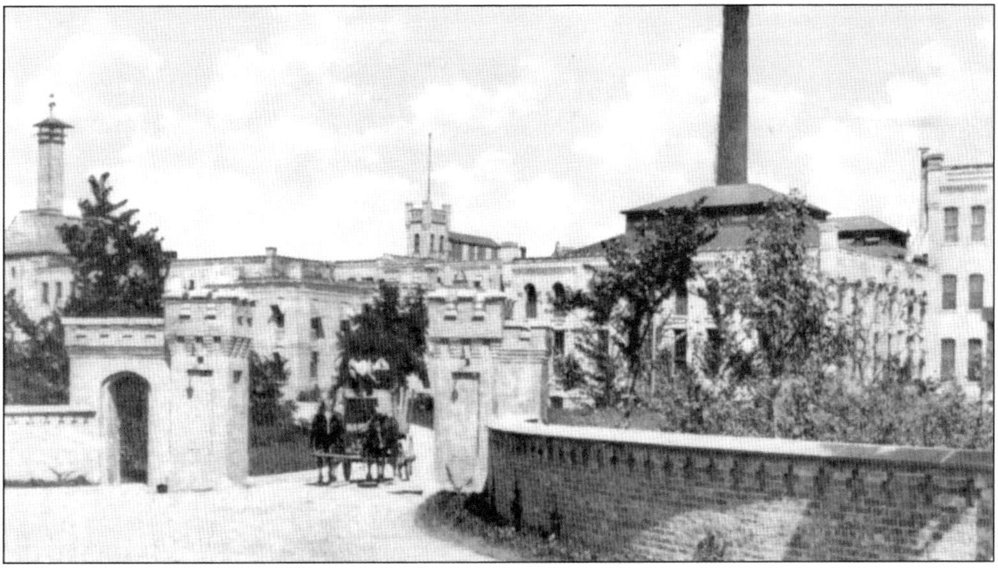

THE MAIN GATE, HORLICK'S MALTED MILK. William Horlick visited Racine in 1869 and then went back to England. He returned to Racine in 1872 to work at the Horlick stone quarries operated by his uncle. In 1873, he was in Chicago selling train carloads of lime and stone after the Great Chicago Fire. His brother James, who was a chemist, visited him from England and the two brothers teamed up to start a company in the Town of Mt. Pleasant just northwest of Racine, making prepared infant and invalid food. In 1877, the partners built a small frame building on Northwestern Avenue and moved the manufacturing to Racine. In 1883, William patented a mixture that was considered the first powered milk in the world. He added this to his infant food and renamed the product Horlick's Malted Milk. Soon people all over the world were whipping up the new American drink—simply called a malted milk. William wanted his new brick factory buildings to remind him of his home in England. So he had them designed and built like old English castles. The Racine plants closed in 1975; however, the stately cream brick buildings are still standing. It is interesting to note that Horlick's Malted Milk went to Antarctica and also into outer space as a food supplement.

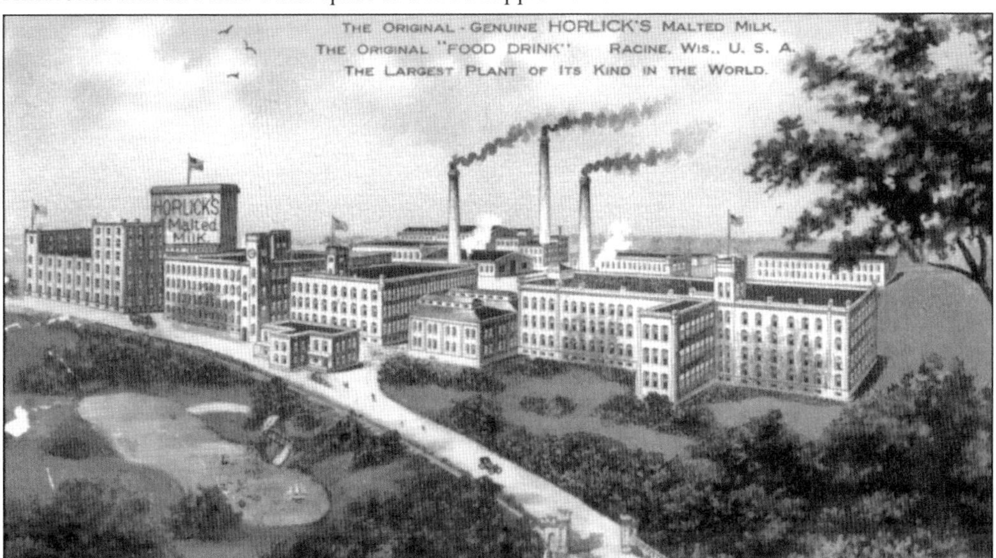

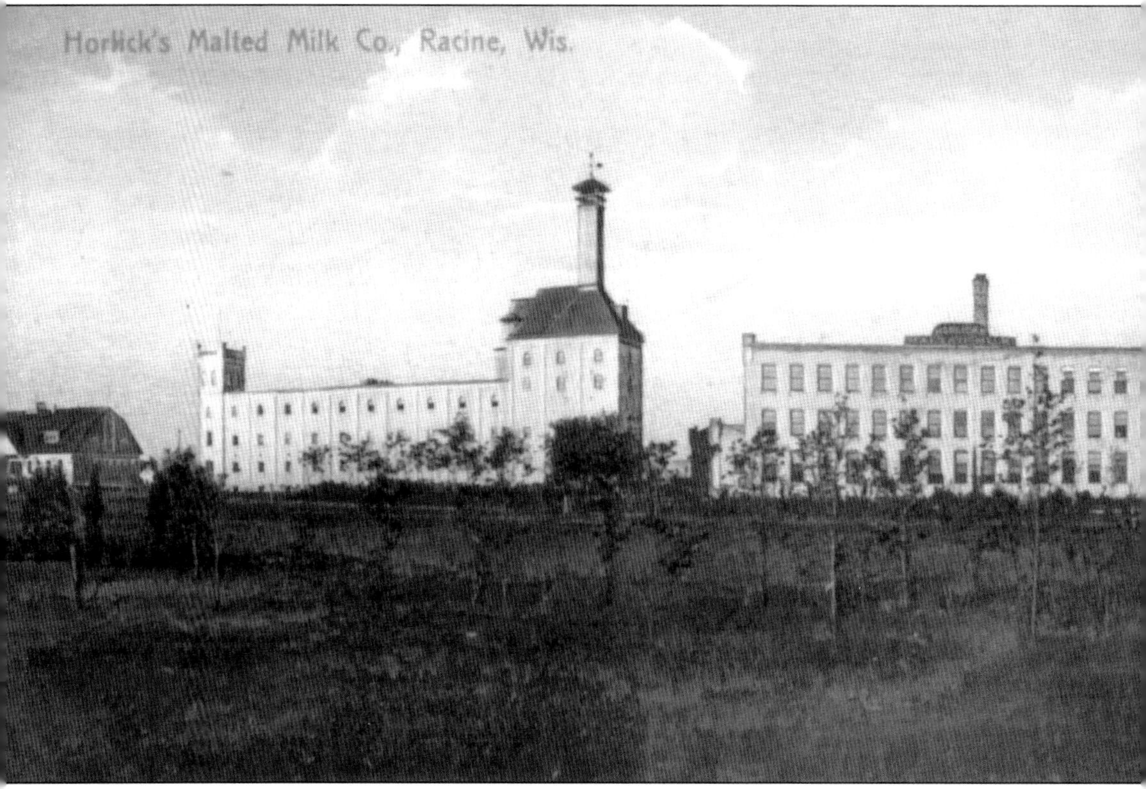

HOME OF THE ORIGINAL GENUINE HORLICK'S MALTED MILK. The site on Northwestern Avenue, where the Horlick brothers built their original one-story, frame Racine plant, was picked because the pure water of the natural springs that flowed there could be used to manufacture the food products. When William Horlick designed the first brick buildings, his small sketch was the only guide followed by contractors in constructing the castle-style buildings. Memories of the British Isles and its castles guided Horlick as he added buildings. Soon there was an entire complex, with a brick drive and courtyard, carefully arranged on the 15-acre site. The factory was a showplace in Racine. When the late Henry Bacon, designer of the Lincoln Memorial in

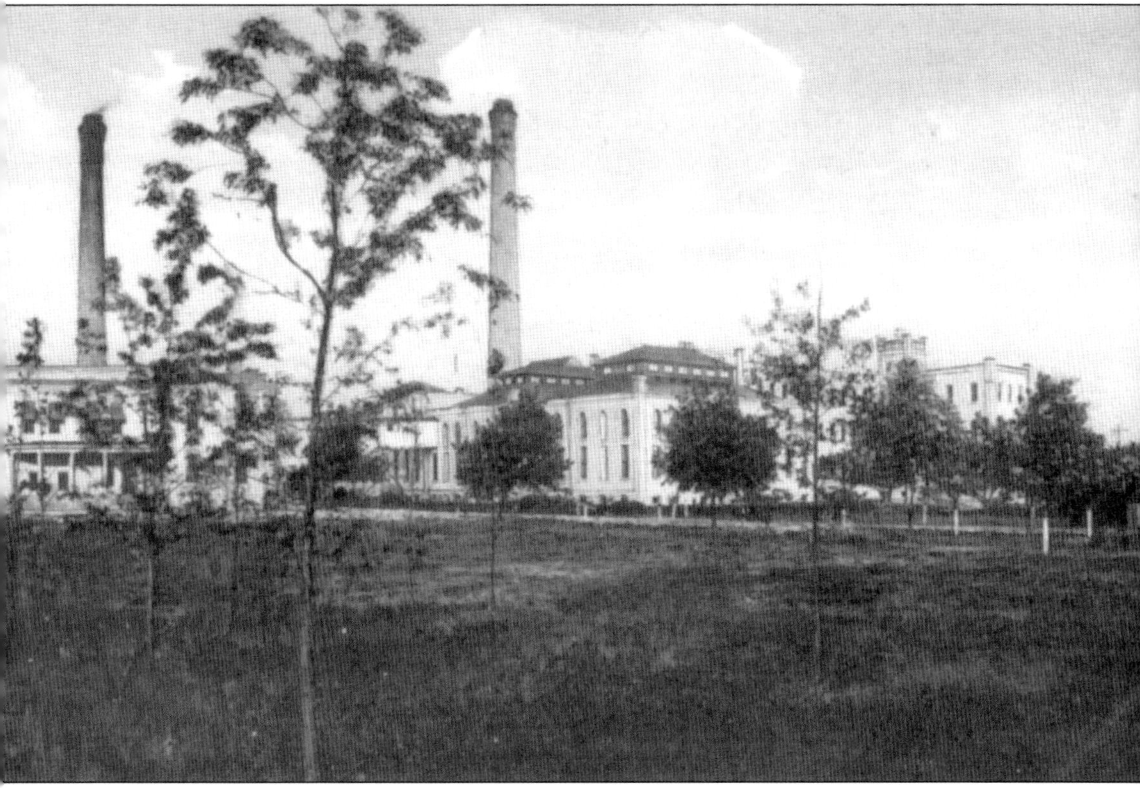

Washington, D.C., visited the buildings, he pronounced them as some of the most beautiful he had ever seen. In 1936, Horlick died and left a fortune of $17 million. As a token to his long-term employees, he left a year's salary to every one of his employees that worked for the company for 20 or more years. The firm was sold to Horlick's Limited of England in 1946. In 1969, it was again sold to Beecham Incorporated of New Jersey and the Racine operations were totally shut down in 1975. The buildings still stand as a reminder of the men and the company that helped make Racine the city it is today.

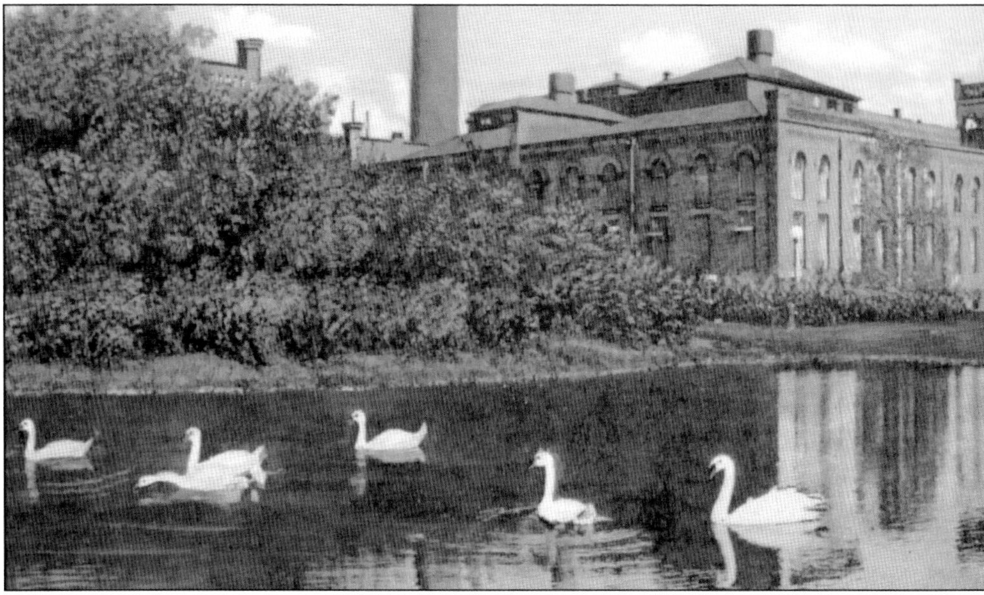

LAGOON, HORLICK'S MALTED MILK CORPORATION. About 1910, the grounds around the Horlick's factory buildings and William Horlick's mansion became a parklike setting. The area was beautifully landscaped with trees and shrubs, and a small lagoon was dug in front of the buildings on Northwestern Avenue. For decades, Horlick stocked the lagoon with fish, and swans could be seen there every summer. The mansion was razed in 1952 and later a gas station was built on the site. Most of the historic buildings are still standing.

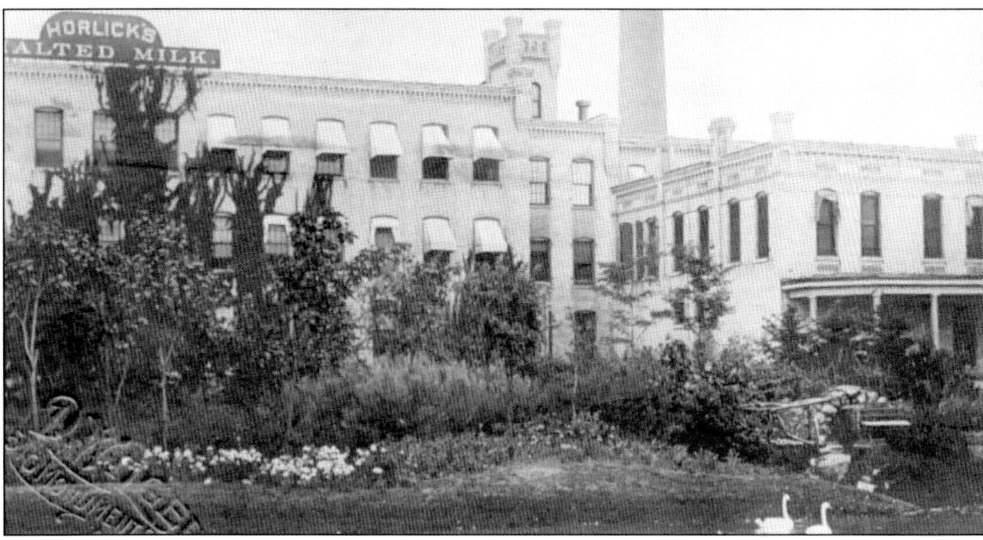

HORLICK'S MALTED MILK COMPANY. The name "Racine, Wisconsin, U.S.A." was carried to every city and village in the civilized world by the 1920s. Through advertising and worldwide distribution, Horlick's became a household name. William Horlick always longed for a life of adventure and exploration and, as his wealth grew, he contributed heavily to arctic expeditions with merit. When Capt. Robert Perry discovered the North Pole in 1909, he carried Horlick's Malted Milk with him. A few years later, Raoul Amundsen took boxes of the tablets to the South Pole. Malted Milk tablets also went into outer space with John Glenn Jr., on his epochal flight on February 20, 1962.

Eight

PARADES AND SPECIAL EVENTS

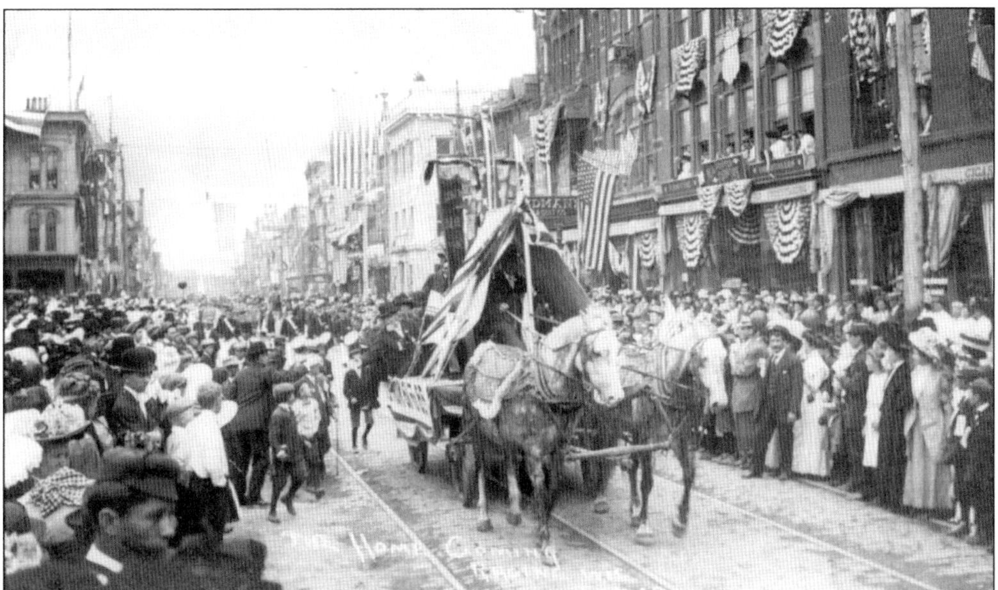

HOMECOMING FLOAT PASSING THE SQUARE. The float decorated in American flags and banners was entered in the 1909 homecoming parade by the veterans of the Civil War. Here is Mayor A. J. Horlick's proclamation: "Hear Ye! Hear Ye! Hear Ye! The time has arrived for all citizens to cease their labors and welcome to their former abode those of their brethren who have ceased to abide among us. Now Therefore Be It Proclaimed, That Monday, July the fifth, and Tuesday, July the sixth be declared Festal Days, when no man shall work. Come all ye who have traveled afar, and join with those of us who have remained at the hearth! Let us all be glad and make merry, for by so doing will life's burdens be materially lightened and our joys increased."

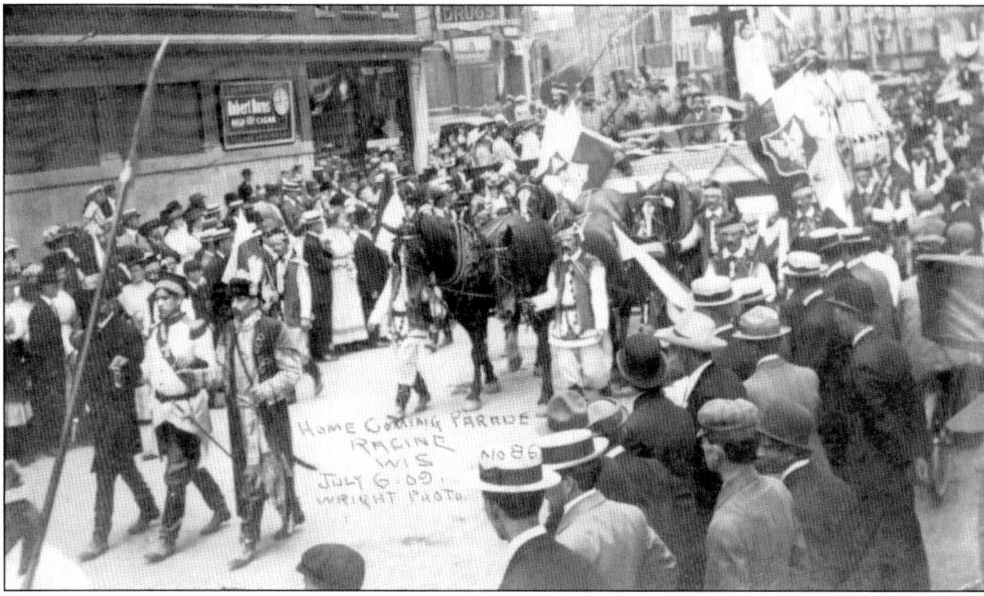

HOMECOMING PARADE. This float, passing the corner of Sixth and Main Streets during the 1909 homecoming parade, appears to be related to a religious group. The unique part of the homecoming was that all ethnic groups were able to display their unique contribution to Racine's diverse makeup. Also interesting is the assortment of head coverings, including not only the women's elaborate hats of the time, but the boaters (straw hats), caps, and derbies worn by the male spectators.

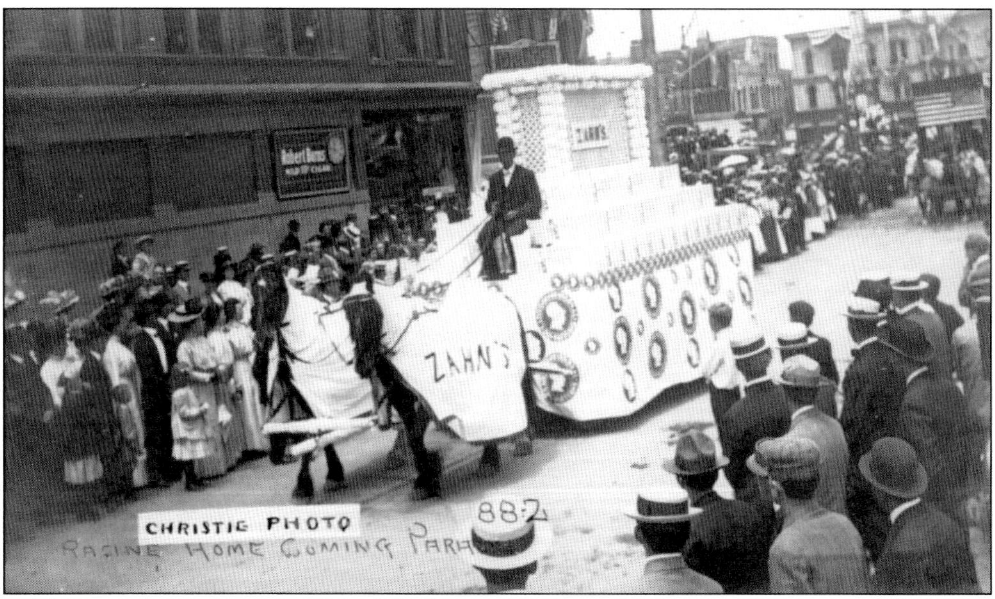

RACINE HOMECOMING PARADE. By 1909, Racine was growing at a rapid pace. New buildings, homes, and factories were being constructed everywhere. Local civic leaders and businessmen planned a homecoming celebration and invited all residents past and present to join in the festivities. The celebration was held July 5 and 6 with parades each day, band concerts, and activities for all ages. Zahn's Department Store, one of the city's largest and most popular dry goods and clothing stores for many decades, entered this horse-drawn float.

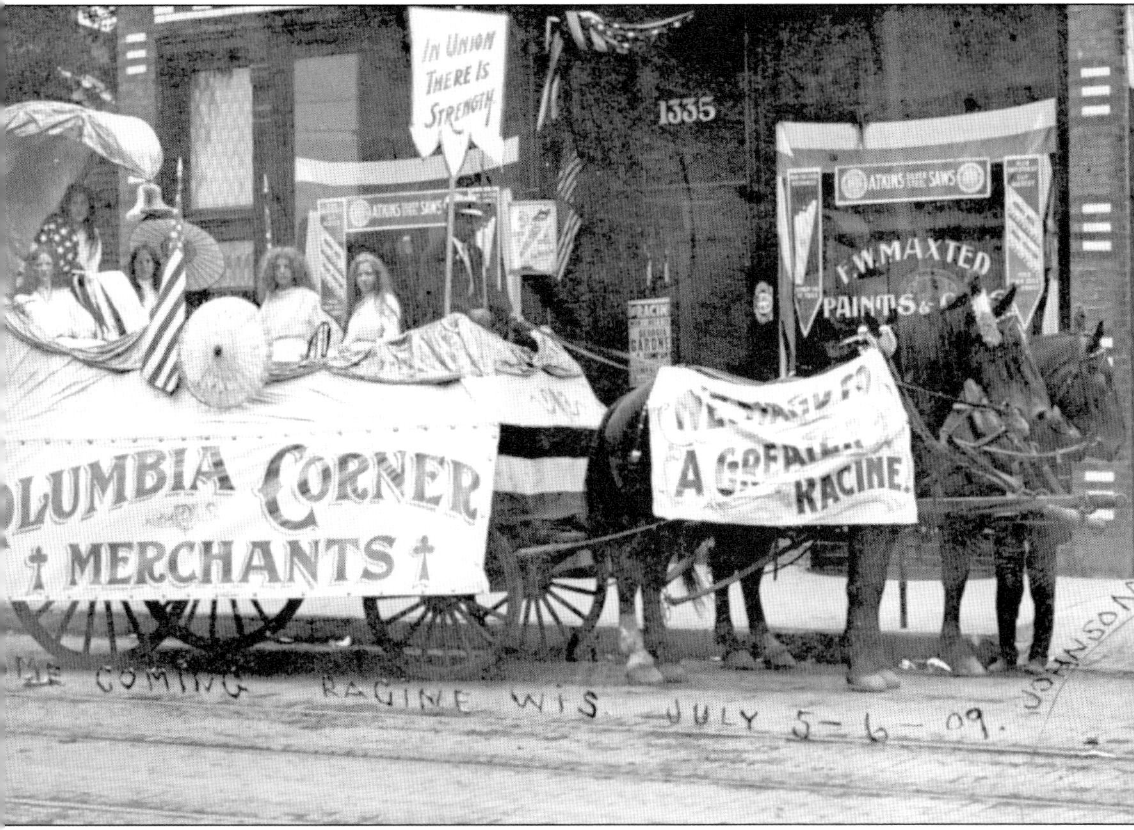

Homecoming Float. The Columbia Corners Merchants (Uptown) float in the 1909 homecoming parade is parked in front of F. W. Maxted's Hardware Store at 1335 Washington Avenue. During the celebration, the new statue of Columbia and a drinking fountain were dedicated at Fourteenth Street and Washington Avenue. The cover on the horse reads "We Stand for a Greater Racine."

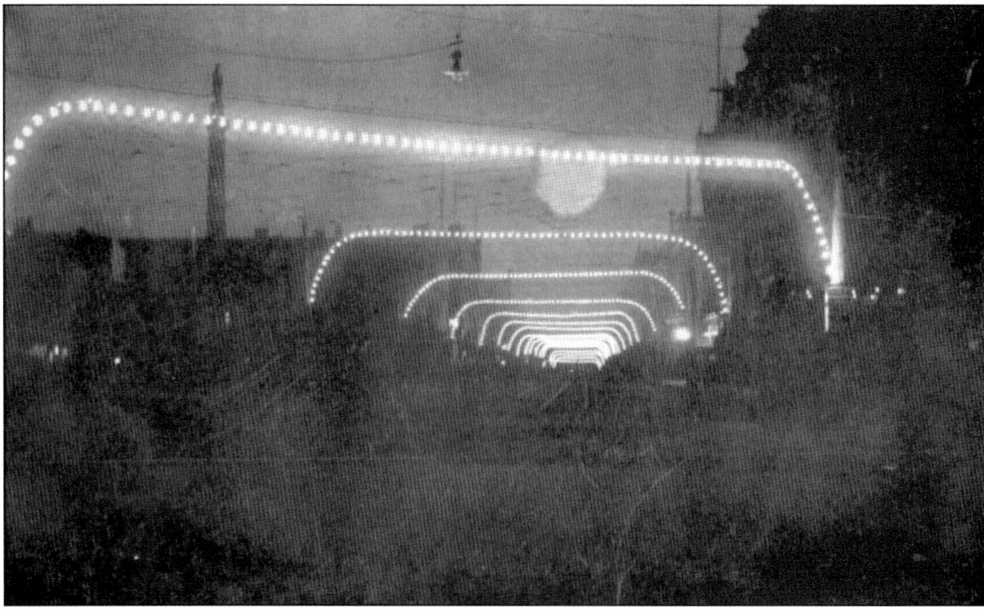

MAIN STREET AT NIGHT. Main Street was lighted with strings of bulbs arching over the roadway during the 1909 homecoming celebration. The effect was called the "White Way." This photograph looks north on Main Street from Sixth Street. In 1910, the city removed the arched lights and new Corinthian-style lights were placed along Main Street. The new streetlights were beautiful fixtures consisting of a number of white round globes on cast iron pedestals.

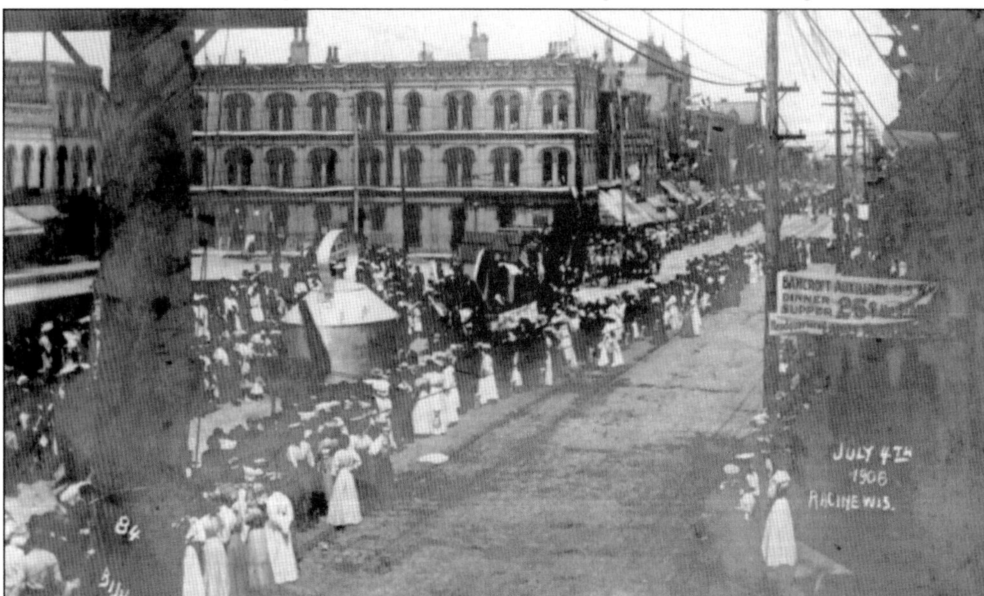

JULY 4, 1906. One of the most spectacular parades ever held in Racine was in 1906. Racine's businessmen concocted a plan to put on a mock circus parade. There were lion tamers, clowns, and 65 wagons with all kinds of animals and freaks. It was called the Lingring Cousins Circus, "The Greatest Show On Any Earth." After the parade, the circus gathered on Monument Square so showmen could continue their performances. This view shows a giant tea kettle making its way past Monument Square.

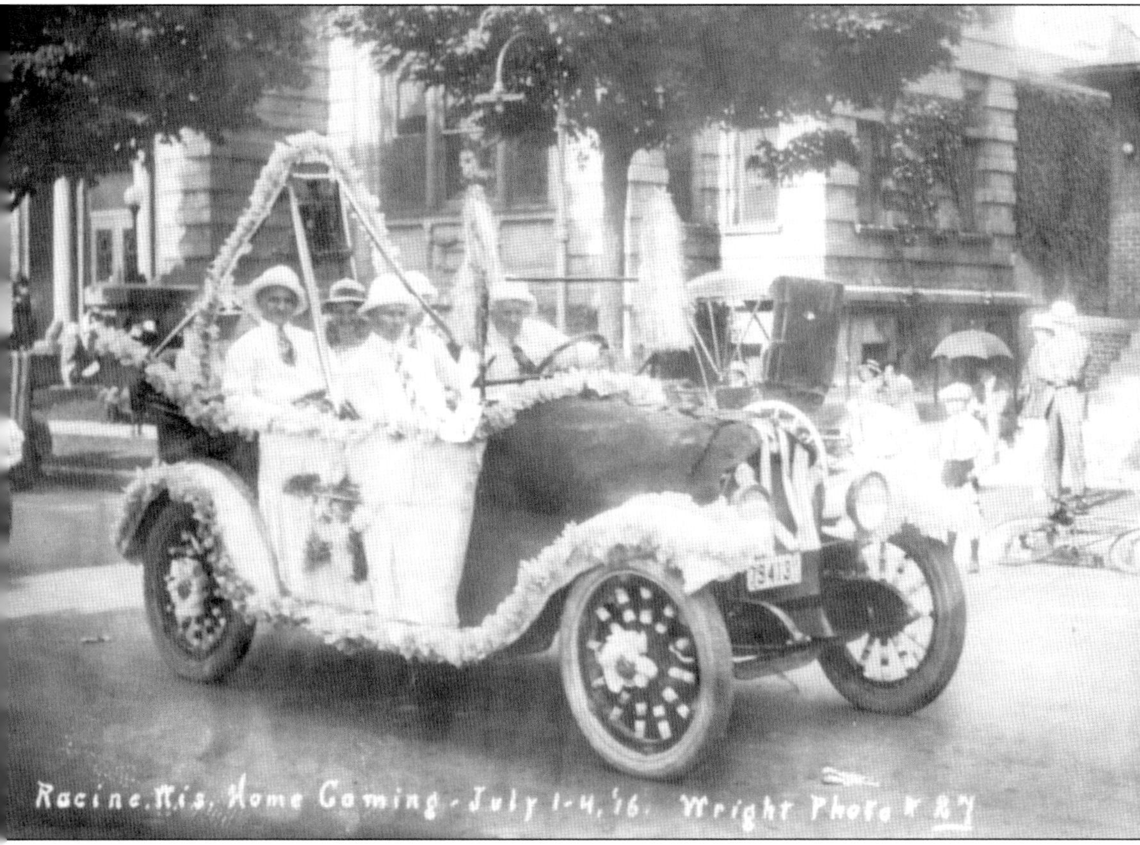

HOME COMING, 1916. This decorated car poses for the camera just south of the Racine Public Library at Seventh and Main Streets during the 1916 homecoming parade. At the time, there were no television sets, few radios, and no computers, so folks were always interested in joining any celebration. Racine continues to host one of the finest community parades each year with hundreds of entries and thousands of spectators. Carloads of people and dignitaries are still common in parades today.

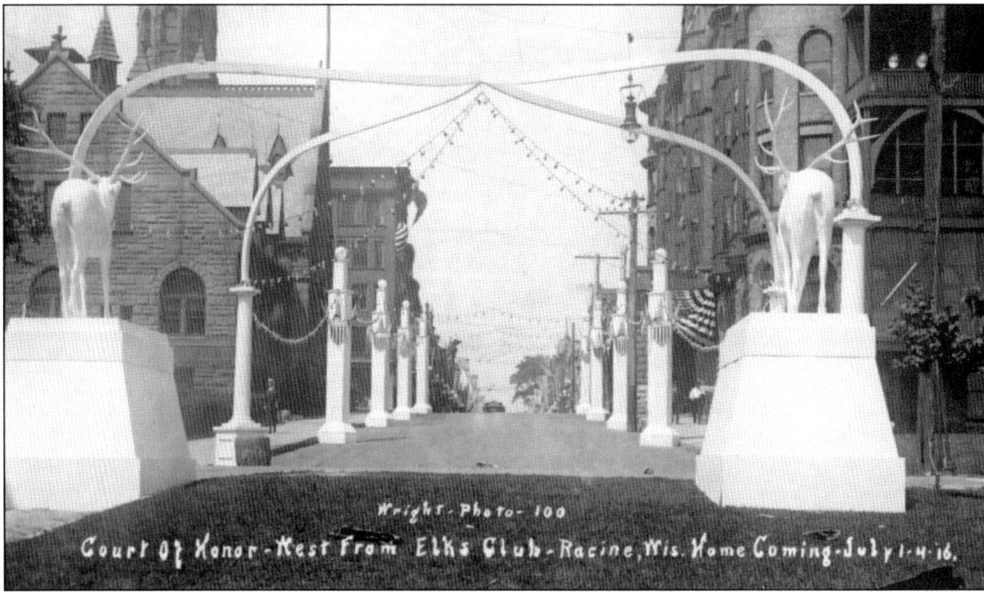

Court Of Honor. This has to be considered a classic example of civic pride. The people of Racine displayed outstanding enthusiasm and creativity during the city's homecoming events. This Elk's lodge court of honor was located on Sixth Street between Main Street and Lake Avenue in 1916. It led to the beautiful Elk's lodge at the foot of Sixth Street with two elk statues on pedestals to greet visitors. The view also shows the back of the old Racine United States Post Office (left) and the Hotel Racine (right).

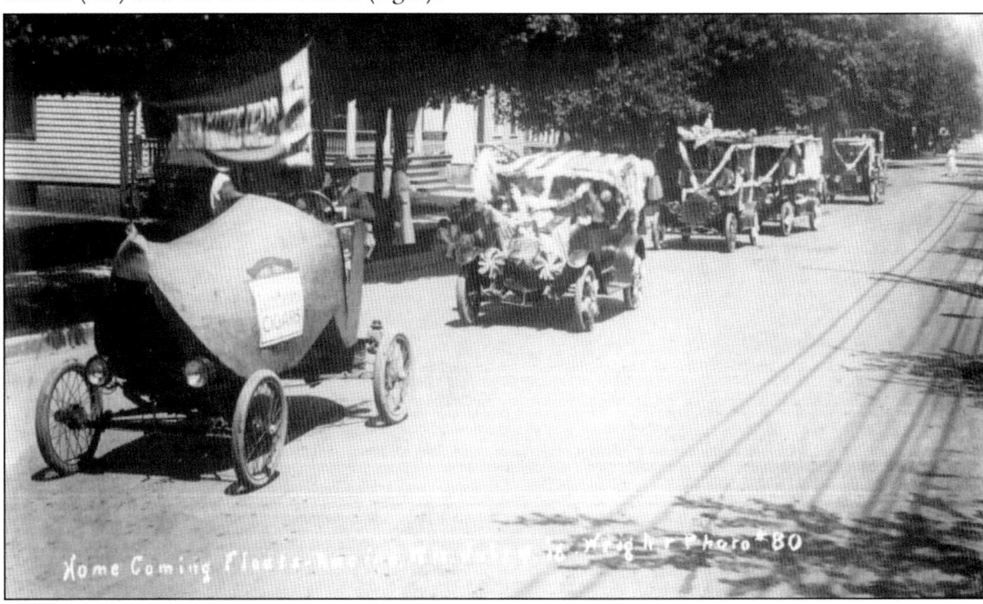

Home Coming Floats. During the 1916 homecoming celebration, a rather unique car was decorated as a wooden shoe advertising Dutch Masters Cigars. Although automobiles were no longer a novelty, they still were major attractions in parades. It is interesting to note that Fred L. Wright photographed and documented many local events during the early 1900s and sold the views. Unlike the printed postcards, only a limited number of these real-photo postcards were manufactured.

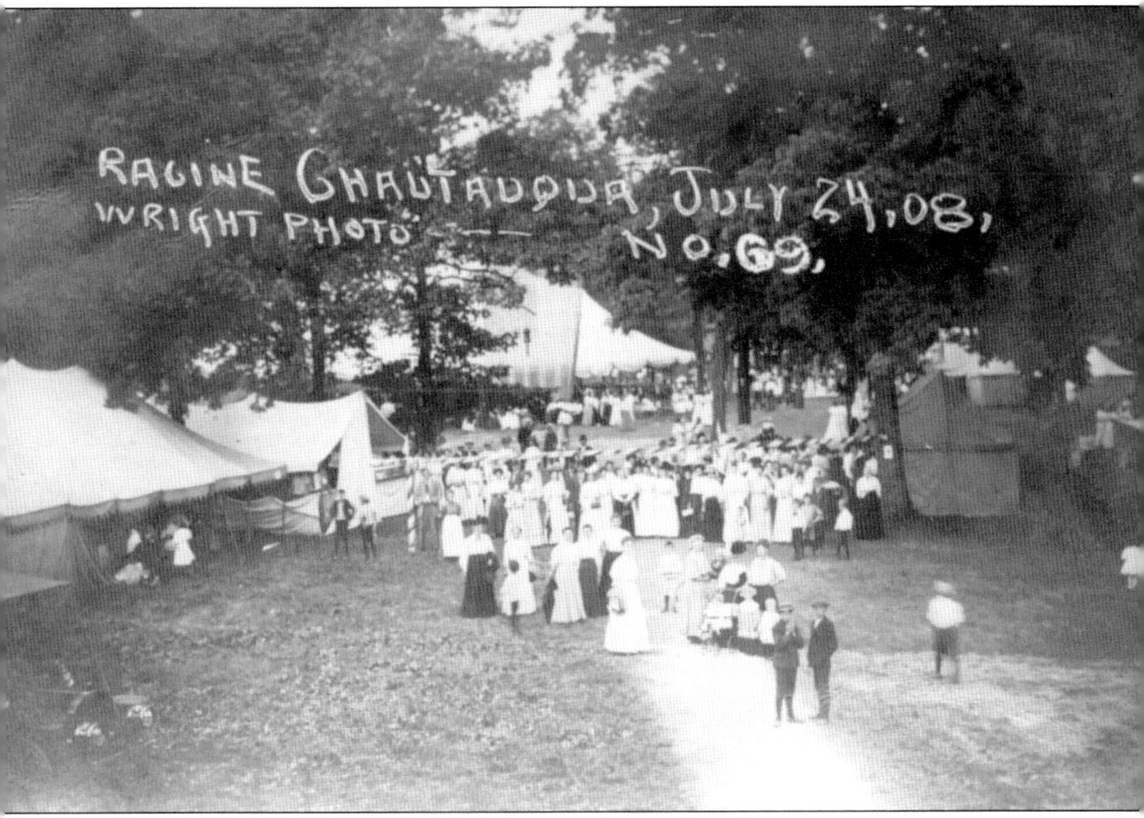

RACINE CHAUTAUQUA. Chautauqua, an early 1900s version of a culture festival, traveled to Racine each summer for several years and set up a tent city where entertainers and speakers would perform daily for up to a week. The Chautauqua campgrounds were located in a area called Kinzie Heights on the high ground where West Sixth Street and Kinzie Avenue intersect.

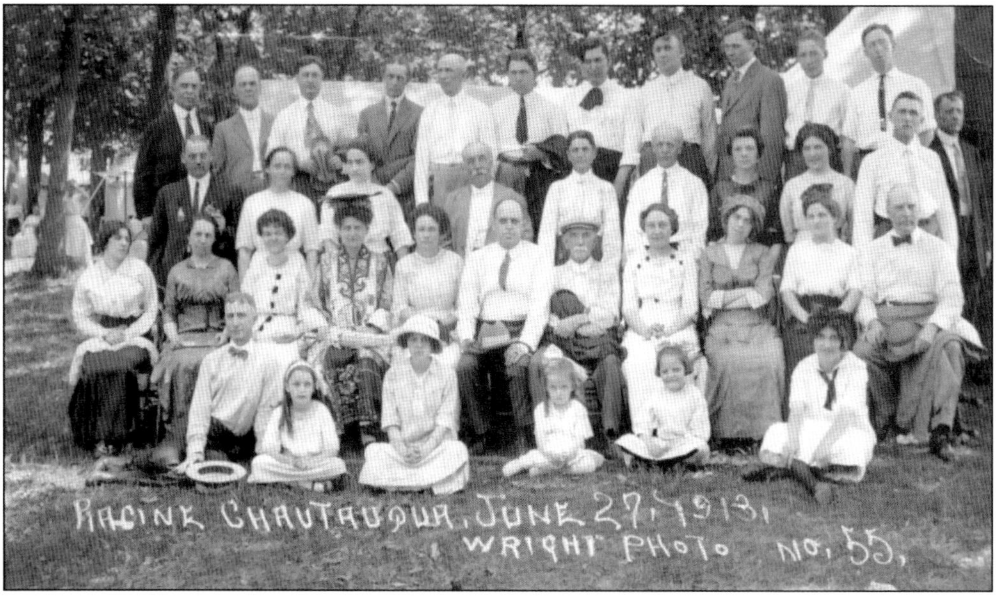

RACINE CHAUTAUQUA, 1913. Chautauqua began in 1874 when young minister John H. Vincent and his friend Lewis Miller started a church summer school at Lake Chautauqua in New York. Soon the pair broke away from strictly denominational study and decided that culture was important too. The movement mushroomed and soon similar camps were spread throughout the country. In 1903, the tent Chautauqua was created. This unidentified group posed at the Racine Chautauqua on June 27, 1913.

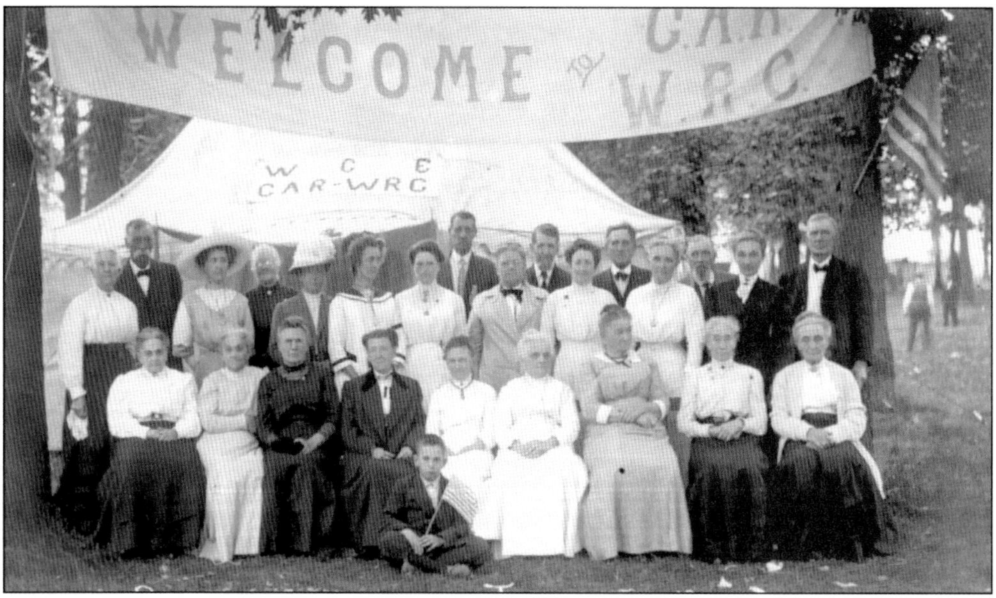

AT RACINE CHAUTAUQUA. "Chautauqua is here!" Banners draped on wagons, posters hung in store windows, and pennants fluttering from street posts proclaimed its approach. Dozens of Racine's young men gathered to help erect the Chautauqua's tent city. Each group posed in front of its tent to be photographed, documenting another exciting year at the annual event. This view shows a group in front of the Grand Army of the Republic (GAR) and Woman's Relief Corps (WRC) tent in 1912.

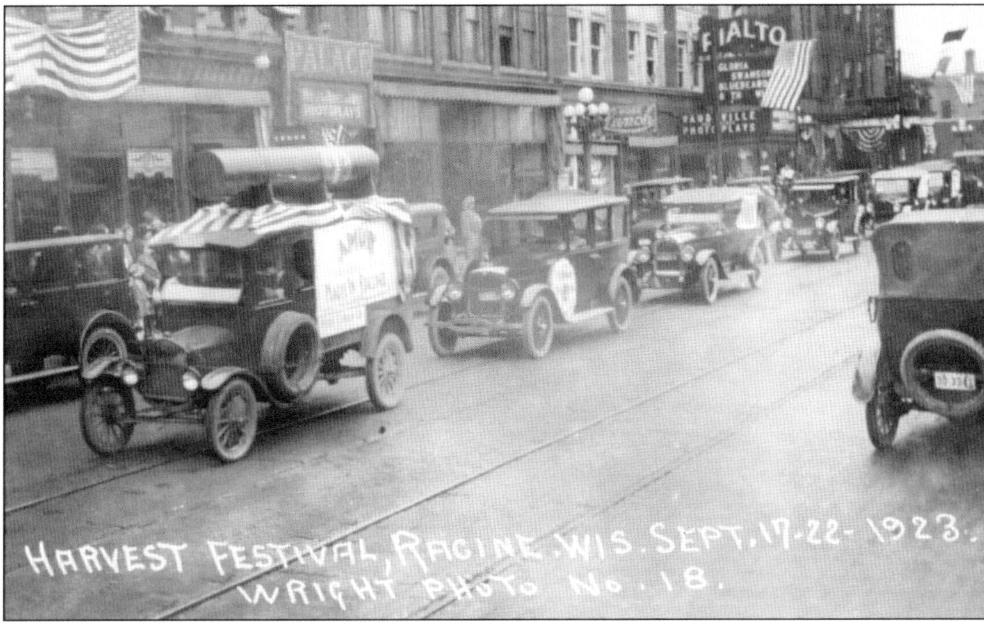

HARVEST FESTIVAL. The 1923 Harvest Festival parade is shown as it passes the 500 block of Main Street. Fred Wright, a local photographer, documented hundreds of Racine events for decades. This was photograph No. 18 taken during this event. James Hebblewaite, a Racine cigar manufacturer, entered the first truck pictured. It featured a large cigar on the roof of the vehicle. One of Hebblewaite's best selling brands was named Amur.

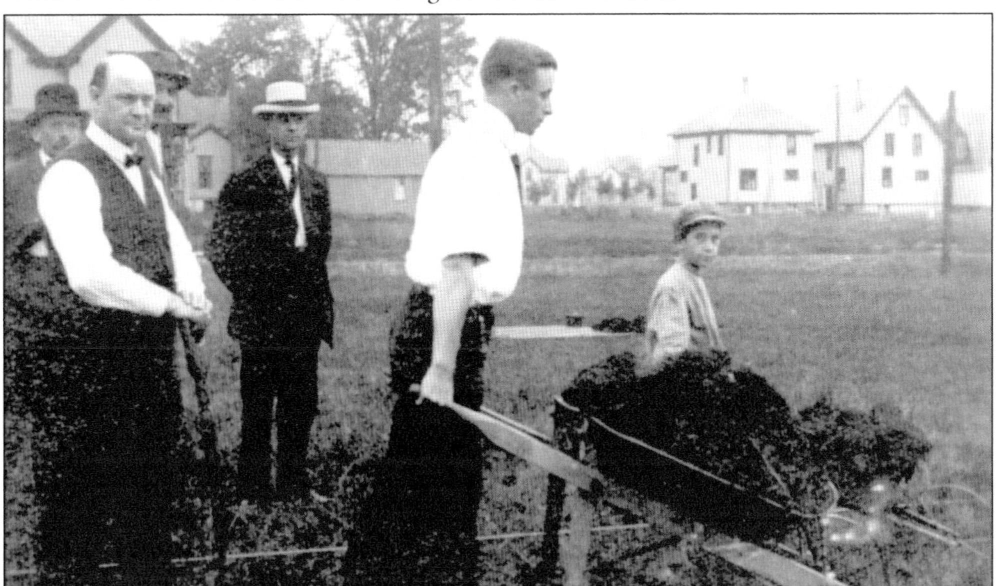

BREAKING GROUND GRANGE AVENUE METHODIST CHURCH. Following a March 3, 1911, meeting at Thomas Hay's home, a new Methodist church group was formed in Racine. By May 1911 the group adopted plans to build a new church. At a social gathering held on the grounds at 2713 Fifteenth Street on August 15, 1911, the contractor's bids were opened and announced. On August 22, 1911, ground was broken by William Leek, while Thomas Hay Jr. and Frank T. Cartwright wheeled away the dirt. This view was taken to commemorate the occasion.

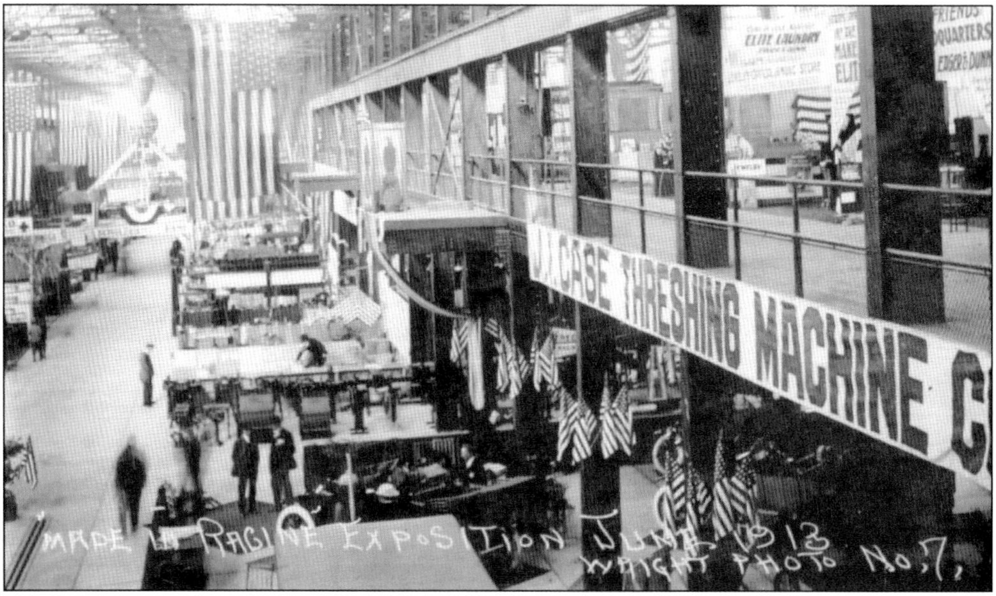

Made In Racine Exposition. Racine business leaders held a gigantic industrial exposition at the newly built J. I. Case Threshing Machine Company's south works factory south of the city on June 13, 1913. Racine had grown to be a leading manufacturing city in the Midwest and community pride was at its peak. Over 165 manufacturers, both big and small, displayed their "Made in Racine" products. The show was a huge success, drawing thousands of spectators from all over the country.

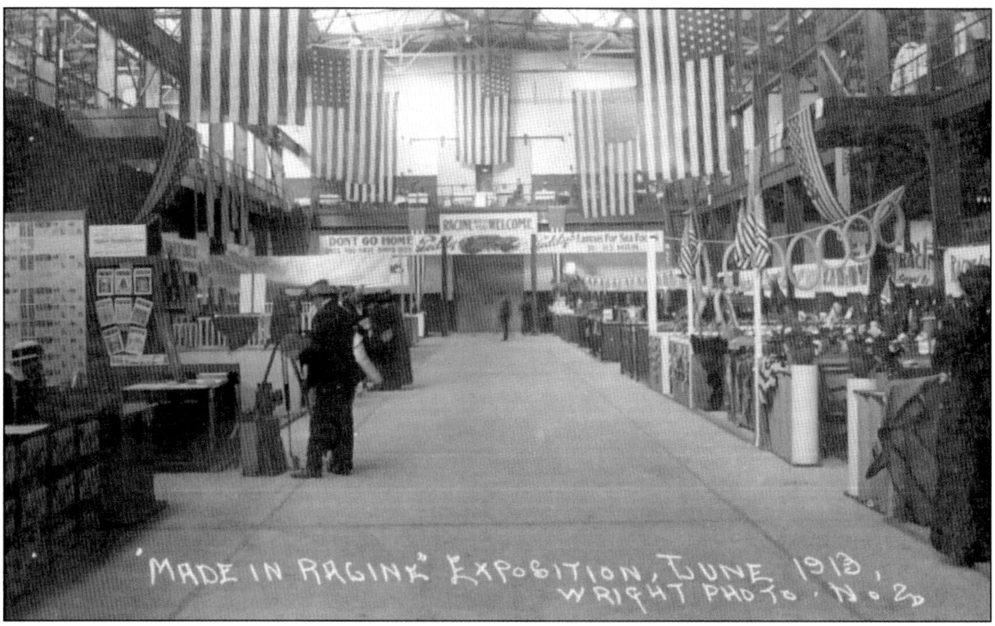

Racine Exposition. This postcard shows another view of the "Made in Racine" exposition at the newly constructed J. I. Case south works in June 1913. The event featured exhibits of Racine's diverse manufactured goods, with everything from automobiles, to malted milk, to woolen shawls, to patent medicine being displayed. This view was taken at the far east end of the machine shop building.

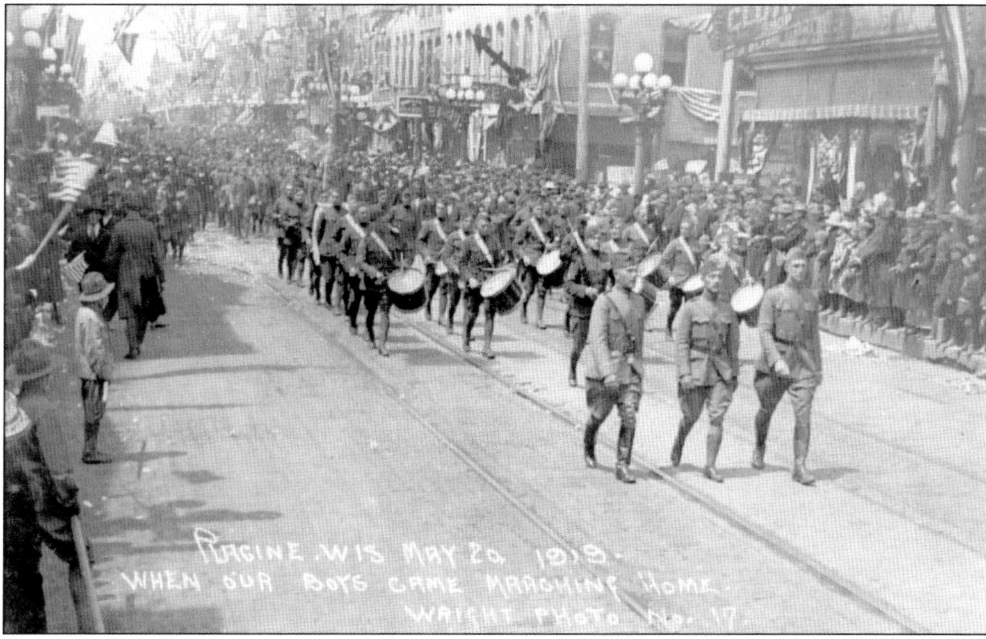

DAY THE BOYS CAME MARCHING HOME. On May 20, 1919, two of the three Racine outfits arrived home from France after almost two years of service there. The troops were part of the U.S. Army's 32nd Division—the Red Arrow Division. The entire city turned out to greet the troops and businesses were closed for the day. A parade of 1,500 marching soldiers, including some men from other Wisconsin cities, were led by the regimental band. The procession began at the railroad depot at the Junction (now Uptown), made its way along Washington Avenue, Sixth Street, Main Street, and ended as the troops marched through the 50-foot high arch of triumph that was built to honor them at Third and Main Streets. From there they were dismissed to join their families and friends.

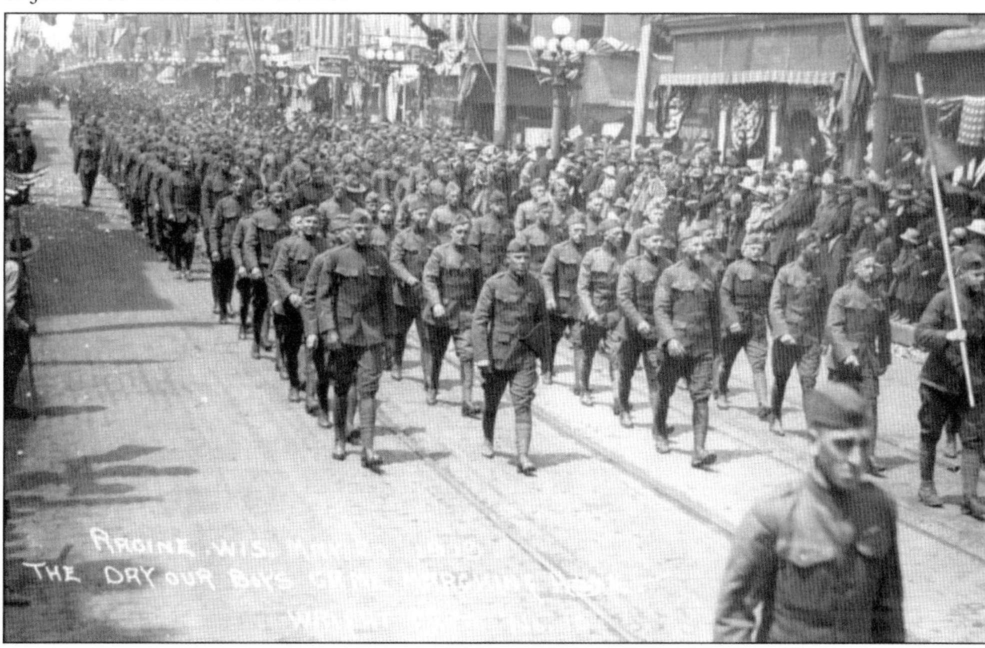

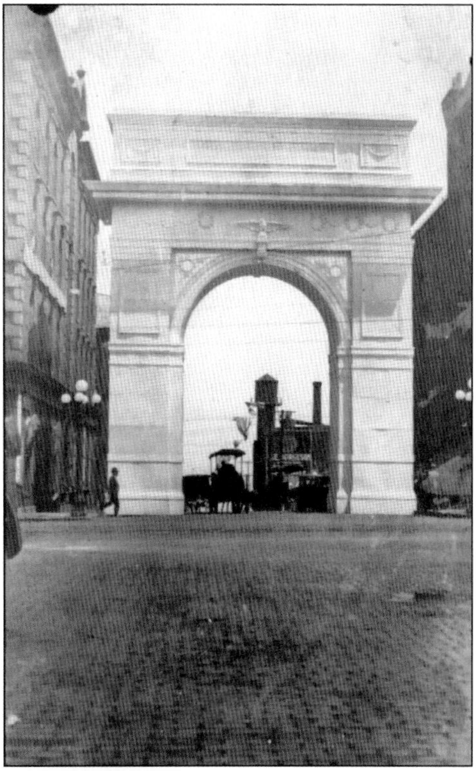

The Arch of Triumph. When the news was heard on November 7, 1918, that the war was over, crowds made their way to downtown and the city celebrated the event. May 20, 1919, however, may have been a day of even greater relief and jubilation as Racine's young men returned home. One can only suppose that tears formed in the eyes of the troops of the U.S. Army's 32nd Division (Red Arrow Division) as they turned the corner at Third and Main Streets to march under the massive 50 foot arch of triumph built to honor their sacrifices and return home. Local craftsman were among the finest in the world and their skills are documented in photographs like these. The view at left shows the arch as it looked from Main Street and the lower view shows what the soldiers viewed as they turned the corner. The arch with the Court of Honor looked west on Third Street from Lake Avenue. The old buildings of the Miller Shoe Company and Hotel Nelson are seen to the right.

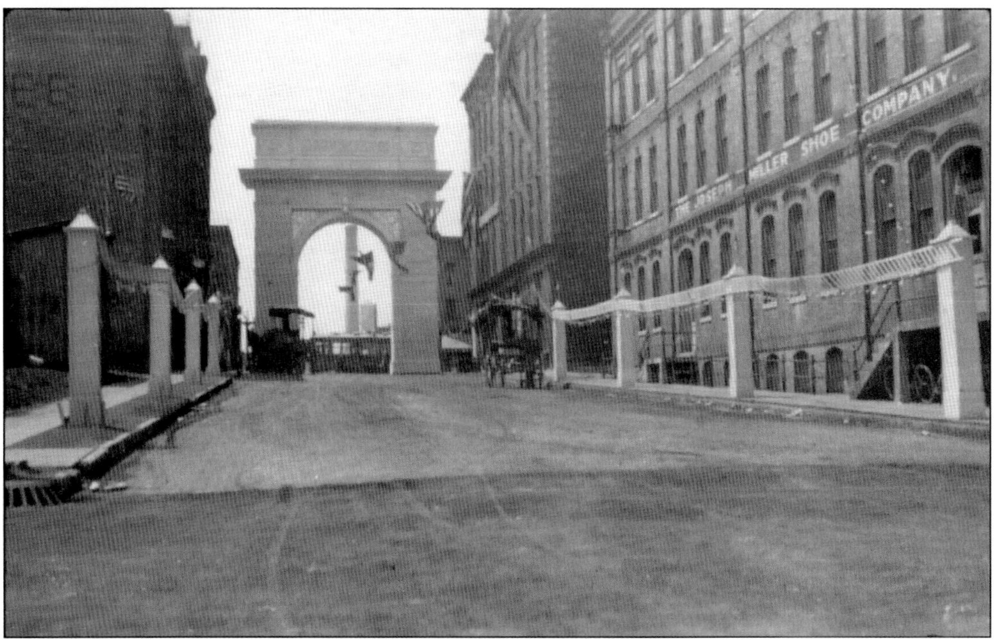

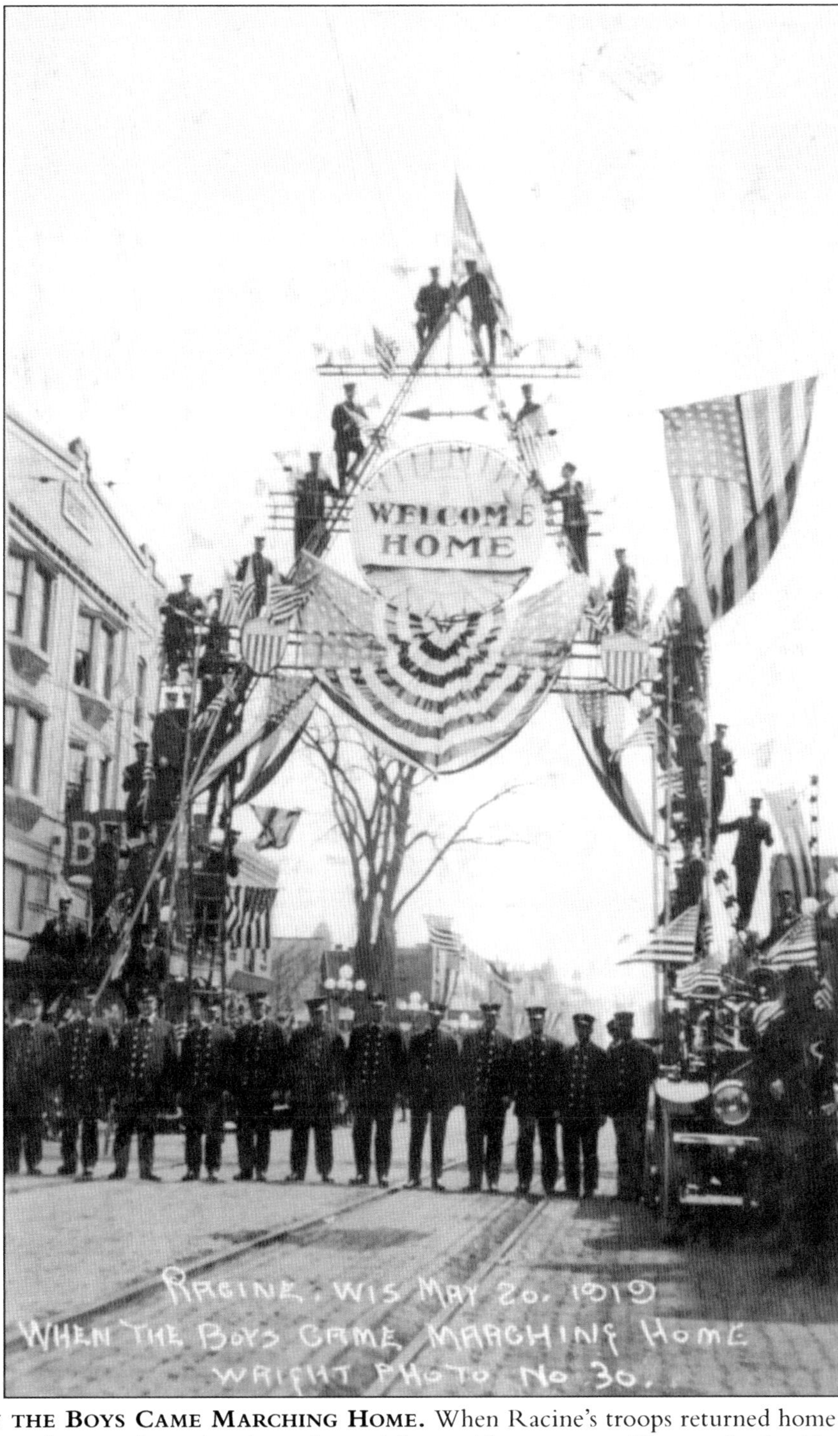

WHEN THE BOYS CAME MARCHING HOME. When Racine's troops returned home in May 1919 from the war, the entire city welcomed them with open arms. Thousands of residents lined the streets to cheer and honor the young men and women as they made their way to downtown. As the parading soldiers marched down Sixth Street, they were greeted by this creative arch of ladders constructed by the Racine firemen.

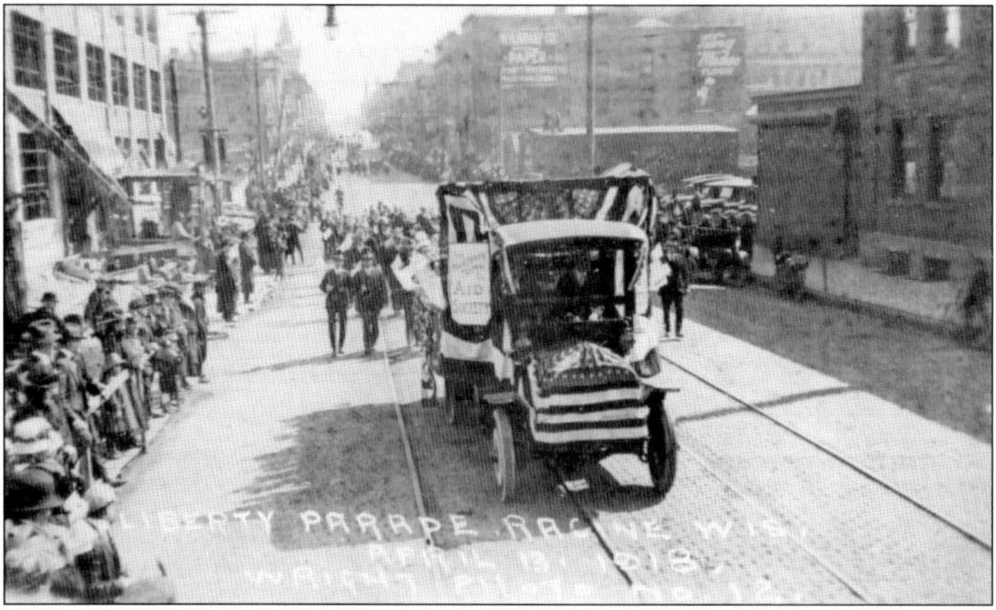

LIBERTY PARADE, 1918. Like cities, towns, and villages throughout the United States, Racine threw its total support to the war efforts. Many large parades were held in support of the young men and women serving in the war. An enormous parade took place on May 29, 1917, as an estimated 30,000 marchers turned out to show the Kaiser. The next year, on April 13, 1918, the liberty parade, another massive show of support, was held. The above photograph, looking south on Main Street from the Root River Bridge, shows a truck decorated in American flags that was entered by the Hartmann Trunk Company Aid Society. The bottom photograph shows a group of Racine American Red Cross nurses marching at the same location.

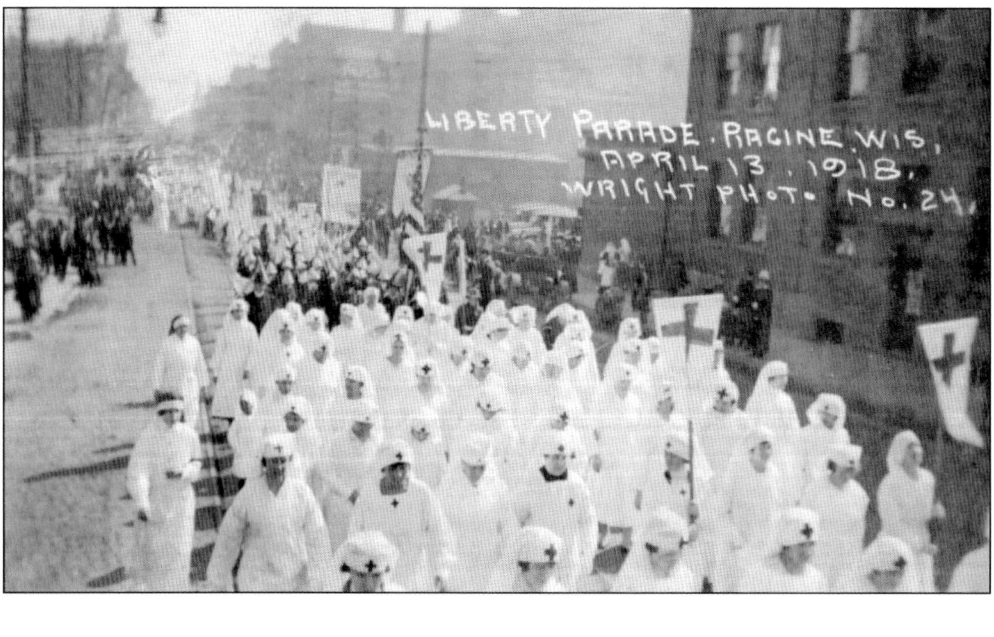

Nine

SCHOOLS

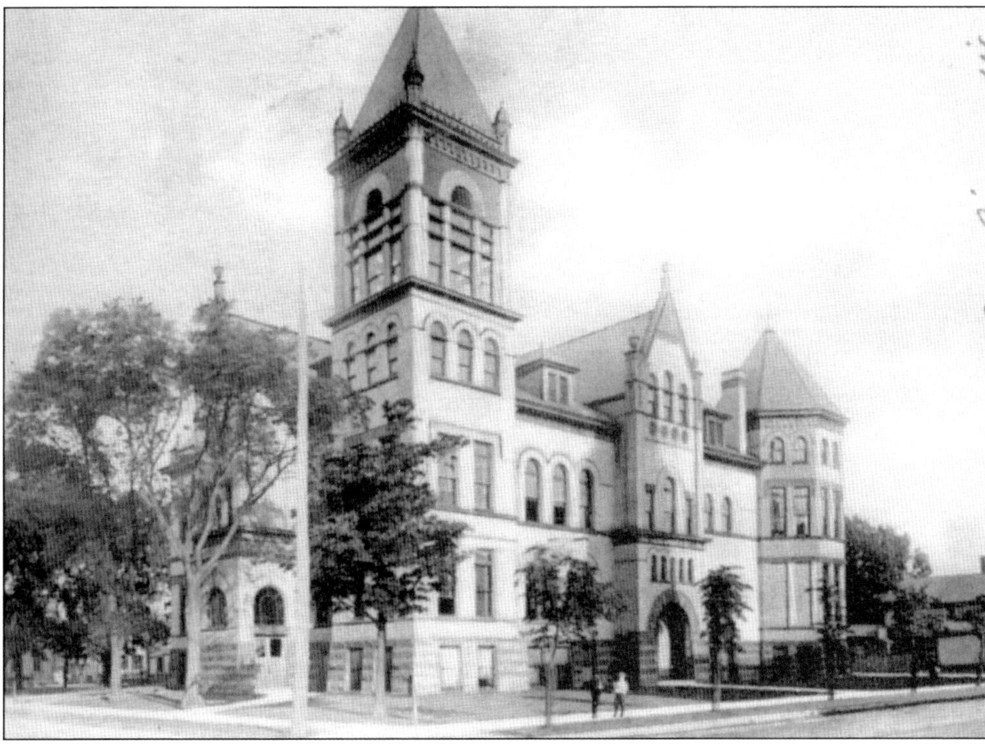

RACINE HIGH SCHOOL. In the 1890s, Racine built this high school building on the corner of College Avenue and Seventh Street where the Racine County Courthouse stands today. Although Kenosha is credited for having the first high school in the state of Wisconsin, Racine had the first graduating class in the state—the class of 1857. One of Racine High School's most famous graduates was Fredrick McIntyre Bickel, who became movie star Fredric March. During his career March matured into one of the best actors in America, winning two Oscars and two Tony awards for best actor.

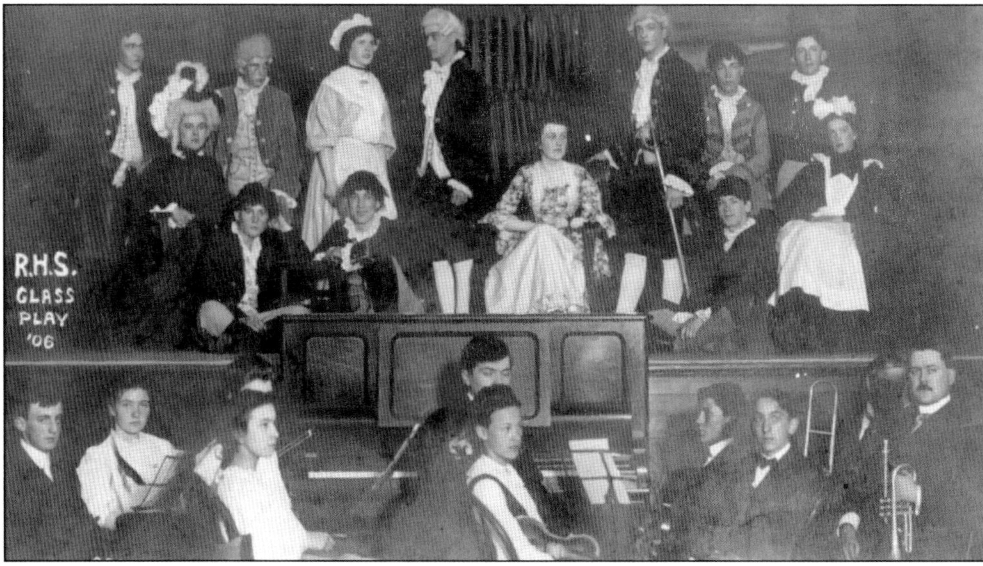

RACINE HIGH SCHOOL PLAY. The cast and orchestra of the class playing *She Stoops to Conquer* posed for this keepsake photograph postcard in 1906. Racine High School published a yearbook starting in 1909. The first book listed all the graduates back to 1857. Many of the yearbooks, called the *Kipikawi*, had photographs of plays, sports teams, and students. After Washington Park High School opened in 1928, it continued publishing its annual yearbook as the *Kipikawi*. The famed statue of Joan of Arc and other Racine High School artifacts were transferred to the new school.

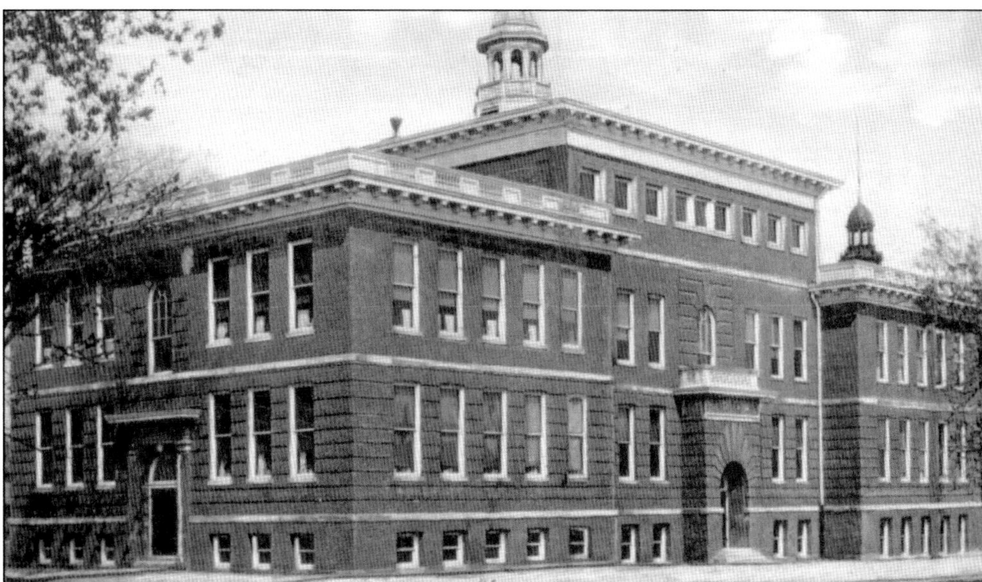

MCMYNN SCHOOL. McMynn School, located at Seventh Street and Lake Avenue, was named for Col. John G. McMynn, the first principal of Racine High School. McMynn also served as superintendent of city schools and state superintendent of schools. The building was used for other educational purposes including by Racine Vocational School in the 1960s. The school building and other smaller structures on the block were razed in the late 1970s and the McMynn Towers and a parking structure were built on the site.

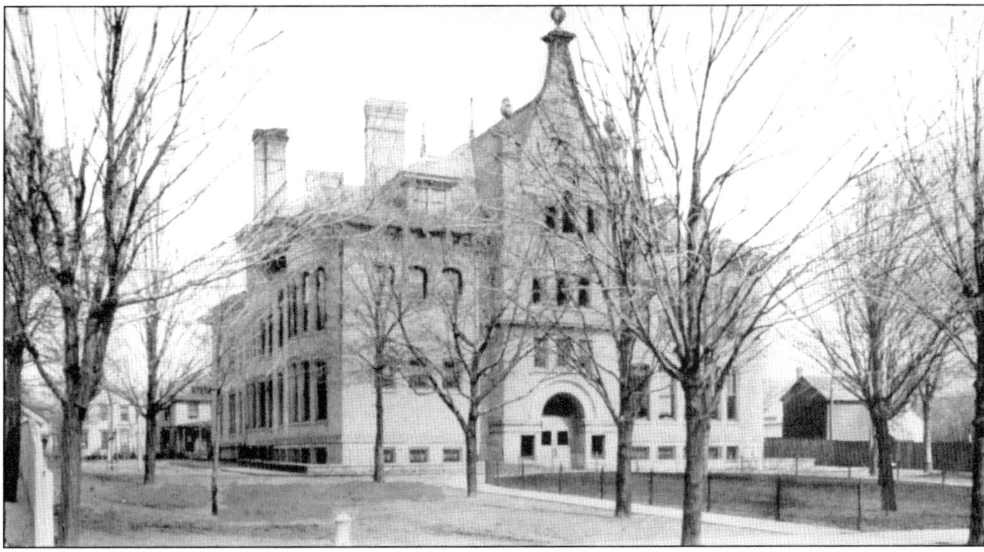

WINSLOW SCHOOL. Originally called the Third Ward School, this cream brick building, located at 1325 College Avenue, was built in the 1850s from the same plans as two other Racine schools. It was later named for Horatio Gates Winslow, a Racine superintendent of schools. The school was built on the site of one of Racine's first cemeteries. According to legend, children digging marble holes were warned not to dig their holes too deep, and boys taunted girls about drinking "skeleton" water. This school and others were redesigned in 1897 by local architect James Gilbert Chandler.

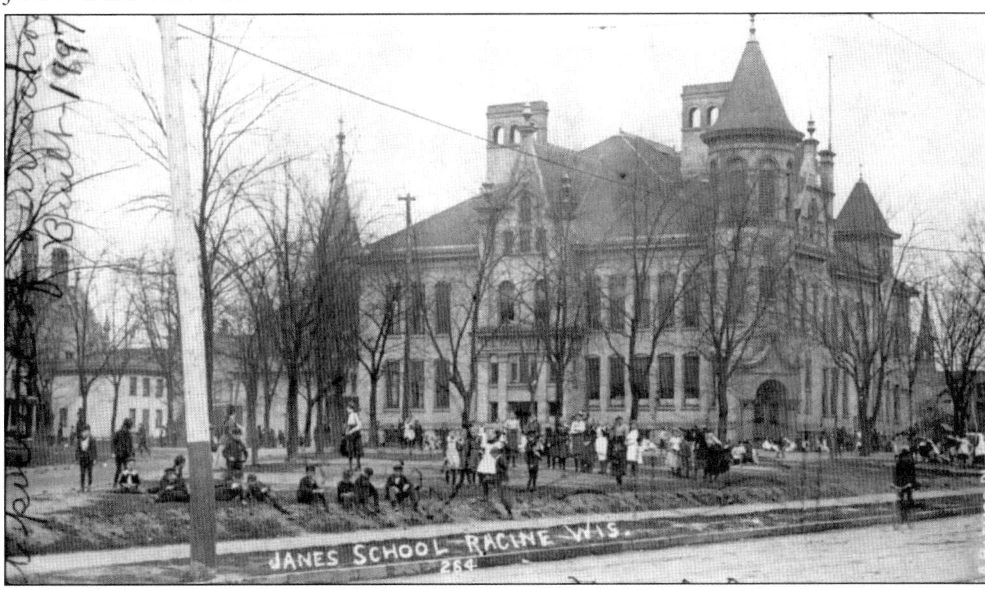

JANES SCHOOL. Built in the 1850s as the Fourth Ward School, this cream brick school was later named for Lorenzo Janes, a pioneer Racine attorney and newspaper publisher. Like other Racine schools, it was extensively remodeled in the 1890s. It is still used today as a public school. Located at 1425 North Wisconsin Street, the school occupies a square block, which was originally set aside for park purposes like East and West Parks. Inadvertently, the land was used for a firehouse and school. When a new north side firehouse was built, the old building was moved to a lot on Erie Street just north of High Street.

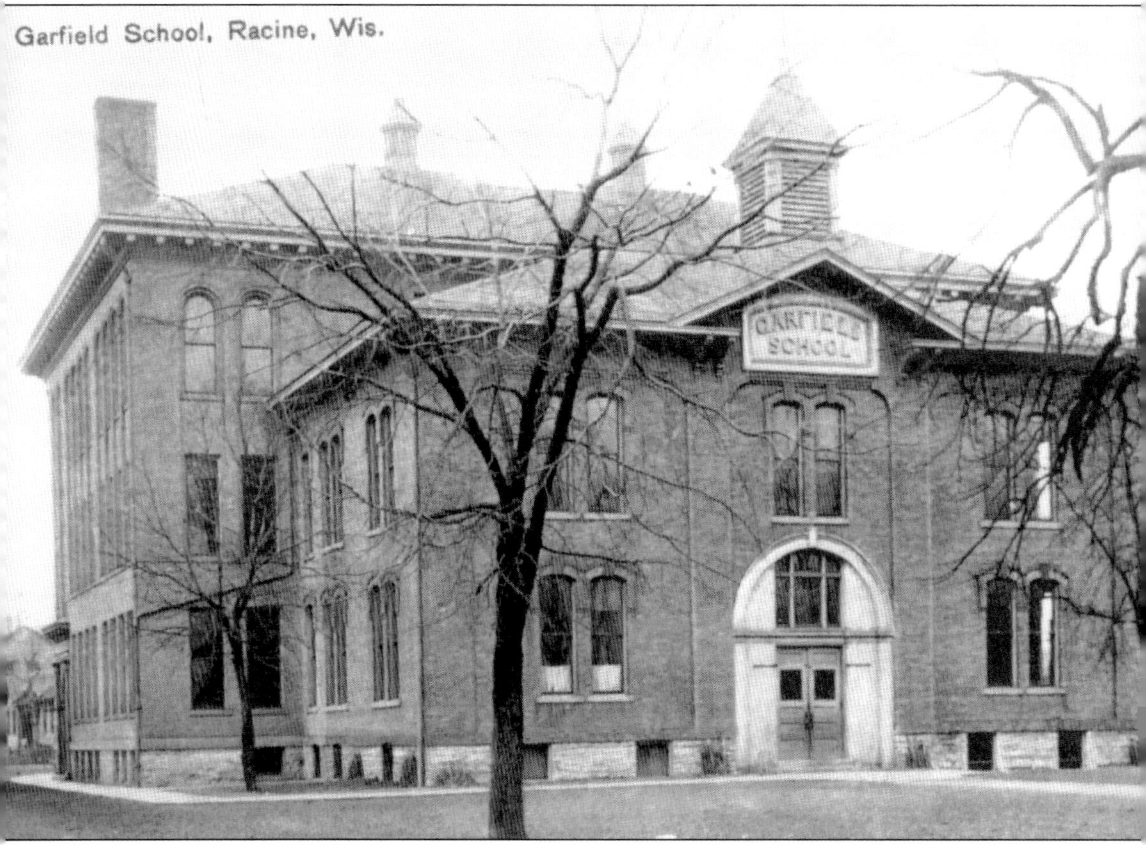

GARFIELD SCHOOL. Now called Julian Thomas Elementary school, this cream brick school was known as the Fifth Ward School when it was built in 1855. It was later named for assassinated Pres. James A. Garfield. The building plans were drawn by Lucas Bradley, Racine's foremost pioneer architect. The building was redesigned a number of times in the 1880s and after 1900. A major addition was completed in 2003. The school was recently renamed and rededicated in tribute to Julian Thomas, a Racine activist and African American leader who was instrumental in desegregating Racine public schools. Thomas died April 6, 2003.

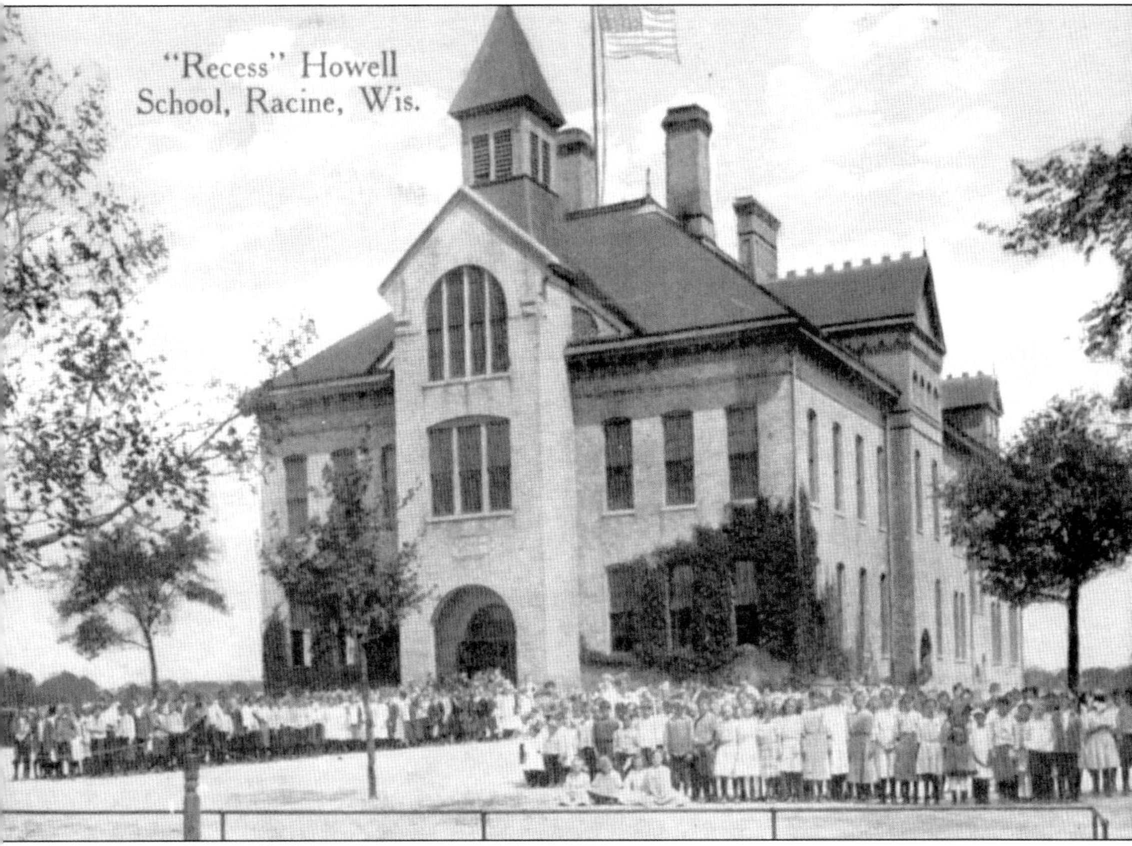

HOWELL SCHOOL. When Howell School was built on Washington Avenue and Valley Drive, the area was considered the outskirts of town. Originally planned as a four-room school plus an office, only two rooms were ready for use when it was first occupied in September 1888. But its first enrollment filled it to overflowing capacity and the next two rooms were completed. By 1891, four more rooms were added. In January 1970 the doors were closed. The school deteriorated so badly that it had a number of rods pulling the opposite outer walls together so the building would not collapse, and the splitting beams were held intact by braces. In July 1970 the cream brick building was razed.

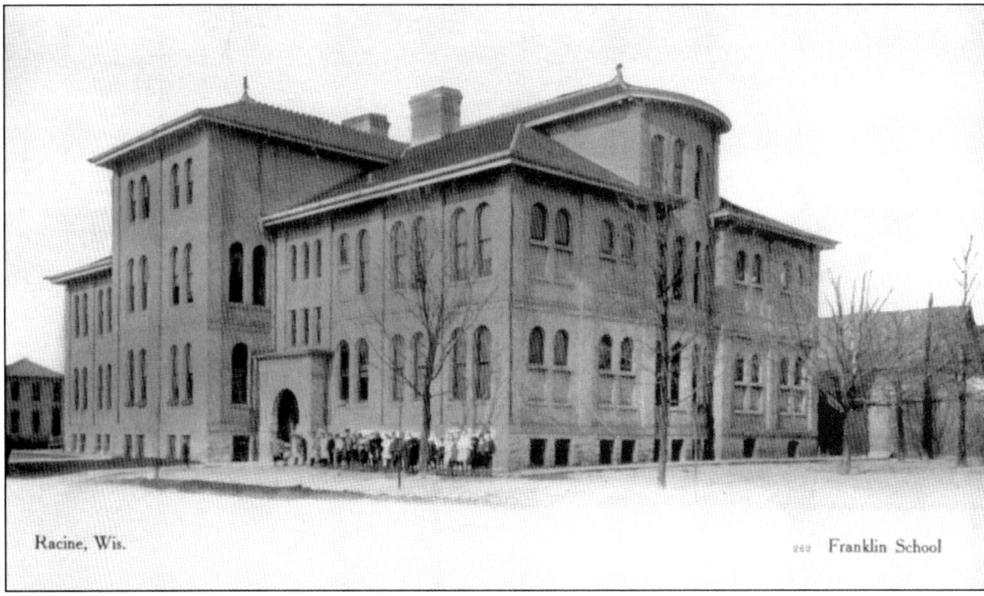

Franklin School. Originally built as the Sixth Ward School serving Racine's south side, the school was later renamed Franklin School. The first structure built of cream brick was completed in January 1870 at a cost of $21,132, including the land. In 1875, the school consisted of an upright building of six rooms. In 1899, the school was remodeled and a large addition doubled the capacity. Other additions followed through the years to keep up with the growing class sizes. In later years the building was used to house Walden III School.

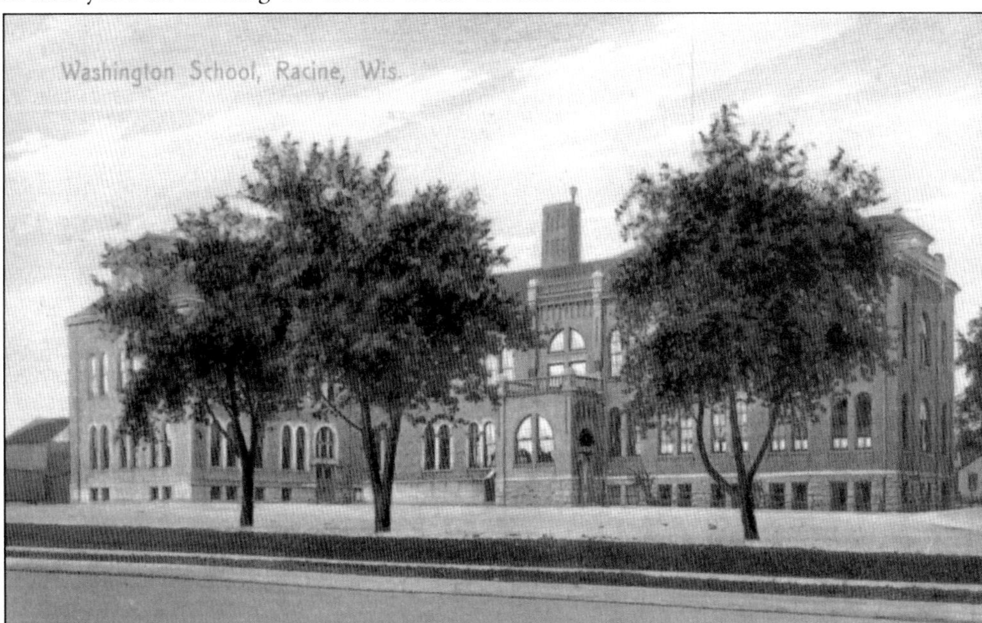

Washington School. This school, originally built as the Seventh Ward School, served Racine's north side. This view shows the school as it looked about 1909, before a 1920s addition wrapped around the south end. Built of cream brick with additions in a plain design similar to Garfield School, there were no fancy turrets or heavy decor like the Janes and Winslow Schools.

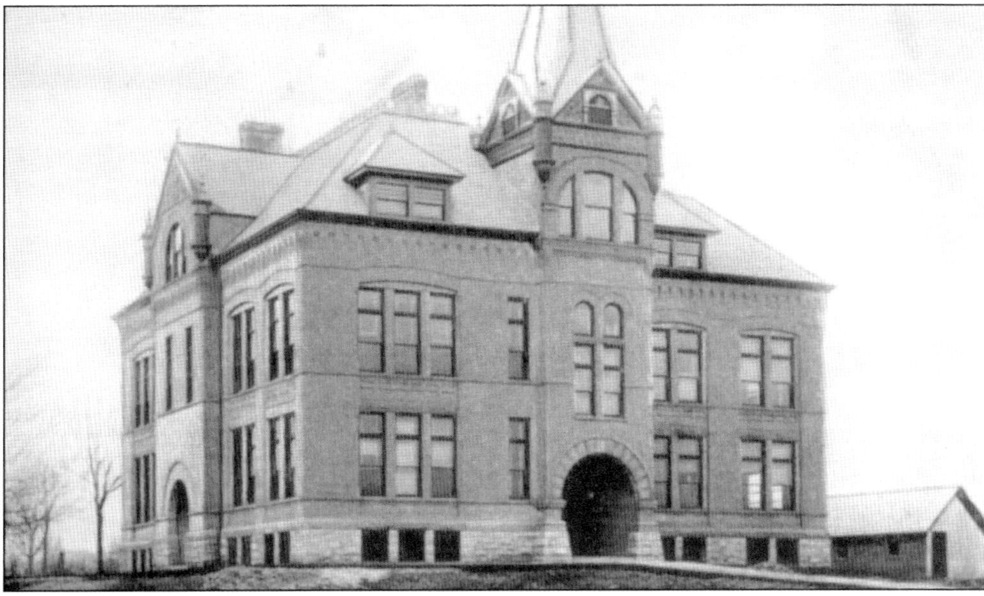

LINCOLN SCHOOL. Serving Racine's northwest side was beautiful Lincoln School. When it was built in the 1890s on a high point at the corner of Carlisle Avenue and Hamilton Street, the school was considered to be out in the country. The massive building constructed of cream brick with stone trim has its grand, towered entrance facing east. When the school was closed in the early 1980s, the building was restored and remodeled into Lincoln School Historic Apartments. The building is a fine example of adaptive use of a historic structure.

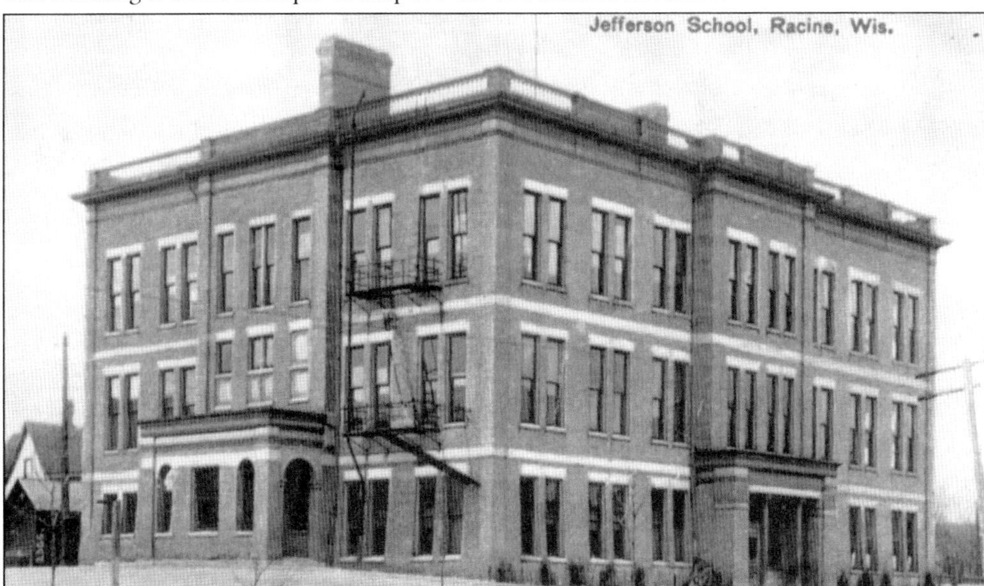

JEFFERSON SCHOOL. When Jefferson School was built in the late 1890s, it was at the edge of the city that was expanding and overflowing to the west. Its transitional design reflected a departure from Victorian styles toward newer and more utilitarian schools like Fratt, Knapp, and McKinley. Although schools like Jefferson no longer have cast iron desks, ink wells, and hanging globe lights, they still serve their purpose as temples of learning. The squeaky wooden floors still entertain young students.

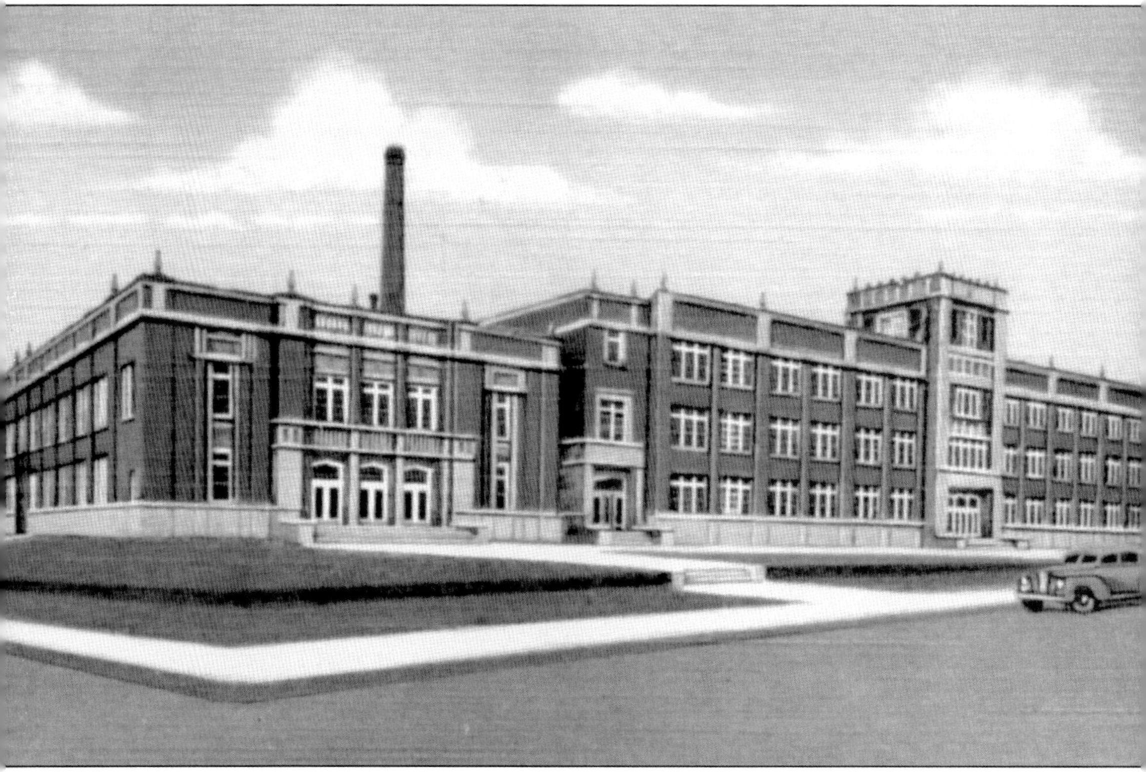

WILLIAM HORLICK HIGH SCHOOL. By the 1920s Racine High School, which had been built in the early 1890s, was bursting at the seams and some classes had to be held in rented rooms and buildings throughout the city. The city found its infrastructure unprepared for the major expansions of industry in the second and third decades of the 20th century. Thousands of new jobs appeared and with them new employees and their families. To alleviate the overcrowding, two high schools were opened in 1928. This one was on an 11 acre site on Rapids Drive, which William Horlick had donated to the city in 1918.

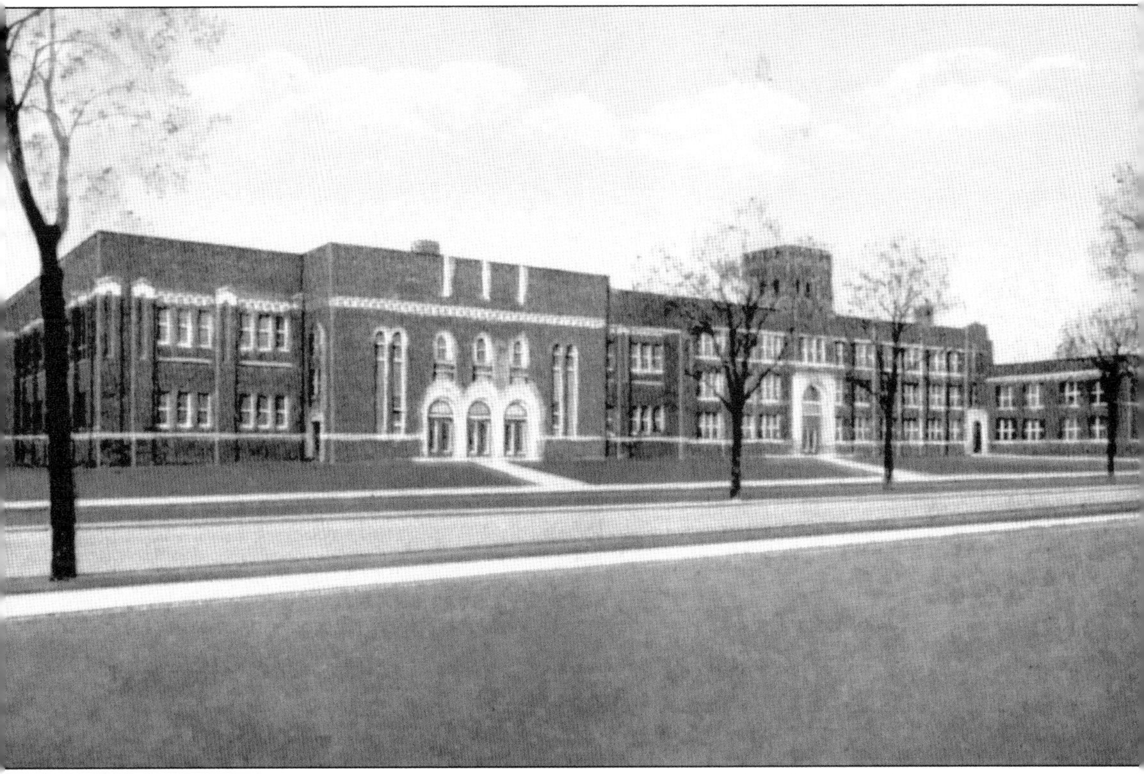

WASHINGTON PARK HIGH SCHOOL. This school was named after the beautiful Washington Park where the building was constructed between 1927 and 1929 on a bluff overlooking the park. The school was built larger than Horlick High School because of the higher concentration of population on Racine's south and west sides. When the old Racine High School was vacated many of its artifacts were moved to Washington Park High School. These included a statue of Joan of Arc which stood in the Racine High School library for many years. The statue now stands in the main entry of Washington Park High School.

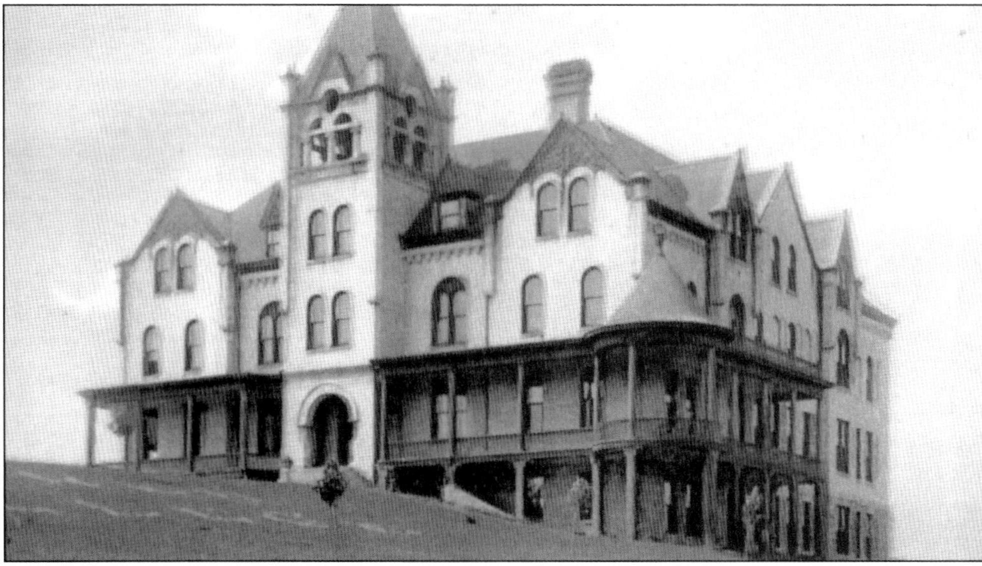

LUTHER COLLEGE. Standing like a fortress on a high bluff overlooking Island Park at West Sixth Street and Kinzie Avenue is the old Luther College. Rev. Christ H. Jensen, pastor of the Emmaus Danish Lutheran Church of Racine, conceived the idea of establishing a high school and college for Midwestern Danish Lutherans. On July 4, 1902, the cornerstone was laid. The three-story structure was built in a Romanesque design. Arched windows and pressed tin panels highlight the upper floors and gables. Above the main entrance at the base of the tower an inscription reads "M. Luther College."

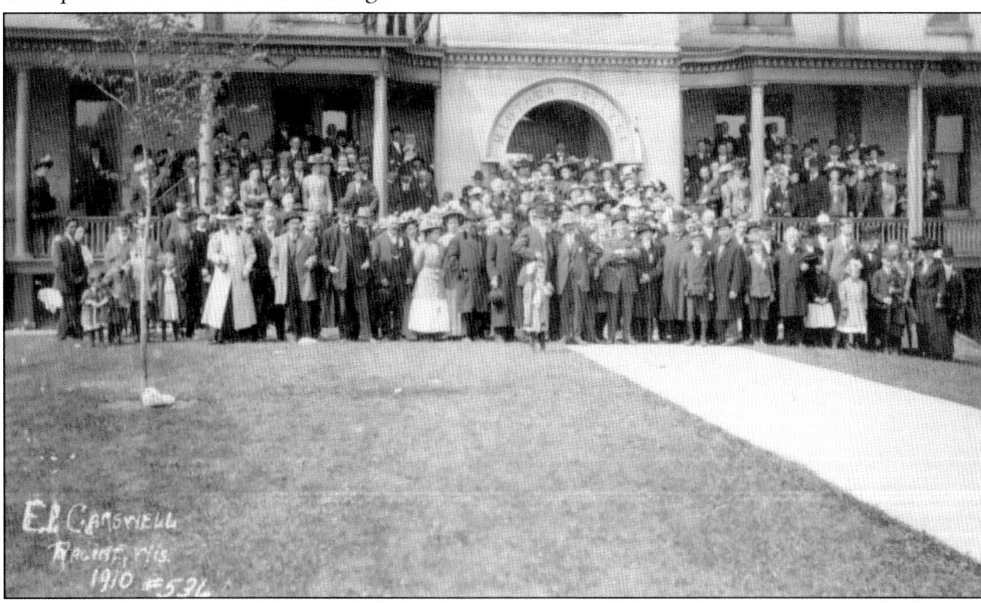

LUTHER COLLEGE, 1910. In 1908, Rev. Christ H. Jensen, president of Luther College, was appointed pastor of a church in Waupaca. In 1909, the college was sold to the United Danish Evangelical Lutheran Church. Rev. John A. Larsen, who succeeded Jensen as college president, invested $50,000 of his own money to keep the school open. But his efforts were in vain and the school closed in 1914. This 1910 photograph shows a large group assembled in front of the college building.

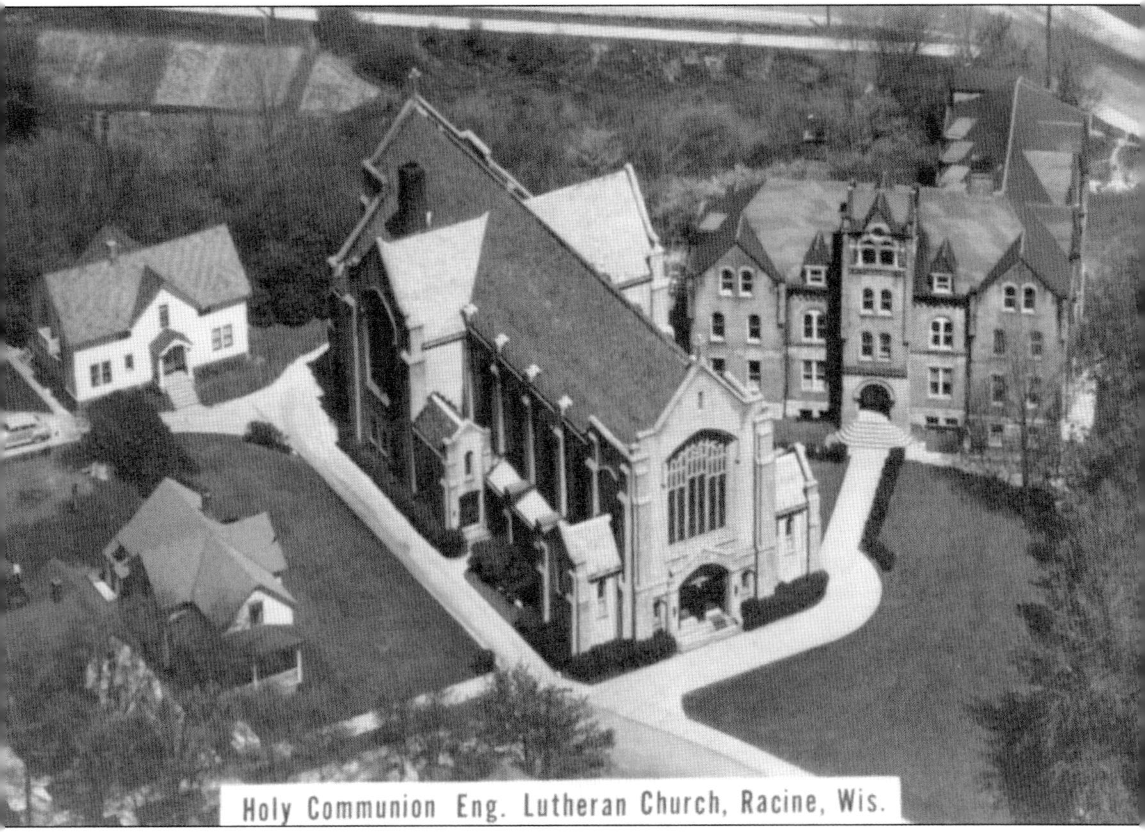

HOLY COMMUNION ENGLISH LUTHERAN CHURCH. Holy Communion Church purchased the Luther College property in 1927 and in 1928 built a fine cathedral-style perpendicular Gothic church of limestone next to the former college building. The college building was converted into a parish house with rooms for church use. Today the old college building is in good condition. A few changes have been made, including lowering the high tower roof and removing the two veranda porches and the corner gazebo-pavilion.

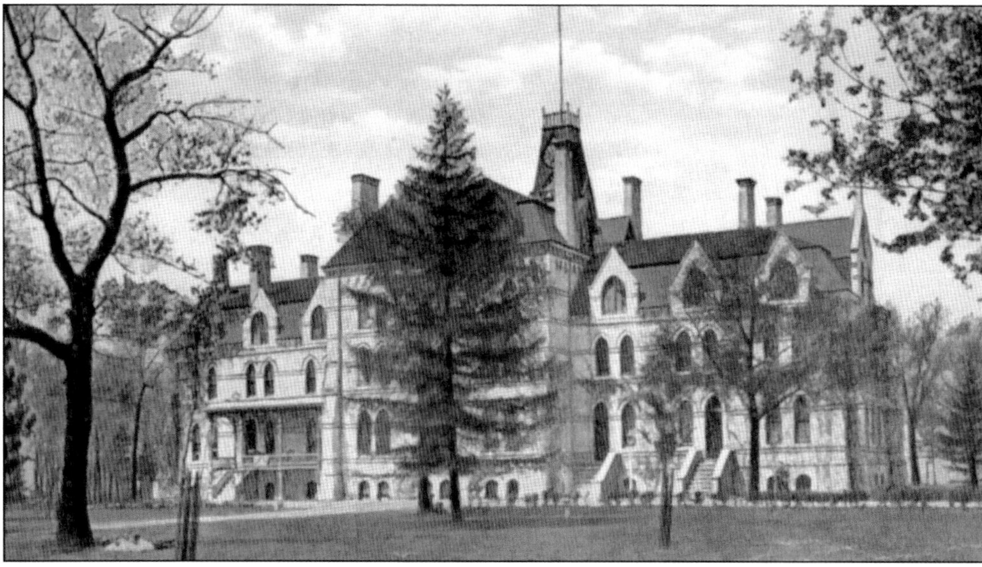

TAYLOR HALL, RACINE COLLEGE. Racine College opened its doors as an Episcopal College in 1852 after Racine had won a contest with Milwaukee by raising $6,000 and offering six acres of land for its site. The buildings occupying about 40 acres of woodland on Racine's lakeshore were designed in a Gothic Revival style. Emerline Taylor, who died in October 1866, bequeathed $65,000 to the college, $30,000 of which was used to build Taylor Hall in 1867. Without a doubt, this complex of Gothic-style cream brick buildings are the finest in Racine and possibly in Wisconsin.

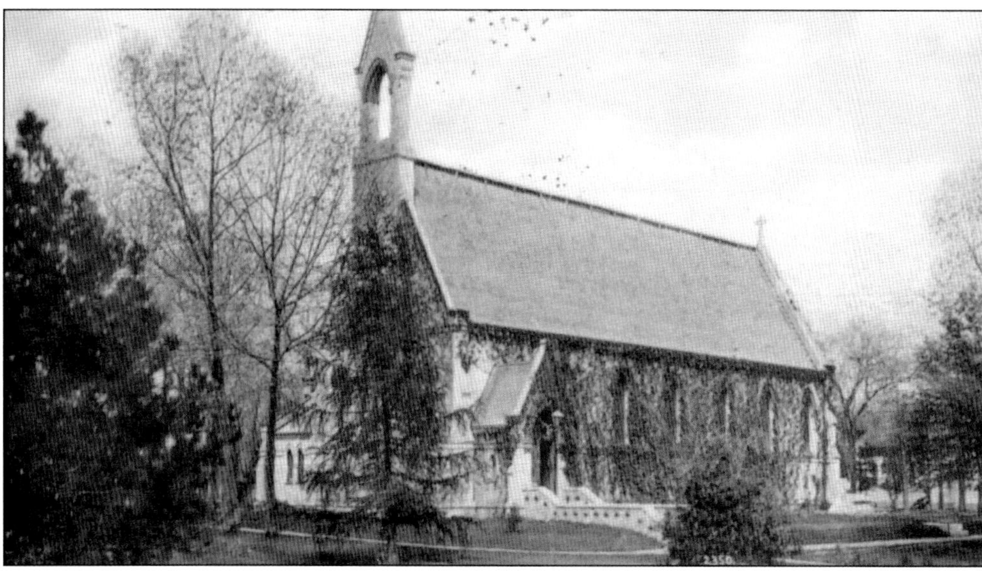

COLLEGE CHAPEL, RACINE COLLEGE. Another fine example of Gothic Revival style architecture is St. John's Chapel built on the Racine College grounds in 1864. The tomb of Rev. James DeKoven is near the chapel. DeKoven served as rector and warden of the college between 1859 and 1879. He is now regarded by some as perhaps the single most important figure in the history of the Anglican Church in the United States. All the buildings of the college complex were built between 1853 and 1876 of cream brick on limestone foundations with a red-orange brick trim.

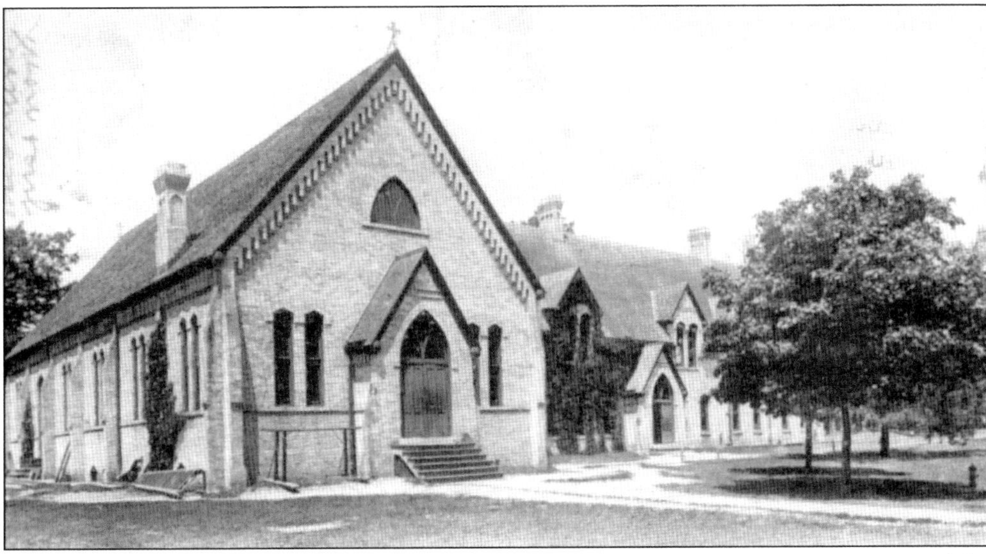

GYMNASIUM, RACINE COLLEGE. The gymnasium building constructed in 1875 was remodeled around 1912 or 1913. Still standing with it on the Racine College campus are Park Hall, Kemper Hall, St. John's Chapel, Taylor Hall, dining hall, assembly hall, and the Gate house. After serving at different times as a prep school, a junior college, and a military school, the complex was finally closed as a school in 1933. For many years it was known as the DeKoven Foundation.

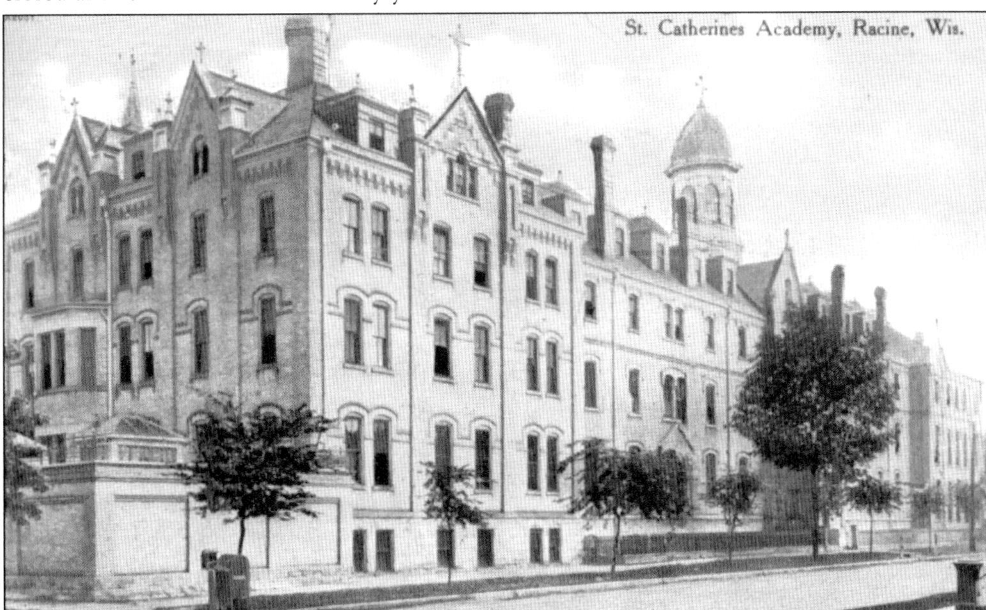

ST. CATHERINE'S ACADEMY. St. Catherine's Academy at Twelfth Street and Park Avenue was founded by Mother Benedicta Baur, fulfilling her hopes of establishing a Dominican Foundation in the new world. Originally a humble two-story convent building that housed the Racine Dominicans, it was expanded in 1864 when a three-story wing was added to the south side. Five years later another wing, measuring 75-by-33-feet, completed the building. In 1884, a chapel was added. As the number of nuns decreased into the 1970s, most of the building became vacant and by 1973, it was razed.

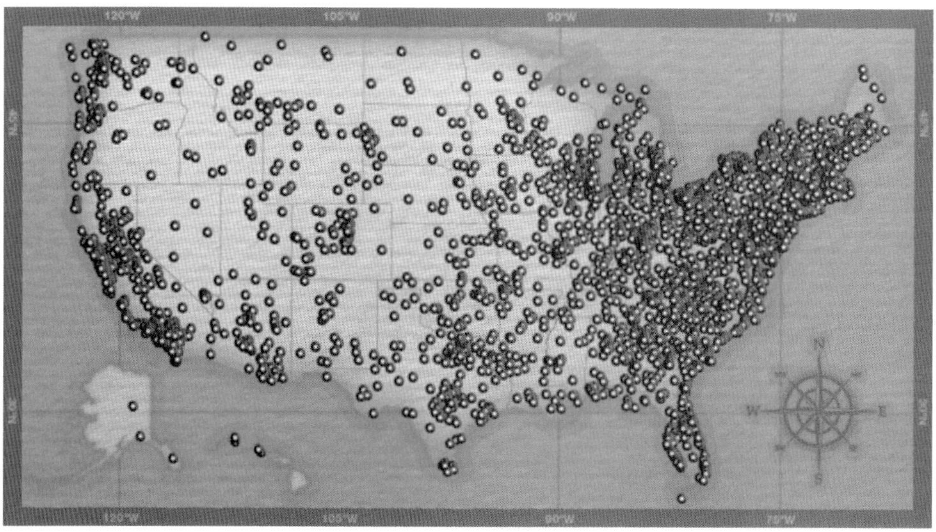